D0348964

Lois Hole's
PERENNIAL
FAVORITES

Lois Hole's
PERENNIAL
FAVORITES

By **Lois Hole**
With **Jill Fallis**

Photography by Akemi Matsubuchi

LONE
PINE

Copyright © 1995 by Lois Hole and Lone Pine Publishing

Printed in Canada

First Printed in 1995   20 19 18 17

All rights reserved. No part of this work covered by the copyrights hereon may be reproduced or used in any form or by any means—graphic, electronic or mechanical—without the written permission of the publisher, except by reviewers, who may quote brief passages.

The Publisher: **Lone Pine Publishing**

206, 10426 - 81 Avenue	202A, 1110 Seymour Street	1901 Raymond Ave. SW, Suite C
Edmonton, Alberta	Vancouver, British Columbia	Renton, Washington
Canada T6E 1X5	Canada V6B 3N3	USA 98055

Canadian Cataloguing in Publication Data

Hole, Lois, 1933–
Lois Hole's perennial favorites

(Lois Hole's gardening guides)
Includes index.
Previous ed. has title: Lois Hole's northern flower gardening:
perennial favorites.
ISBN 1-55105-076-5

1. Perennials—Canada. 2. Flower gardening—Canada.
I. Fallis, Jill, 1960– II. Matsubuchi, Akemi. III. Title.
IV. Title: Perennial favorites. V. Title: Lois Hole's northern
flower gardening. VI. Series: Hole, Lois, 1933–
Lois Hole's gardening guides.
SB434.H64 1996   635.9'32'0971   C96-910057-4

Editor-in-chief: Glenn Rollans
Editing & Proofing: Jennifer Keane, Roland Lines
Design: Bruce Timothy Keith
Production & layout: Bruce Timothy Keith, Greg Brown
Printing: Quality Colour Press, Edmonton, Alberta, Canada
Colour Separations & Prepress: Screaming Colour
Photography, including cover: Akemi Matsubuchi
Additional photography: Marney Allen 193, 210; David Askan (Garden Picture Library) 280, 282; Liz Ball 63; Linda Burgess (Garden Picture Library) 260; Brian Davis 169; Jill Fallis 28; Derek Fell 131, 155, 195, 255, 283; Steve Nikkila 77, 85, 228; Photos Horticultural Picture Library 84, 89, 119, 129, 165, 217, 245, 257, 256, 260; Carol Spring 234, 290; Jean Wieprecht 235, 330, 331.

The publisher gratefully acknowledges the support of Alberta Community Development, the Department of Canadian Heritage and the Canada/Alberta Agreement on the cultural industries.

To all those who share my love of gardening. *Dedication*

Acknowledgements

This book was made possible through the collaborative effort of many people: family, employees, customers and friends. We would particularly like to thank our Perennials people — Bob Stadnyk, Stephen Raven, Ernie Onyskiw, Murray Aspden and Jan Goodall. A heartfelt thank-you also goes to Janelle Grice and Cheryl Johnson for their creative floral arrangements; Sheryl Walker for her boundless enthusiasm and invaluable gardening experience; Michelle Kieser for her splendid garden and dried flowers; and Norm Tardif for his keen eye and helpful hands.

Also thanks to Mike and Carol Coursaux for sharing their extensive knowledge of perennial propagation, and to all the gardeners who allowed us to photograph their gardens and told us many gardening tips and tales. Finally, to all the gardeners who said that they couldn't wait to get their hands on this book, thank you for your enthusiasm.

The Perennial Plant Association is a North American organization dedicated to raising standards within the perennial plant industry and to promoting the use of perennials. Each year, a single plant or variety is recognized as being outstanding, and is promoted as the 'Plant of the Year.' Several of these perennials are included in this book.

Contents

Dedication 5
Acknowledgements 5

INTRODUCTION 9
THE PERENNIAL FLOWER GARDEN 9
What Is a Perennial? 10
  Biennials 11
Learning by Doing 12
A Glorious, Hassle-free Garden 14
What's in a Name? 15
PLANNING THE PERENNIAL GARDEN 17
Six Essential Questions 18
CHOOSING TO PLANT PERENNIALS 21
Experimenting with New Varieties 21
Hardiness Ratings 23
WHERE TO PLANT PERENNIALS 25
Perennials for Shady Spots 26
Perennials for Wet Spots 26
Perennials for Hot, Dry Spots 27
Perennials for Shady, Dry Spots 27
Soil pH 28
  Perennials for Acidic Soil 28
  Perennials for Alkaline Soil 29
HOW TO PLANT PERENNIALS 30
Four Ways to Get Started 30
  Starting Seeds Indoors 31
  Direct-seeding the Garden 32
  Growing Perennials from Roots and Bulbs 34
  Buying Perennials 35
Hardening Off 37
BEFORE YOU PLANT 38
  How to Transplant 38
Container Gardens 40
Rock Gardens 41
  How to Create a Rock Garden 42
WHEN TO PLANT 43
HOW TO CARE FOR PERENNIALS WITH A MINIMUM OF EFFORT 44
Watering 44
  Easy Ways to Reduce your Water Bill 44
Fertilizing 46
Deadheading 48
Supporting Plants 49
Mulching 49
Weeding 50
Pest Control 52
Dividing Perennials 53
  How to Divide Perennials 54
WINTER PROTECTION 57
What to Do in Fall 58
  Additional Care Required for Tender Perennials 58
What to Do in Winter 59
What to Do in Spring 59
  Additional Care Required for Tender Perennials 60
FLOWERS *(see facing page)*
APPENDIX 332
Chart of Plants by Blooming Period 336
SELECT GLOSSARY 344
SELECT INDEX 347

List of Flowers

ANEMONE	62	JACOB'S LADDER	194
ASTER	64	JOE PYE WEED	196
ASTILBE	68	LADY'S MANTLE	198
BABY'S BREATH	72	LAMIUM	200
BEARDTONGUE	76	LIATRIS	202
BEEBALM	78	LILY	204
BELLFLOWER	80	LILY-OF-THE-VALLEY	210
BISHOP'S HAT	84	LUPIN	212
BITTERROOT	86	MASTERWORT	214
BLACK-EYED SUSAN	90	MEADOW RUE	216
BLANKETFLOWER	92	MEADOWSWEET	218
BLEEDING HEART	94	MONKSHOOD	220
BLUE FESCUE	98	MOOR GRASS	222
BLUE HIMALAYAN POPPY	100	OBEDIENT PLANT	224
BLUE OAT GRASS	102	ORNAMENTAL ONION	226
BLUE SAGE	104	OSTRICH FERN	230
CAMPION	106	PAINTED DAISY	232
CANDYTUFT	108	PASQUEFLOWER	234
CATMINT	110	PEONY	236
CHECKER MALLOW	112	PHLOX	242
CLEMATIS	114	PINK	246
CONEFLOWER	120	PLUME POPPY	250
CORALBELL	122	POPPY	252
CORNFLOWER	126	POTENTILLA	256
CRANESBILL	128	PRIMROSE	258
CREEPING JENNY	132	PULMONARIA	262
DAYLILY	134	RAYFLOWER	266
DELPHINIUM	138	ROCKCRESS	268
ELEPHANT-EARS	142	RUSSIAN SAGE	270
EVENING PRIMROSE	144	SAGE	274
FALSE-SUNFLOWER	146	SAXIFRAGE	280
FLAX	148	SEA HOLLY	284
FLEABANE	150	SEA THRIFT	286
FLEECEFLOWER	152	SHASTA DAISY	288
FOXGLOVE	154	SHOOTING-STAR	290
FOXTAIL LILY	156	SNAKEROOT	292
GARDEN MUM	158	SNEEZEWEED	294
GASPLANT	162	SNOW-IN-SUMMER	296
GENTIAN	164	SOAPWORT	298
GLOBE THISTLE	166	SOLOMON'S SEAL	300
GLOBEFLOWER	168	SPEEDWELL	302
GOATSBEARD	170	SPURGE	304
GOLDENROD	172	ST. JOHN'S WORT	306
GOUTWEED	174	STATICE	308
HENS & CHICKS	176	STONECROP	312
HOLLYHOCK	180	STRAWBERRY	316
HONEYSUCKLE	182	THYME	318
HOPS	184	TICKSEED	320
HOSTA	186	YARROW	324
IRIS	190	YUCCA	328

Introduction

Gardening has always been of great interest to me. As a child, I looked forward to helping my mother tend almost every plant she grew. Most of my mother's garden was dedicated to growing vegetables to help feed the family, but she always set aside a small, highly cherished area for flowers.

Her hobby became my passion. I loved to choose and plant the limited variety of flowers that were then available. We had only about a half-dozen options in flowers, and it was difficult to find the plants and information on how to grow them. Today, listening to people at the greenhouses and at my gardening talks, I hear the need for good information repeated over and over. Gardeners tell me that what they want is a smaller book with easy-to-follow information, of a size perfect for toting out into the garden for on-the-spot reference. Their requests led to the creation of the gardening series. This book, the third in the series, is dedicated solely to perennials. I hope you enjoy reading it as much as we loved writing it.

The Perennial Flower Garden

'... there are literally thousands ...'

Many splendid flower gardens contain a mixture of plant types—perennials, bulbs, roses, shrubs and annuals. The wide range of plants available can make it difficult to decide what to include in your garden.

There are literally thousands of perennials, and deciding which ones to include in this book took a lot of discussion. The final decision was to include only the ones that are the least demanding to grow, but which are beautiful and tough. I wanted the ones that have proven to survive extreme conditions— hot summers and cold winters—and which combined would provide a wide range of heights, blooming seasons and colours. There had to be something for every corner of the garden.

The result is what we determined to be the 100 best perennials for northern gardens. Each perennial, however, may include two or more species and a few recommended varieties, so, in total, there are probably closer to

Black-eyed Susans, Shasta daisies and delphiniums in a summer garden (opposite).

200 different plants to choose from. Some are my favourites, and some are the favourites of other gardeners; all of them are loved because they grow successfully season after season, year after year—and that, in a nutshell, is the reason for having a perennial garden.

WHAT IS A PERENNIAL?
'... simply said, they come back year after year ...'

A perennial is any plant with a life-cycle of more than two years. This means that trees and shrubs are technically perennials, but few of us think of them in those terms. To most people, perennials are simply the plants in the garden that come back year after year.

The term 'herbaceous perennial' describes a plant with non-woody stems that dies to the ground each year—usually, in our part of the world, at the onset of winter. The following spring, new shoots poke through the earth and the plant returns to grow another season. Most perennials fall into this category.

An evergreen perennial keeps its leaves over winter, and still appears green when the snow melts in spring. Pinks, elephant-ears and yucca are a few examples. This type of plant should never be cut back except to remove finished flowerstalks, because it is from the evergreen leaves that the new season's flowers will grow. Heavily pruning leaves and stems prevents flowers from forming, and may kill the plant.

For the purposes of this book, 'perennial' is a catch-all term for plants that, with proper

Woolly thyme is a low-growing, evergreen perennial which blooms with pink flowers in spring.

care, come back year after year. It is their longevity, glorious flowers and attractive foliage that make these plants so fascinating.

Biennials

Biennials are often thought to be perennial because they produce seed so enthusiastically that once you plant them, you will likely have them in your garden for years. The demise of the original plant is almost unnoticed in the abundance of new offspring plants.

11

Technically, biennials are plants that need two years to bloom, set seed and die. In theory, they are supposed to grow a green cluster of leaves in the first year and bloom in the second. In reality, some do this in just one year and others take three. Most of them put on their most spectacular floral show in their second year of life.

Canterbury bell blooms in summer; its tall flowerstalks are lovely in bouquets.

To keep a constant supply of biennials in your garden, allow some blooms to go to seed. The following spring, you will find seedlings around the mother plant. Allow some to remain in place, transplant others and discard the rest.

Many biennials are evergreen: rather than dying to the ground in the fall their foliage remains green under the snow. It is important, therefore, to make sure that they have lots of snow piled on them throughout the winter. Snow acts as a protective blanket and shelters the plants over winter.

Biennials included in this book are:

Canterbury Bell
(see Bellflower)

Foxglove

Hollyhock

Iceland Poppy (see Poppy)

Learning By Doing

'...we started with a few easiest to grow...'

When I was growing up in Buchanan, a small Saskatchewan town, almost every garden had the same perennials—delphiniums, Shasta daisies, Iceland poppies, peonies and hollyhocks.

My mother grew a glorious garden, but her choice of plants was limited: the plants she grew were raised easily from seed or were shared between friends and neighbours. My passion for gardening began in childhood, when I excitedly searched the bare soil in spring for the first green shoots of perennials to appear, and, in our family, the love of gardening has passed on through generations. My six-year-old granddaughter, Katie, would, if permitted, happily slice off every flower in the yard to give away in bouquets, while my mother, Elsa, at 88, still produces a splendid garden.

Hollyhocks bloom all summer.

We are lucky, because our passion for plants has been transformed into a family-run greenhouse business that allows us all to be involved every day in something that we truly enjoy.

My husband Ted and I started out as growers of fresh vegetables for farm-gate sales. Ted has a university degree in agriculture, but neither of us had a background in farming. We built our first greenhouse to grow vegetable seedlings for our own gardens, to gain an earlier harvest. The greenhouse was visible from the road, and people driving by would stop to ask if they could buy the young plants.

One year we grew a few annual bedding plants, again only with the intention of planting them in our own flower gardens. When customers asked to buy them, annual flowers became part of our business.

It was my daughter-in-law Valerie who first suggested that we sell some perennials. We started out with a few that were easiest to grow from seed: hollyhocks, Iceland poppies, delphiniums, bellflowers and Shasta daisies. For a few years, the perennials occupied only a small corner of our greenhouse.

It wasn't until we expanded the business into a full-fledged garden centre with nine large greenhouses that we seriously got into perennials. Growing perennials is different from growing annuals and vegetables because perennials have widely varying needs. We hired specialized staff to run the area, and our selection of perennials soon grew from a half-dozen to ten times that.

When we first ventured into the world of perennials, things were pretty simple. People would ask for a red or pink peony, or a Shasta daisy. Now, however, gardeners are asking for particular varieties of peony by name, and we no longer sell just Shasta daisies, but a selection of short and tall plants, with single, double or semi-double flowers, and plain or variegated leaves! We now carry more than 1500 different types of perennials, few of which are raised from seed in our greenhouses because many perennials take years to reach flowering size. In order to provide plants that will bloom the first or second year in the garden, we bring in cuttings, bare roots and full-grown plants.

Bob Stadnyk, our Perennials Manager, has passion and an innate instinct for these plants, and because of this, he pretty much has free rein in his department. His

The colour blue in flowers is a curiosity. Many plants described on plant tags and in catalogues as having blue flowers actually bloom in a hue more closely related to purple. Only those with 'true blue' petals, such as blue Himalayan poppy (above right), speedwell, iris and peachleaf bellflower (above left), are listed in this book.

Things didn't always run smoothly. One year, we decided to try raising blue Himalayan poppies, and because of their notoriously poor germination, we seeded far more than we thought we'd need. Well, almost all of the darn things grew, and we had enough blue poppies to fill a field, but far more than we could sell at that time. The next year, feeling rather smug, we planted only as many seeds as we thought we'd need. Only about 10 of 150 plants came up! Over the next few years, we had better results. Never, though, in the years since, have we been able to figure out exactly what we did right the first year to have such a stupendous outcome. I attribute it to beginner's luck.

The more you learn about plants, the more fascinating they become. Some information is not essential to growing the perfect garden, but it does make it more interesting, as you cut irises for a bouquet, to know that these plants were named after a Greek goddess, or, as you water your ferns, to contemplate that their ancestors lived long before humans walked on the earth.

knowledge is hands-on, self-taught and so thorough that he has been able to successfully challenge horticultural-certificate exams without taking formal courses or training. Bob says the best way to learn is the way he did, by reading, growing the plants, and talking to old-time gardeners and horticultural people who have 'done it for years.' Luck has played a great part in our success over the years, and it was sheer luck that brought us Bob.

Bob's right-hand man is Stephen Raven, who has an equal passion for and awareness of plants' needs. Stephen has been gardening since he was a young boy; at the age of 14, he had his own garden plot with almost 600 gladioli, numerous perennials and small shrubs. His dedication has resulted in many gardening awards over the years. In the yard of Stephen's present home, garden area outdoes lawn by a ratio of more than two to one—he grows more than 300 types of perennials! I'll tell you about some of his plants, and how to grow your own as successfully, on the pages that follow.

A Glorious, Hassle-free Garden
'... sit back and enjoy ...'

Everyone wants a garden that provides non-stop beauty and maximum results for minimum effort. But how do you obtain that, and where do you begin? The array of plants categorized as perennial can seem overwhelming at first, but after you 'meet' the plants individually on the following pages, you'll know which ones to bring home to your garden.

Through the individual plant portraits, we'll introduce you to each plant and tell you all you need to know about it, from seeding to maturity, as well as ways to extend the garden into your home.

Remember, too, how important it is to spend time just enjoying your

Bob Stadnyk divides a perennial.

14

Stephen Raven gives the garden a final fall cleaning.

garden. Take a meal or afternoon tea outdoors, or simply sit back and enjoy the sights, scents and sounds. Some of my best memories are of times spent with my friend Shirley Munro after hectic school-board meetings. Sitting in her garden, surrounded and soothed by glorious flowers, dappled sunlight, chirping birds and gentle breezes, it is easy to laugh and regard the world as a wonderful place to be.

WHAT'S IN A NAME?
'... a hollyhock is a hollyhock ...'

Perennials are an enigma to many people, especially to those just starting out in gardening. Many gardening books, and people who work with the plants, tend to discuss them in technical terms—botanical terminology and nomenclature that sounds like a foreign language.

To me and to many other gardeners, a hollyhock is a hollyhock and not *Alcea rosea*, so I expect to find it listed under the letter 'H.' I want to know if a plant has pretty flowers, and don't really care about technical details of stamens and sepals. Judging by feedback from customers, readers and guests at my gardening talks, I am not alone. Most people ask only when it blooms, what colour are the flowers, whether it is happiest in sun or shade, and what other information is vital for the plant to grow well.

And so, in this book, you will rarely find horticultural terms, except when essential. Even then, they are translated into easy-to-understand language. If you do want to know

Common plant names often include the suffixes '-wort' and '-bane.' 'Wort' simply means 'plant'; moneywort is a plant with coin-shaped leaves and lungwort is a plant whose leaves were once believed to cure lung diseases. 'Bane,' in plant names, means 'poison,' hence the name 'fleabane' for a plant reputed to be an effective flea-repellent, and 'wolfsbane' for a plant whose roots were, in olden days, used to poison meat for killing wolves.

16

the difference between an inflorescence and a panicle, refer to the glossary at the end of the book.

I admit that there are very valid reasons for using botanical plant names. A salesperson at a greenhouse may ask you for the botanical name, just to be certain that the two of you have the same plant in mind, and botanical names can tell you a lot about a plant's characteristics. Sprinkled throughout the book you will find explanations of Latin names, with further details in the appendix section 'Botanical Names: Learning a Little Latin,' on page 343.

In an effort to keep it simple, though, we have departed from the standard format of gardening books, by listing perennials by their most commonly used names rather than strictly by their botanical or Latin names. A bleeding heart, for example, will be found under 'B,' rather than under 'D' for *Dicentra*. More gardeners know *Astilbe* by that botanical name than by its 'common' name of 'false spirea,' so it can be found under 'A.'

I realize that this method has its limitations. You may know a certain plant as bergamot, while I refer to it as beebalm: we both mean *Monarda*. A 'coneflower' to one person may mean *Echinacea*, while to another it means *Rudbeckia*. Other plants have a variety of common names. The names elephant-ears, leather-leaf, saxifrage and rockfoil all describe *Bergenia*!

It is impossible to create a list of plant names that will be perfect for every person. To solve this problem, we have thoroughly cross-referenced the index in case you're having difficulty locating a particular plant.

Coneflowers are named for their protruding centres. Grow these plants in sunny borders to have flowers all summer.

I often talk to people about planting perennial gardens, and I always say that it is best to begin with a plan. This plan can be altered over time, as your tastes and needs change, but, as with any project, it helps to know where you are headed.

The best gardens contain a mixture of plants. Ideally, these plants are a carefully coordinated blend of shapes, sizes, textures and colours, with glorious bursts of bloom and foliage throughout the season. Regardless of varying garden styles, most gardeners share three common goals:

1. to create a continuous show of flowers

2. to keep the different types of perennials from overgrowing one another

3. to get maximum results with minimum work.

Planning the Perennial Garden

'...three common goals...'

17

If your flower garden is situated so that it is seen only from one side (against a fence, for example), the general rule is to plant tall-medium-short, from back to front. Keep in mind, however, that too-strict adherence to this rule can result in monotonous repetition. Put a few tall plants in the middle row, and some medium-height ones toward the front.

With island beds, which can be seen from all sides, the general rule is to put taller varieties in the centre, with medium-height varieties surrounding the tall plants and short perennials around the edges. A more effective show can be created by gently sloping the bed from a central high-point to the outer edges.

Even within rock gardens, which contain mainly plants listed as short, there will be varying heights. You might choose, for example, a 12-inch-high (30 cm) cranesbill, a 6-inch-tall (15 cm) sea thrift and a low-growing rockcress.

Refer to page 332 for a list of perennials by height.

The mature size of a plant dictates how many to include in your garden. As a general rule, to create a pleasing show you need five of each small plant, three of each medium-sized plant, and only one of each large plant. Large, bushy plants, such as peonies, bleeding hearts, daylilies and Oriental poppies, are often planted individually because they are striking by themselves and need to be spaced 3–4 feet (90-120 cm) apart. Do not, however, allow this to stop you if you want an entire bed of daylilies at the side of the house, or a hedge of peonies lining the driveway (above).

Six Essential Questions
'... prepare yourself ...'

Attaining these goals requires a fair bit of planning. You can make it easier by consulting someone who knows the plants. Go to a garden centre that specializes in perennials. Discussing your needs with a person who is well-versed in the growing and use of perennials will save you time and money. But before you head off, prepare yourself by answering some questions:

1. Where will the flowerbed be located?

Along a walkway, in front of the house, beside a patio? Backed by a fence or in the middle of the lawn, like an island? The location can help you decide which plants are most suitable.

2. How much sun or shade does it receive?

Yes, it's either sunny or shady, but to what degree? How many hours of sun? Sunny all day or only in the morning? Is the entire bed sunny or is it shaded by a tree at one end? What direction does it face? Southern exposures are generally the hottest, while north-facing beds receive less warmth. By being aware of when the sun shines on your garden, you will be better able to decide which plants are best.

3. Do you prefer tall or short plants?

There is no right or wrong answer; it's a matter of personal preference.

High fences and tall trees protect plants from wind, but also restrict the amount of moisture and sunlight they receive (right).

Repetition can really pull a flowerbed together. Consider using your favourite plant in more than one spot—at both ends of the bed, perhaps, and somewhere in the middle. Several clumps of liatris brighten this garden.

4. What colours do you like?

Here too, there are no rules. If you like purple, orange and pink together, then choose flowers in those colours. Go with whatever makes you happy.

5. What size of flowerbed do you want?

Measure the flowerbed not only for length, but also width. Most perennials grow 2–3 feet (60–90 cm) wide, so, in a narrow bed, you may have to put plants in a single row.

6. Which plants do you like?

Make a list. Look at the neighbours' gardens. Flip through this book. Take notes. If you see a picture of a plant or garden that you like, bring it with you to your garden centre.

If your flowerbed runs along the side of the house, note any windows that open. You may want to reserve the spot directly under the window for a plant with fragrant flowers. Refer to page 338 for a list of fragrant perennials.

I always like to see a mixture of plants in a garden— all types of flowers along with shrubs and roses. Many annuals mix well with perennials and provide continuous colour in the garden all season long. I often advise allotting a central area of the flowerbed for annuals, with the perennials coming into and out of bloom behind. Asiatic lilies are a fine backdrop for annual geraniums.

Curved edges for flowerbeds often provide a more pleasing, natural look than do square ones.

If you have an established garden, take note of the breaks between blooming periods. Perhaps your garden performs gloriously in spring, then sulks until midsummer. You need to add plants that will bloom in between those times. Refer to pages 336–337 for a list of perennials by blooming period.

If you always take summer holidays at the same time, remember to take that into account. Don't, for example, plant Siberian irises if you are always away in mid-July, or they will put on their best show without an audience.

Remember to think of foliage when planning your garden. A mixture of plants with different leaf shapes, textures and colours is more interesting than a group which is all the same. Irises, for example, have attractive, sword-like leaves that enhance other flowers when the irises are not in bloom. Perennials such as hostas and deadnettle are added to the garden primarily for their handsome foliage. Silvery-leaved plants like sage lighten heavy or monotonous masses of dark green leaves. See page 342 for a list of perennials with interesting foliage.

Many gardeners are worried about matching flower colours, but it is no more difficult than matching the curtains with the wallpaper when redecorating the house. If, for example, you like bright colours, go for brilliant scarlet and butter yellow. If you prefer pastel shades, choose plants in rose-pink, pale blue, lavender and white. Remember too that flower colour changes—petals are often brightest in light shade and opening buds or fading flowers may take on different shades from the flowers at their peak. Refer to pages 333–335 for a list of perennials by flower colour.

Spring-flowering bulbs brighten gardens when few other flowers are in bloom. Although perennial in nature (they live year after year), bulbs fall into a category of their own. They spend most of the year in dormancy, hidden under the ground, after producing a splendid but short-lived show of flowers.

Tulipa tarda is a species-type tulip with starry, yellow and white flowers in spring.

You can extend the blooming season of your garden by adding early-blooming bulbs. The bulbs on the following list look wonderful in any perennial flowerbed, including rock gardens. All of them naturalize, meaning that they spread from a single plant into many, producing more flowers each year.

Checkered Lily (*Fritillaria meleagris*)
Crocus (*Crocus*)—species types are hardiest and bloom earlier than larger-flowered Dutch hybrids
Daffodil & Narcissus (*Narcissus*)
Glory-of-the-Snow (*Chionodoxa*)
Grape Hyacinth (*Muscari*)
Siberian Squill (*Scilla*)
Snowdrop (*Galanthus*)
Snowflake (*Leucojum*)
Star-of-Bethlehem (*Ornithogalum umbellatum*)
Striped or Lebanon Squill (*Puschkinia*)
Tulip (*Tulipa*)—only the species types naturalize; they are also known as wild or botanical tulips
Winter Aconite (*Eranthis*)

Ever since I was a child, the thing I've loved most about perennials is the excitement they bring each spring, when little sprouts suddenly appear in the bare soil like a promise of the warm, sunny days to come. Gardeners often tell me that these flowers bring memories of carefree childhood days spent in their parents' or grandparents' gardens. Perhaps this is one of the best reasons to include perennials in your garden—to colour your children's memories, so that one day they add these plants to their own gardens in a nostalgic salute to happy days.

Choosing to Plant Perennials

'... flowers bring memories of carefree childhood days ...'

EXPERIMENTING WITH NEW VARIETIES

'... but it died, you might say ...'

Plant breeders are constantly improving existing varieties, and seed companies introduce new ones each year. Be willing to experiment in your own garden; it's fun! I get a real charge from successfully growing a plant that everyone said would never survive here.

We constantly test new plants.

✿ Occasionally, someone asks me about the danger of poisonous plants. In all the time that I spent in my mother's garden as a child, I was never tempted to eat a delphinium, nor have I, in all my years in the gardening business, ever run into any person who has actually been poisoned by a plant. Many of the most common garden and house plants are poisonous, in part or in whole, but quite honestly, the risk to children is very low. You would have to eat quite a bit of most poisonous plants to be harmed, and since they generally taste dreadful this would not be very easy. That being said, children should always be discouraged from eating any plant that could harm them.

Every year we test many new plant varieties in our show garden and trial beds, to ensure that they will perform well. We try out new perennials from Agriculture Canada's Morden Research Station, and some that we have seen or heard of growing in other regions with winters similar to our own—Denver, Colorado, the Czech Republic and Hungary. We watch the plant's performance during the growing season, and then wait to see if it survives the winter. If it survives several harsh winters, it gets the green light and we usually offer it for sale the following season.

Our show garden contains many open, exposed beds with very little shelter from the weather. The plants that grow there are not pampered. We just plant, water and fertilize them, and then wait to see how they do. If they survive, great; if not, we try something else. The idea is to find those that perform well without fussing, because the average gardener doesn't fuss. Through this process, and as new or improved varieties become available, we update, change and add to our list of recommended plants and varieties.

Taking a gamble has often paid off handsomely by proving that perennials that are not supposed to survive here actually do. Until recently, we had a Zone 7 California Fuchsia (*Zauschneria garrettii*), which bore beautiful scarlet trumpet flowers for three summers before succumbing to a sudden cold snap early last fall.

But it died, you might say. Well, yes it did, but not until three years after planting, and with no winter protection. An initial investment of only a few dollars provided me with something beautiful that lasted three seasons—I feel the money was well spent!

HARDINESS RATINGS

' ... general guide rather than absolute rule ... '

The accepted standard to determine the hardiness of a particular plant is its zone rating. Both the Canadian and American zone maps, which divide North America into areas based on the average annual minimum temperatures, were created by plant scientists and meteorologists as standards for rating plant hardiness.

These ratings should be used as a general guide rather than an absolute rule. It's true that there are only so many species of plant that can be grown in northern gardens. The problem is that there is no guaranteed way of determining precisely which ones will survive in your garden, and which ones will not. Zone ratings may not accurately reflect the conditions specific to your backyard.

In the Edmonton, Alberta area where I live, for example, there are, on average, only about 140 consecutive frost-free days in the

Although Cholla cactus (Opuntia imbicata) is not supposed to grow here, this one has survived two winters without any dieback at all.

If you see something you like in a catalogue that is not recommended for your area, don't be afraid to try it. When experimenting with out-of-zone plants, try these tips to increase chances of success:

• Choose a protected area of the garden, such as a flowerbed on the south or west side of the house, that is sheltered from wind.

• Water the plant well in the late fall, shortly before the ground freezes. Leave all leaves and stems standing, to help trap snow over the plants during winter.

• Consider mulching the plant in the fall, for at least the first winter (see 'Winter Protection' on pages 57–59).

• Ensure that the plant has a good snow-cover throughout the winter. Throw snow overtop when you shovel the driveway, unless you use salt.

• Buy two of the same plant. Give one a protective mulch for winter, and leave the second uncovered. Compare the two in spring, and decide on that basis whether the protective mulch is really necessary.

The candy lily (Pardancanda norisii) is one of the plants currently being tested for hardiness at our greenhouses.

Some wildflowers have become endangered species, and by taking away even a single specimen, you could be assisting in their extinction.

If you see a wildflower or alpine plant that appeals to you, take a photograph. Bring your snapshot to your local greenhouse and ask for assistance in identifying the plant, and whether it is for sale.

year. This is Zone 3A; in theory, a plant that can survive temperatures of -37°C (-35°F), but will suffer or die at temperatures below that, is considered hardy for this area. In reality, however, we can successfully grow many 'out-of-zone' plants—ones that are listed as Zone 4, 5 or 6. This has been proven time and again over the years, with plant trials in our show gardens, and in the gardens of many of our customers.

Even areas with the same zone rating are different. Part of southern Manitoba is also rated as Zone 3A, but conditions there are far more humid than other areas of the Prairies. Most of southern Alberta is Zone 3A too, but that part of the province is prone to erratic winters and less snow-cover due to chinook winds, which occur less frequently in areas further north.

The only way to be 100 per cent sure that a particular perennial will survive in your garden is to try it yourself, keeping a few principles in mind. Go with the advice of experts who have actually grown these plants. Whether or not a perennial survives comes down to how well it is prepared for and looked after during winter, how much snow-cover it has, and where in your yard it was planted. For example, clematis is readily accepted as hardy for northern gardens, but a hybrid variety, such as 'Jackmanii,' will not survive winters planted in the middle of the yard. It will, however, flourish for years in a south- or west-facing bed alongside the house.

The same theory holds for out-of-zone plants. If you have lots of snow throughout the winter, provide what each plant needs to be happy and follow the recommended procedures for winter protection on pages 57–59, you are likely to have great success. That is why, in this book, you will not find zone ratings listed for each plant. We *know* that they are hardy in northern gardens, because we have grown them for years, and can tell you what you need to do to keep them in your own garden.

One cold winter day years ago, our dog, Sparky, gave birth outdoors in the snow. It was about -40°, so she chose to have her pups in the warmest spot she could find—the flowerbed up against the south wall of the house. That spot is an example of a microclimate: an area that is distinctly different in its climate from the surrounding areas. (We did, of course, bring Sparky and her pups indoors as soon as we discovered them!)

A microclimate may be either warmer or colder than other parts of your garden. On a fall morning after a freezing night, you will sometimes notice that frost has hit only certain spots in your yard—usually exposed, low-lying areas. The warmest parts of your garden will be those near fences, walls, trees and tall plants; these 'obstructions' trap heat and provide shelter from the wind. Choose protected spots for the more tender, and reserve exposed areas for hardier varieties.

Every plant has its ideal spot in the yard. Under similar conditions of care, plants that receive more shade tend to produce fewer flowers and 'stretch'—be taller and less bushy—than the same plants grown in sun. Even the time of day that the sun shines directly on the garden makes a difference; morning sun is less intense than afternoon sun. We have two gasplants in our garden: the one on the south side receives sun all day long, and is a wide, compact plant covered in flowers. The other grows in an east-facing flowerbed where it is shaded in the afternoon; this plant is taller with fewer flowers.

Where to Plant Perennials

'... every plant has its ideal spot ...'

Hybrid clematis does best on the south or west wall of the house, with its roots shaded by a shorter plant like baby's breath.

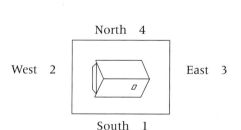

North 4

West 2

East 3

South 1

The areas are numbered 1 to 4 from sunniest to shadiest. Southern exposures receive the most sun. Shade is intensified by obstructions such as decks, fences, tall plants, trees and shrubs, which may also reduce the amount of moisture received from rainfalls. Microclimates in your yard affect how well plants grow in each location.

PERENNIALS FOR SHADY SPOTS

These plants grow well in shady gardens. The ones marked with an asterisk (*) are the best choices for more heavily shaded areas.

Anemone

Astilbe

Bishop's Hat

Bleeding Heart

Blue Himalayan Poppy

Coralbell

Creeping Jenny

Elephant-ears*

Gentian

Globeflower

Goatsbeard

Goutweed*

Honeysuckle

Hosta*

Lady's Mantle

Lamium*

Lily-of-the-Valley*

Masterwort*

Meadowsweet

Monkshood

Ostrich Fern*

Primrose*

Pulmonaria*

Rayflower

Shooting-star

Snakeroot*

Solomon's Seal*

Use plants with various foliage textures, such as snakeroot, goatsbeard and hostas, in shady gardens.

PERENNIALS FOR WET SPOTS

Low-lying, wet areas are often the most frustrating parts of the garden. In these areas, only a limited number of plants will do well. An asterisk (*) indicates those plants that also like shade.

Creeping Jenny*

Elephant-ears*
(either sun or shade)

Fleeceflower

Globeflower*

Goatsbeard*

Goutweed*
(sun or shade)

Iris (Siberian ones)

Meadowsweet*

Ostrich Fern*

Rayflower*

Snakeroot*

Creeping Jenny makes a beautiful groundcover alongside a pond.

PERENNIALS FOR HOT, DRY SPOTS

Some sunny areas of the garden are extremely warm and dry, such as those near heat-radiating brick walls or sun-reflecting surfaces such as white, stucco walls. Choose drought-tolerant plants for these flowerbeds.

Remember, though, that even drought-tolerant plants need to be well-watered when young, at least once a week, until their root systems develop to the point where they can sustain the plants through periods of drought. After their first season of growing, you need water them only occasionally, but more often during spells of unusually hot, dry weather. 'Drought-tolerant' does not mean the plant is like a cactus, which survives in a desert. Drought-tolerant plants still need to be watered, but less often than other plants.

The following plants, once established, have excellent heat and drought tolerance:

Baby's Breath	Foxtail Lily	Sea Holly
Bitterroot	Gasplant	Snow-in-Summer
Blanketflower	Globe Thistle	Soapwort
Blue Fescue	Hens & Chicks	Spurge
Blue Sage	Liatris	St. John's Wort
Coneflower	Potentilla	Stonecrop
Cornflower	Russian Sage	Yarrow
Daylily	Sage	Yucca
Fleeceflower		

PERENNIALS FOR SHADY, DRY SPOTS

Dry shade can be a difficult area for plants. Remember to keep young plants well-watered until they are established, and add large amounts of organic matter, like compost or peat moss, to improve the soil's moisture retention.

The following plants are more tolerant of dry shade conditions than most.

Bishop's Hat

Elephant-ears

Fleeceflower

Goatsbeard

Goutweed

Lady's Mantle

Lily-of-the-Valley

Pulmonaria

Solomon's Seal

Lady's mantle, elephant-ears and goutweed are great plants for dry, shady gardens. The latter two also do well in acidic soil.

SOIL pH

The ability of plants to absorb nutrients depends, to a large extent, on the soil pH. This is measured on a scale from 1 to 14. Low numbers indicate acidity and high numbers indicate alkalinity; 7.0 is considered neutral. Most perennials grow best in soils with a pH between 6.0 and 7.0, and garden soils generally fall into that range. Soil tests are useful if you have difficulty growing plants, because they may indicate an imbalance that can be corrected easily.

Perennials for Acidic Soil

In extremely acidic soil, few plants will grow well. Areas near evergreen trees such as spruce and pine are usually quite acidic. Either add a fair amount of dolomitic lime and bone meal to the soil, or choose plants that do well in acidic conditions. An asterisk (*) indicates plants suited for shady locations.

Anemone*

Astilbe*

Beardtongue

Bishop's Hat*

Blue Himalayan Poppy*

Daylily

Elephant-ears* (either sun or shade)

Gentian (Chinese)*

Goatsbeard*

Goutweed*
(sun or shade)

Hosta*

Lily-of-the-Valley*

Meadow Rue

Meadowsweet*

Moor Grass

Ostrich Fern*

Primrose*

Pulmonaria*

Shooting-star*

Snakeroot*

Solomon's Seal*

Goatsbeard is a shrub-like perennial; it has showy plumes in summer.

Perennials for Alkaline Soil

In alkaline soil, either add lots of peat moss, or choose plants that do well in alkaline conditions. Plants marked with an asterisk(*) are suited to shady areas.

Baby's Breath

Blue Sage

Campion

Elephant-ears* (either sun or shade)

Goldenrod

Hens & Chicks

Hops

Lady's Mantle*

Lamium*

Lupin

Plume Poppy

Poppy

Potentilla

Sage

Saxifrage

Soapwort

Statice

Stonecrop

Yarrow

Yucca

Blue sage produces plenty of blooms even in poor soil.

How to Plant Perennials

'... essentially, four options ...'

🌺 As a general rule, the smaller the seeds, the longer the plants take to grow, and the more difficult the seed is to handle. Find out how long it takes for the plant to bloom; certain ornamental onions, for example, take as long as two years to germinate, and another three to five years to flower. With any perennial that takes so long to reach maturity, you are better off to buy a plant that, within a year or two, will grow to its maximum size. At that point, you can divide the original plant into two or three separate plants.

There are, essentially, four options for starting your garden. Refer to individual plant listings for recommendations and details on the best methods for each species.

Four Ways to Get Started

Which method is best for you? Here are some things to consider:

1. Starting plants from seed indoors

- Starting seeds indoors may save money in the long run, and eliminates problems with outdoor pests.
- Starting seeds indoors gives plants a headstart on the season.
- The seeds of some perennials will not germinate readily indoors.
- Most homes do not have ideal conditions for growing seedlings. Some plants are so challenging to raise to the seedling stage that many greenhouses purchase their young plants from specialist growers.
- Starting plants from seed takes a lot of time.
- Few perennials bloom in their first year of life. Most put on a satisfactory show in their second year, but others take five or more years from seed to flower.

2. Sowing seeds directly into the garden

- This is the cheapest way to get started.
- It takes longer for perennials to bloom from seed. Very few produce flowers their first year.
- The choice of plants that grow easily from seed sown outdoors is limited.

3. Planting roots and bulbs

- Roots and bulbs are usually fairly inexpensive.
- Most roots and bulbs produce plants that bloom their first season.
- Only certain perennials can be started in this manner.

4. Buying established plants

- Buying established plants is the simplest route for immediate results.
- This approach offers the widest selection of plants. Professional growers often have access to varieties which are not available as seed through retail outlets.
- Established plants are more costly than seed.

Starting Seeds Indoors
'... some need cold, others warmth ...'

I often hear from gardeners who have difficulty starting seeds. Seeding perennials is not as simple as seeding either annuals or vegetables, because not all perennials' seed germinates readily. Before they will sprout, some types of seed must be scarified (scratched or scraped), stratified (a process of alternate freezing and thawing), or exposed to either light or dark, in order to simulate natural processes that break dormancy. Some need cold, others need warmth. Most need high humidity (often attained by covering the seedling flat with plastic wrap).

The easiest perennials to start from seed indoors are those which do not require difficult special treatment, germinate within a month and grow quickly once seedlings are up:

Bellflower	Jacob's Ladder
Blanketflower	Poppy (Iceland)
Campion	Potentilla
Candytuft	Shasta Daisy
Catmint	Snow-in-Summer
Flax	Soapwort
Foxglove	Thyme
Hollyhock	Yarrow

When we first started raising plants, we had an unheated greenhouse, so in the late winter and spring, the living room floor of our small farmhouse became our germination area and was often covered with seedling flats. Nowadays the plants are relegated to the

This is what you will need in order to grow top-quality plants from seed indoors: seeds, potting soil, seedling trays, fertilizer, grow lights, vermiculite, pest-control products and a misting bottle.

greenhouses, and I am very happy to keep my living room just for family and friends!

Here's how to successfully start seeds indoors:

- Fill a seedling flat to within a $^1/_2$-inch (1 cm) of the top with a good-quality seedling mixture (a potting soil with a high percentage of peat moss and perlite). Never use garden soil! It always becomes hard and inhibits rooting of seedlings. Garden soil may contain insects and almost always has disease organisms that cause root-rot.

- As a general rule, plant seeds no deeper than the thickness of the seed.

- Water just enough to moisten the soil. Use a misting bottle with a fine spray so you don't wash seeds away as you water.

- Never allow the seedling mix to become dry. Germinating seeds will not tolerate dry soil and often die if the soil becomes dry for even a short time.

- To get the best possible germination, use a fungicide shortly after planting to prevent 'damping off' (rotting of seedlings).

- Cover the seedling flat with plastic wrap or a plastic dome to increase humidity. Make a few slits in the plastic wrap to allow ventilation and prevent over-heating. Remove the plastic covering once seedlings have fully emerged.

Lupin seed needs to be scarified (scratched or scraped) because it has a hard coat that inhibits germination; these seeds will not sprout until moisture can penetrate the seed coat. Carefully scrape the seeds with fine sandpaper before sowing. Alternatively, sow seed as late as possible in fall, even in mid-

November. The action of frost on the fall-sown seed will then break down the hard seed coat.

- Tag each container with the date planted and the variety of seed.
- Use grow lights to enhance germination and growth.
- When seedlings produce their second set of leaves, fertilize with a 'plant starter' fertilizer, such as 10–52–10, at one-quarter strength, once a week. If your seedlings are crowded, transplant them into larger containers at this point.

Plants vary greatly in their seeding-to-maturity intervals. Most perennials should be started in February or early March. Transplant them into the garden once the risk of spring frost has passed.

Direct-seeding the Garden
'... as a general rule, sow in late spring ...'

As a general rule, direct-seeding should be done in late spring. Starting seeds at this time is important to allow enough foliage to be produced during the growing season for the plants to survive the winter. Some perennials can be sown in fall, but this must be done late enough that the seeds will not germinate until spring. Certain seeds need a prolonged freeze-thaw period (stratifying) in order to germinate. Refer to individual plant listings for recommendations.

If you sow seeds in fall, sow them thickly, because germination will be poorer than with spring seeding. Be sure to mark the area so you don't mistakenly cultivate it in spring. Label the plants so you know which variety is growing.

An area of the garden designated as a 'seedling bed' is ideal. You may be able to use a corner of your vegetable garden for this purpose. Seedlings are ready to be transplanted once they have produced two or three sets of leaves.

Refer to individual plant listings to determine which perennials grow most successfully from seed sown in the garden.

Indoor light is weaker than outdoor light, so exposing some types of seed to light indoors improves germination, and we recommend just pressing the seed on top of seedling mix and not covering it with soil. Outdoors, the same type of seed must be covered with soil to prevent it blowing away, drying out or being eaten by birds.

33

You can collect seed from non-hybrid plants when it is brown and ripe. Sow at once or store inside an envelope in the refrigerator.

✿ The best time to plant bulbs in fall is when the leaves of native trees are at their peak fall colour. Earlier, it is still too warm and bulbs may begin to sprout right away. Later, there is usually not enough time for roots to adequately develop before the ground freezes.

Growing Perennials from Roots and Bulbs

'... top quality is your best choice ...'

Some perennials are available as packaged bulbs or roots. These are graded for quality, as meat and eggs are, and top quality is always your best choice. Grade No. 1 hosta roots, for example, will have three or more 'eyes' (where the sprouts come from; like those on a potato), and will quickly grow to form a good-sized plant.

Lower-grade roots, on the other hand, will have only a single eye and usually come from a year-old plant. Because they are younger, they take longer to produce a good-sized plant and probably won't bloom the first year in your garden. With clematis, for instance, you need three-year-old roots in order to have a profusion of flowers that season.

For the best quality, buy roots and bulbs as early as possible, because the climatic conditions in most stores are not ideal. Indoor areas are usually too warm and dry, so roots or bulbs that are on sale toward the end of the season are generally not a good buy.

Always choose the largest ones you can find. It's okay to buy them if they are starting to sprout, as long as the shoots are thick and small. Avoid any with long, pale sprouts and more than 2 inches (5 cm) of growth.

Plant roots and bulbs into the garden as soon as possible after taking them home. If it is spring and too early to get into the garden, plant them into a pot at a shallow depth, so that they are just barely covered with soil. Keep the pot in front of a sunny window. When spring temperatures have warmed, gradually acclimatize plants to outdoor temperatures (see 'Hardening Off' on page 37). Potted plants are ready to be transplanted into the garden when their roots are visible to the edges of the pots. Most good-quality roots and bulbs will produce plants that bloom the first season.

Plant ornamental onion bulbs in the fall.

In either spring or fall, plant roots or bulbs of foxtail lilies, bearded irises, Asiatic lilies and peonies.

In spring, plant roots and bulbs of the following perennials:

Astilbe	Hosta
Bleeding Heart	Iris (Siberian)
Clematis	Liatris
Coneflower	Lily-of-the-Valley
Cranesbill	Ostrich Fern
Daylily	Painted Daisy
Elephant-ears	Phlox (garden phlox only)
Globe Thistle	
Globeflower	Solomon's Seal

Buying Perennials
'... a spring ritual ...'

One of the best reasons to buy potted perennials is that more mature plants will very often bloom the first year. For some people, shopping for new plants is a spring ritual, celebrating the end of another long winter. For others, it is an opportunity to get something new and different, a plant that nobody else on the block has in his or her garden, or one that they happen to particularly love.

Look for large, healthy rhizomes when shopping for bearded irises. The large rhizome on the right will result in one or more good stalks of large flowers this year, while the smaller rhizome on the left is likely to produce only sparse blooms the first year, or may not bloom at all until the second season.

Most garden centres keep their best selection of perennials at flowering time in spring and summer. Usually these plants are sold in pots, which means that they can be planted at any time during the growing season, up until two to three weeks before the ground freezes in late fall.

For the best selection of perennials, shop early in the season.

When buying perennials, look for plants that are healthy and bushy. Don't necessarily choose those with the most flowers; look instead for those with plenty of new growth at the base.

Shopping for perennials late in the season often results in great savings—most garden centres are offering plants at sale prices then, in order to clear out their stocks—but your selection of plants will be reduced. Many of these plants will be 'pot-bound'; they've been growing in pots all season long, with nowhere for their roots to go but around and around the inside of the pot. Before planting pot-bound perennials, gently untangle and snip off up to the bottom third of roots. After you have enabled their tangled roots to grow out and down into the soil, they will do just fine.

What size is the best buy? It's up to you. Small pots are cheapest, but only some plants this size will bloom the first season. Larger plants cost more, but quickly reach mature size and peak performance.

Buying perennials by mail-order is another option and often a good way of getting exactly the varieties you want. Order as soon as you receive the catalogue for the best selection. It is best to unpack your parcel as soon as it arrives and plant promptly.

If you need to store perennials for a few days before planting, keep the plants in a shaded area and thoroughly soak them. Check plants daily to see if they need watering; do not allow soil to dry out. If you are worried about frost, cover plants overnight. Never store plants in a dark location or in the garage longer than a single night or day. Even a garage with large windows will not provide enough light to support plants.

A plant that looks stretched, diseased or as if it has been neglected is never a good buy, no matter how low the sale price. Some perennials, however, such as pasqueflower (right), go into a dormant stage at some point later in the growing season, and, although they look less than ideal, they are still perfectly healthy plants.

HARDENING OFF
'... to withstand all types of stress...'

Hardening off simply means to gradually acclimatize plants from indoor to outdoor temperatures over a period of several days before planting. Plants that have been hardened off are usually sturdier, bushier and better able to withstand all types of stress than are those that have not been through this process.

If you buy your perennials from an outdoor sales area, they will likely not need this treatment, but any plant that has been growing inside a warm greenhouse or was raised from seed in your home requires a period of hardening off before being planted into the garden. To harden off plants, simply place the pots outdoors in a warm, but not hot, sunny area for at least a week prior to planting. A site that receives morning sun is ideal. Don't forget to water every day, because most plants that dry out in their pots do not fully recover.

If there is a risk of frost, cover the pots with an old sheet, towel or blanket, a roll of burlap, sheets of newspaper or a cardboard box. Never use plastic; it provides virtually no insulation. Don't bring the plants back into the house or into a heated garage, because if you do, you'll need to begin the hardening off process again, from the starting point.

The phrase 'well-drained soil' is often used to describe optimum conditions for plants, but what does it actually mean? Well-drained soil is neither too wet nor too dry; water percolates through very easily. Most (but not all) plants are happiest in well-drained soil.

If you are starting a garden from scratch, use this recipe for the best soil mix: 3 parts soil, 2 parts peat moss and 1 part coarse sand. I have found that this also works well to revitalize an older garden, where the soil has turned rock-hard.

37

Before You Plant

'... enough good topsoil ...'

Before planting anything into the garden, try a couple of things to greatly improve the show of plants. The first is to ensure that there is enough good topsoil. I always recommend about 8–12 inches (20–30 cm) of topsoil for flowerbeds. The second is to mix in some bone meal or a granular fertilizer with a high middle number, such as 10–20–5, along with some organic matter.

Organic matter improves the ability of the soil to retain water and nutrients, resulting in impressive plant growth and vigour. It also loosens clay soil, making it easier for air and roots to penetrate, and binds sandy soil so that it dries out less quickly. We get our best results by adding lots of compost or well-rotted manure mixed with peat moss to the garden twice a year, once in spring and again in fall.

How to Transplant

1. *Before you start planting, ensure that you know the mature size of each variety, so you can allow sufficient space between plants. If you have a garden plan, have the drawing beside you. Plant the back row first.*
2. *Add 3–4 inches (7.5–10 cm) of organic matter to the soil surface. In hot, dry areas, add even more— an additional 2–3 inches (5–7.5 cm). Dig the organic matter in about one spade's depth.*
3. *Each planting hole should be twice as wide and twice as deep as the size of the pot the plant is growing in. To aid root development, toss in a handful or two of bone meal, and lightly stir it into the bottom of the planting hole.*
4. *Remove the plant from its pot. Gently untangle the rootball to enable roots to spread into the soil as the plant grows.*
5. *Refill the planting hole with fresh soil so the plant will be sitting at the same level as it was when growing in its pot. Stir the soil some more to mix the bone meal into it. Now place the plant in the hole, and firmly pack the soil around it, leaving a small depression around the base of the plant. Water until the soil is completely soaked.*
6. *New plants should be watered regularly and thoroughly twice a week, for the first year after planting. Fertilize once a month with 20–20–20 until the first of August.*

1.

2.

3.

4.

5.

6.

The crown of a plant is a thickened junction between stem and roots. Most perennials prefer to have their crowns at or barely below the soil surface. With its crown planted either too shallow or too deep, the peony shown here is unlikely to bloom.

Certain perennials have specialized planting needs. A peony, for example, must have its crown from 1¹/₂–2 inches (3.5–5 cm) below the soil surface, or it will not bloom. Bitterroot, on the other hand, may rot unless coarse sand is provided when planting. Before you plant, check individual plant listings for specific recommendations.

CONTAINER GARDENS

'... glorious growing in containers ...'

Perennials look absolutely glorious growing in containers. We often plant clematis in a large tub with a trellis, and, at the base, we add trailing plants like deadnettle, creeping Jenny or pink-flowered strawberries. The inspiration for this came from Raymond Evison, a British gardening authority and author, who visited our greenhouses to talk to staff about clematis. After seeing his slides of marvellous clematis planters, someone asked whether they would survive here. His immediate answer was that of course they would, but he then hesitated and said, 'How cold does it get here?'

The answer to that, for gardeners in most parts of Canada and the northern United States, is that it gets cold enough that plants will not survive winter in a container. Even so, do not let this stop you if you like the look of perennials in containers. Go ahead and

Brighten patios and balconies with perennials in containers. Choose those with long blooming periods or interesting foliage for the most effective display. Both the clematis and catmint in this container will bloom all summer long.

experiment with any variety of plants that you choose. Enjoy your container gardens throughout the summer, but remember that, in the fall, the entire planter must be laid on its side and buried underground, or the perennials must be transplanted into the garden. Do this at least two to three weeks prior to freeze-up, and water well in either case to ensure the plants' survival.

Rock Gardens

A properly planned rock garden is an attractive, low-maintenance addition to the home landscape. By coordinating the varieties, you can have an unending show of flowers, beginning with a burst of colour in spring and continuing non-stop throughout summer and into fall.

The following plants are those we have found to be most suited to growing in rock gardens. Most of these plants prefer sun; those marked with an asterisk(*) are more tolerant of shade.

Anemone*	Gentian*	Shooting-star*
Aster (alpine types)	Hens & Chicks	Spurge
Baby's Breath (creeping types)	Hosta* (dwarf types)	Stonecrop
		Strawberry
Beardtongue*	Moor Grass	Thyme
Bellflower (some)	Ornamental Onion (Turkestan)	Tickseed
Bishop's Hat*		
Bitterroot	Pasqueflower	
Bleeding Heart* (fernleaf types)	Phlox (creeping types)	
Blue Fescue	Pink	
Blue Oat Grass	Poppy (Iceland)	
Candytuft	Potentilla	
Catmint	Primrose*	
Coralbell*	Rockcress	
Cranesbill	Sage (some types)	
Creeping Jenny*	Saxifrage	
Elephant-ears*	Sea Thrift	
Flax		

How to Create a Rock Garden

1. It is best to prepare a rock garden in fall and leave planting until spring. This allows time for soil to settle. Weeding is difficult in a rock garden and must be done by hand, so do your utmost to get rid of all weeds at this stage.

2. Rock gardens are most pleasing when you prepare a slope, because the plants are low-growing and a slope permits a better view. Build a retaining wall if your garden area is flat. Fill the bottom third with gravel for improved drainage—most rockgarden plants will die in wet soil—and the remaining two-thirds with good-quality topsoil.

3. Add the largest rocks. Choose similar rocks for the most natural appearance, and place them so that their strata lines (or grain) run in the same direction. Try to bury them so that it looks as if the bulk of their surface were underground.

4. In the spring, add soil as needed to areas that have settled over winter. Gather your plants and smaller rocks. Set them on top of the soil to experiment with placement. Move them around until you like the overall effect.

5. Put the remaining rocks into their permanent positions, and plant the plants according to the directions on page 38. Add a handful of coarse sand to the bottom of each planting hole to improve drainage. A gravel mulch on top of the soil will look attractive, and it will reduce heat damage to roots, minimize water loss in the soil and suppress weeds.

Rock gardens provide years of enjoyment with their diversity of flowers, foliage and textures. Add annual flowers for variety, and to fill space until perennials reach mature size.

I generally recommend spring as the best time to plant perennials. This gives the plants the entire growing season to establish themselves and, as a result, they will better withstand stressful conditions. Plant your garden as soon as you can work the ground in spring. Perennials are hardy plants and can withstand frosts. Seedlings are ready to be transplanted into the garden once their roots reach to the edges of their pots.

With seeds and bulbs, however, there are a few exceptions. The seed of lupins, for example, should be sown in fall, as should bulbs of ornamental onions, but as potted plants, both of these perennials can be planted at any time during the growing season. See page 35 for roots and bulbs that can be planted in fall, and refer to individual plant listings for specific recommendations on seeding.

When to Plant

'... as soon as you can work the ground ...'

A container-grown plant can be planted at anytime during the growing season, from early spring until two to three weeks before the ground freezes in fall.

How to Care for Perennials with a Minimum of Effort

'... find what suits your garden ...'

❀ In early spring, plants in south-facing flowerbeds against the house or in other areas where the snow melts most quickly can die if they become too parched. Throw clean snow overtop to add moisture.

Overall, perennials are fairly undemanding. Putting plants in areas that best suit them makes it a lot easier. For example, we have a south-facing flowerbed which is hot and dry. There, we grow yarrow and sage, which thrive in sun-baked locations. If we grew less drought-tolerant plants in that spot, we would constantly be struggling to provide them with sufficient water. Refer to the listings on pages 26–29, and to individual plant listings, to find what suits your garden.

WATERING
' ... Stephen needed to water his garden only twice last season ...'

Improper watering is probably the number-one reason plants die. Spending the time to do it right requires little extra effort, and results in having to water less often. Last summer, our staff member, Stephen Raven, watered his garden only twice. Most of his neighbours had the hose on about once a week, despite frequent rainfalls. This is because they did not water long enough each time.

You need to allow water to soak deep into the soil, to encourage roots to grow deeper. Shallow watering makes for shallow roots, and when the soil surface dries out, the roots do too. Soil always dries at the surface first, so plants with deep roots need watering less often. To check if you have watered enough, poke your finger as far as you can into the soil. It should be moist as far down as you can reach. If there are any dry areas, keep watering. During dry spells, flowerbeds should be watered heavily once a week.

More water less often is better than less water more often, and actually uses a smaller amount of water. An organic mulch of compost or peat moss helps retain moisture.

Easy Ways to Reduce Your Water Bill
' ... a few simple changes ... '

Most gardeners spend about half their total water bill to water lawns and gardens. A great deal of that water is wasted through evapora-

My favourite watering tool is a water-wand. Because it allows me to direct water where it is needed, I find it to be one of the most effective ways to water. This inexpensive tool attaches to any hose. Most water-wands come with a shut-off valve, which eliminates the need to run back and forth to the tap.

tion and inefficient watering techniques. Making a few simple changes to your garden and the way you water can immediately reduce your water bill.

- Use lots of organic matter, like compost, peat moss and well-rotted manure, to help hold water. Add organic matter to soil before planting, and supplement each spring and fall. Organic matter acts like a sponge: peat moss, for example, holds up to 20 times its weight in water.

- Group perennials according to their water needs. Put drought-tolerant plants in one flowerbed and ones that need more water in another. This avoids wasting water on plants that do not really need it.

- Build a rim of soil around plants to create a saucer-like depression that holds water.

Perennials need watering most often:
- while seeds are germinating and during the seedling stage,
- immediately after being transplanted,
- throughout their first year in the garden (even drought-tolerant plants need regular watering during this stage of life, to allow their root systems to become established),
- when planted on slopes and in south-facing beds,
- during extended periods with no rain, and
- in the late fall, just prior to freeze-up. Fall watering is an important step in ensuring that plants have the best chance for winter survival. Plants that enter winter with their roots in dry soil are likely to suffer.

A soft-rain nozzle gives a gentle spray of water that won't wash away soil. Using this attachment, you turn water on low, set your hose down in the garden and walk away. Once that area is sufficiently soaked, move the hose to another area.

- If possible, plant drought-tolerant perennials at slightly higher elevations. Run-off water can then quench the thirstier plants growing below.

- For areas of the garden where soil dries out most quickly, choose perennials that thrive on a minimum of water. Refer to the plant lists on pages 27–28 for 'Perennials for Hot, Dry Spots' and 'Perennials for Shady, Dry Spots.'

- Whenever possible, water early in the morning. Moisture loss through evaporation is far less then than in midafternoon heat. If you can't find time in the morning, water on a calm, cool evening.

- Trap rain in barrels for use in the garden.

- Use a watering system especially designed for flowerbeds. Soaker hoses are great for long, narrow flowerbeds. Set sprinklers so that they won't waste water by spraying over paved areas.

FERTILIZING

'... so why would I starve my plants?...'

In addition to water, plants need constant nourishment to stay healthy. Plants get their nourishment from soil. Most garden soils contain all of the nutrients essential for plant growth, but often in insufficient amounts to suit the needs of each plant. Regularly adding lots of organic matter, like compost or peat moss, helps. Usually, though, we find the healthiest plants are those that are also fertilized on a regular basis.

I firmly believe that plants need regular fertilizing, just as people need three square meals a day. I know how important eating properly is, and I don't allow anyone in my house to skip breakfast, so why would I starve my plants? The results of regular fertilizing are obvious: your plants will be bushier with more flowers and stronger roots.

Because plants have different needs at various stages of growth and at different times of the year, there are specific fertilizers for specific needs. The numbers that you see on fertilizer containers are percentages of the three major plant nutrients, by weight. For example, '10–52–10' means the mixture is 10 per cent nitrogen, 52 per cent phosphate and 10 per cent potash. These elements each help plants in different ways: nitrogen promotes leafy plant growth and lush leaves; phosphate promotes root development and flower production; potash promotes flower quality and disease resistance.

There are two basic types of fertilizer: those you add directly to soil and those you mix with water first. Granular fertilizers, the first type, are usually slow-releasing; they feed plants slowly, over a long period of time. Water-soluble fertilizers, on the other hand, produce quick results by rapidly releasing all their nutrients. Either type is fine. Some gardeners prefer an annual application of granular fertilizer; others like fertilizing as they water. I sometimes use a combination of both.

Whichever type of fertilizer you choose, perennials need two kinds. The first is a 'complete' fertilizer for when they are actively growing. I use 20–20–20 once a month in spring and early summer, to provide a balanced diet that aids all aspects of plant growth and I stop fertilizing perennials in midsummer to give the plants time to slow their growth down before winter. I use August 1 as the cut-off, because having a set date makes it easier to remember.

The second kind is a high-phosphate fertilizer (one with a high middle number) to be applied just after planting and in the spring and fall. Immediately after transplanting, and once a week for three weeks afterward, I feed perennials with a half-strength solution of 10–52–10. Why half-strength? Because I mix a handful of bone meal into each planting hole, which feeds plants over a long period. Bone meal is a slow-release, organic fertilizer that is rich in phosphorous. As you might expect from its name, it is made of crushed animal bones. I sprinkle a few handfuls of bone meal around my perennials in both the spring and fall, and lightly work it into the

A fertilizer applicator on your hose makes applying water-soluble fertilizers far easier; it eliminates the need for repeated refills by supplying the equivalent of up to 25 filled watering cans. Fertilizer dispensers are readily available and inexpensive.

Fertilize your perennials:

- when planting new plants or dividing mature perennials, by adding a handful of bone meal to each hole before setting plants in.
- in the fall or early spring, by lightly working bone meal into the soil around perennials.
- using water-soluble 20–20–20 fertilizer once a month from spring until August 1.

soil to feed roots. Strong roots result in healthier plants and are essential for enabling perennials to survive harsh winters.

DEADHEADING

'... pinching off the finished flowers ...'

Deadheading simply means removing dead flowers. Doing this has become a habit of mine; I can rarely pass a plant by without stopping to pinch off a few finished flowers. Dead-heading not only keeps gardens looking neat and attractive, it also prevents the plants from producing seed, which uses up a lot of the plant's energy. Many perennials respond to deadheading by producing more flowers over a longer period of time, thus extending the blooming period. Some perennials, such as delphiniums and Oriental poppies, can be cut back to a height of 6–12 inches (15–30 cm) after they finish blooming, resulting in a second flush of flowers later in the season. Cut back unsightly foliage from any peren-nial; most respond with fresh new leaves.

Remember, though, that there are reasons to allow certain plants to go to seed. Biennials, such as hollyhock and foxglove, must set seed in order to stay in your garden. Some peren-nials, such as delphiniums, poppies and Shasta daisies, are in the habit of self-sowing. Wait to see where the seedlings sprout; if you don't like their location, uproot and move or

Lilies should always be deadheaded. Allowing them to go to seed detracts from the overall vigour of these plants.

discard them. Poppies and irises produce attractive seedpods that can be used in dried arrangements.

Supporting Plants

'... floppy ones may need support ...'

Many newer varieties of perennials are self-supporting, but tall or floppy ones may need support, particularly in windy, exposed areas. You can buy ready-made supports, like peony rings, or build your own. Place three strong stakes or sticks around each plant and loop with twine or sturdy string.

Put supports in place early in the season before young shoots are too tall. The plants then grow around and through to eventually disguise the support.

Mulching

'... it simply means covering the soil ...'

Mulching is something I mention more and more often; it simply means covering the soil surface around plants. In the perennial garden, there are two kinds of mulch: the one that you lay down in spring to reduce the need to weed and water (which we will discuss here), and the one that you lay in fall to protect tender plants over winter (see 'Winter Protection' on pages 57–59).

Peat moss, compost, shredded bark and other organic materials are the best to use. In rock gardens, gravel is a better and more natural-looking choice. Gravel allows air to circulate under the foliage of spreading plants and keeps them clean.

There are many reasons to use a mulch:

- Mulches help the soil to retain moisture, so you will need to water less often.

- There will be less erosion of the soil during heavy rain.

- Mulches of natural materials slowly decompose over summer, adding valuable organic matter to the soil.

- There are fewer weeds in mulched areas. Those weeds that do manage to sprout are easier to uproot from mulch than from soil.

A grid-topped plant support is best for holding plants upright. The green frame is soon camouflaged by leaves.

A large-rock mulch offsets the foliage of hostas and fernleaf bleeding hearts.

WEEDING

'... I use a stirrup hoe ...'

Few of us like weeding, but it has to be done. Weeds compete for nutrients, sunlight, water and garden space, and they will take over or eliminate less aggressive plants.

The easiest time to get rid of weeds is before anything has been planted. Leave soil in a new garden bare for as long as possible. Rototill or turn the soil over often; germinating seeds and seedlings of annual weeds, such as chickweed, stinkweed and shepherd's purse, will be exposed to the air and die.

Annual weeds produce enormous amounts of seed, which can easily overwinter. The key to control is never to let these plants set seed. Eliminate them before or as they are in flower. Slice them off with a hoe, or pull them out by hand. Don't put weeds that have gone to seed into the composter, because as you use your compost, you will spread their seeds around the garden.

If perennial weeds, such as thistle and quack grass, exist where you are planning to have your garden, save yourself an enormous headache by completely eliminating them before you plant. Perennial weeds will, if

🌼 Weeds are easiest to remove while they are small, and after a good rainstorm even a young thistle or dandelion may submit to a good tug, usually with the whole root intact. Do not, however, be overly enthusiastic in the spring. Young seedlings of all types look surprisingly similar; what appears to be a weed may actually be a desirable plant.

permitted, live for years and years. Their long, tough roots must be entirely removed, which is really hard to do. A Canada thistle's root system is an intricate maze up to 8 feet (2.5 m) deep! Even the smallest bit of broken-off root will grow into a new plant. In tough situations, sometimes the careful use of an herbicide is the only solution.

In an established bed, hand-weeding is the best method. I find a hand-sized garden fork helps, and when there is room, I use a stir-rup-hoe between plants. Waging war on weeds by physical means can require a lot of effort, but using herbicides without damaging desirable plants is difficult in a planted garden and often more trouble than it is worth. If you must use herbicides, ask for advice at a reputable garden centre to ensure that you have the right product for the job, and be sure to read the label instructions carefully before using.

Landscape fabric is a porous, spun-woven plastic material that allows water to penetrate to underlying soil but prevents weeds from growing. Lay it over your garden after first slicing an 'X' for each plant to poke through, and then cover with an attractive mulch. Allow extra-big holes for perennials that you want to allow to spread. Be aware that this material will prevent seeds of perennials like hollyhocks and poppies from sprouting.

Pest Control

' ... I don't mind squishing bugs ... '

52

 Many birds eat both insects and seeds. The seedheads of tickseed, foxglove, coneflower, black-eyed Susan and goldenrod attract birds. Also, keep bird-feeders in your yard to help birds survive the winter. Some of these birds will patrol your trees in search of insect eggs that were laid in the fall.

If you pay attention when visiting your garden, you will likely notice most problems before they become severe. I don't mind squishing bugs, and often just remove affected leaves and stems to prevent insects or disease from spreading onto other plants. A strong spray of water sends spider mites flying from plants, and insecticidal soap works wonders on soft-bodied insects like aphids.

If you are constantly having a problem with the same disease in a particular area, consider replacing the affected plants with disease-resistant varieties of the same species, or with another plant that is rarely afflicted. Gardening practices should also be considered. In my experience, powdery mildew is most likely to strike in areas with poor air circulation, where plants are too crowded and when soil has been allowed to dry out. Improving air movement by dividing plants and spacing them further apart may eliminate the problem.

Beebalm (right) can be prone to powdery mildew, a fungal disease that can weaken a plant enough to kill it. Avoid this problem by growing 'Marshall's Delight' (below) or other mildew-resistant varieties.

Insects often prefer plants that are weak or stressed. Many problems can be avoided by simply keeping the garden clean and the plants in the healthiest state possible. Promptly dispose of any diseased or insect-infested plants. Enlist nature's help: be aware of and encourage beneficial insects, such as ladybugs and lacewings, which feed on 'bad bugs' that destroy plants.

If you do run into a severe pest problem, take a sample of the affected plant parts into a garden centre. Let staff identify the problem and recommend the best and safest method of treatment. Leaf spots or discolouration, for example, may be due to disease, but can also be caused by a nutrient deficiency in the soil, by frost, cold or a severe lack of water.

53

Dividing Perennials

' ... *rejuvenate them...* '

Most perennials eventually need dividing. Some plants reach this stage in a few short years, others are likely to be fine for up to five years, and a few perennials can be left alone for ten or more years. However long it takes, at some point, most perennials should be divided. Dividing your plants will rejuvenate them, increase their health and flower production and provide you with a greater number of plants at no cost—other than a little time and effort.

While you are dividing plants, use the opportunity to replenish soil. Add lots of organic matter and a handful of bone meal before replanting. Refer to individual plant listings for specific information on how often each perennial needs to be divided.

Signs That a Perennial Needs Dividing

- Plants are overcrowded.
- The centre of the plant becomes weak or dies.
- Few or no blooms appear on mature plants that bloomed well before.
- Overall, the plant is smaller this season than in previous years.

Throw out old, weakened centres when dividing plants, and replant only the vigorous sections.

 When to Divide?

- Spring is the best time to divide most perennials.

- Divide them when new growth is at least 1–2 inches (2.5–5 cm), but less than 4 inches (10 cm) tall.

- Divide spring blooming plants when they have finished flowering.

- September is the best time to split and move peonies.

How to Divide Perennials

1. *Cut back foliage of larger plants by two-thirds. This makes plants easier to work with and allows more energy to be devoted to developing new roots. Avoid damaging new growth.*
2. *Carefully loosen the soil around the plants. Soil is easiest to work with when it is fairly dry. Lift out the entire clump, including as much soil as possible.*
3. **Method A: Large Perennials**
   Use a garden shovel to split the plant into two or three pieces. Each piece should have at least three stems and lots of roots.
4. **Method B: Small Perennials**
   Use a sharp knife to divide the root into two or three separate pieces. Make sure each piece has a growing point and some roots.
5. **Method C: Easily Separated Perennials**
   Some perennials can be easily pulled apart with your hands. Ensure that each set of leaves has its own stem and roots.
6. *Loosen the soil in the bottom of the original hole. Add a couple of inches (5 cm) of peat moss or fresh potting soil and mix in thoroughly. A handful of bone meal aids root development.*
7. *Firmly plant one segment into the old hole. Place other divisions elsewhere in the garden. In some plants, the centre portion dies out with age and should be discarded.*
8. *Pack soil firmly by tamping it with your feet.*
9. *Leave a slight rim of soil around new transplants to hold moisture more readily. Water well, and fertilize with a half-strength solution of 10–52–10.*

Sometimes a gardener tells me she is moving to a new house and wants to take some perennials from her old garden with her. I advise following the guidelines for dividing perennials as much as possible. However, a small plant, of a size that allows you to uproot its entire root system with a shovel, can be moved at any time up until 2–3 weeks before the ground freezes in fall. Moving plants later does not permit time for roots to adjust to their new home before winter arrives. Large plants, which are likely to suffer root damage in a move, are best left behind, unless you can move them in early spring.

The following quick-reference list tells you which method to use for dividing each perennial:

Method A

Aster
Beardtongue
Beebalm
Bellflower (tall ones)
Black-eyed Susan
Bleeding Heart
Blue Sage
Campion
Checker Mallow
Coneflower
Cornflower
Cranesbill
Daylily
Delphinium
Elephant-ears
False-sunflower

Fleabane
Fleeceflower
Globe Thistle
Globeflower
Goatsbeard
Goldenrod
Goutweed
Jacob's Ladder
Joe Pye Weed
Lady's Mantle
Masterwort
Meadow Rue
Meadowsweet
Monkshood
Obedient Plant

Painted Daisy
Peony
Phlox (garden type)
Plume Poppy
Poppy (Oriental)
Rayflower
Sage
Shasta Daisy
Snakeroot
Sneezeweed
Soapwort
Speedwell
Spurge
St. John's Wort
Yarrow

Method B

Anemone
Astilbe
Bishop's Hat
Blanketflower
Blue Fescue
Blue Himalayan
    Poppy
Blue Oat Grass
Candytuft
Catmint

Coralbell
Evening Primrose
Garden Mum
Hosta
Moor Grass
Ostrich Fern
Pasqueflower
Phlox (creeping types)
Pink

Potentilla
Pulmonaria
Snow-in-Summer
Solomon's Seal
Statice
Stonecrop
    (upright types)
Tickseed
Yucca

Method C

Bellflower
    (dwarf types)
Bitterroot
Creeping Jenny
Gentian
Hens & Chicks
Iris
Lamium

Liatris
Lily
Lily-of-the-Valley
Ornamental
    Onion
Primrose
Rockcress

Saxifrage
Sea Thrift
Shooting-star
Stonecrop
    (creeping types)
Strawberry
Thyme

Division is not recommended for some perennials, because it is difficult and does them more harm than good.

Do not divide:

Baby's Breath	Honeysuckle
Clematis	Hops
Flax	Lupin
Foxglove	Poppy (Iceland)
Foxtail Lily	Russian Sage
Gasplant	Sea Holly
Hollyhock	Statice

Winter Protection

'... plants are, after all, living things ...'

Most perennials have little trouble surviving winter where snow comes early and stays late. Even hardy perennials, however, may have difficulty when wind and severe cold arrive when the ground is still bare or only a little snow has fallen, and when midwinter thaws are followed by sudden hard freezes. Early warm periods before spring has arrived can also injure and kill poorly protected plants.

'Winter kill' is the result of roots and crowns drying out, or freezing, thawing and freezing again. It makes sense to protect your perennials by using a mulch. Mulching, especially in exposed areas of the garden, helps, as does piling extra snow on plants, especially on bare beds close to the house and under the eaves. Before the ground freezes in fall, be sure to water plants well.

The following points are useful for helping to protect your perennials from winter kill. In extreme conditions, though, even the most carefully protected plants may occasionally suffer or die over winter. Plants are, after all, living things and, like other living things, will eventually die. Sometimes we forget this, and expect plants to perform like machines, remaining in exactly the same state year after year.

What to Do in Fall

- Water frequently throughout the fall, especially during dry spells.

- In early fall, scatter a few handfuls of bone meal on the soil around your plants. This helps to strengthen their roots.

- The volume of soil in most containers is not adequate to prevent roots from freezing and plants dying over winter. In cold winter areas like ours, perennials growing in patio containers should be transplanted into the garden. Allow at least two to three weeks prior to freeze-up for roots to become established.

- Some gardeners cut back their perennials in fall, but we have found over the years that leaving pruning until spring increases plants' survival rates over winter. Growth left standing traps snow, and, for plants and roots, snow is the best protection against cold. Bishop's hat, lilies and peonies are exceptions; these plants should be cut back in fall.

- Just before the ground freezes in late fall, water all plants heavily again to prevent roots from being damaged in cold, dry soil.

Additional Care Required for Tender Perennials

Tender perennials include hybrid clematis and any out-of-zone plants that you are

Clematis vines have masses of flowers.

experimenting with in your garden.
(See pages 23–24 for an explanation of out-
of-zone plants.)

- As the ground starts to freeze in late fall,
  soak plants heavily.

- Once the ground has frozen to a depth
  of 2–4 inches (5–10 cm), cover tender
  plants with a hill of protective mulch
  10–12 inches (25–30 cm) high. An ideal
  mulch is light enough to permit air to
  penetrate, but dense enough to prevent
  severe cold from penetrating into the soil.
  Do not use plastic. Fallen tree leaves and
  grass clippings are not good materials for a

On warm fall days, many gardeners phone our greenhouses,
wondering if it is okay to cut back perennials. The answer is that, with
most perennials, it is better to wait until spring to do this, but if you
insist on cutting back your plants in fall, keep a few things in mind.
The following rules will result in a more spectacular show of flowers
next season:

- *Wait until plant leaves become brown and dry: green foliage helps*
  feed roots, and strong roots are needed for plants to get through
  winter intact. Some perennials, such as peonies, won't turn brown
  until after a hard frost.

- *Never cut back biennials or evergreen perennials, such as pinks and*
  elephant-ears. Cutting these plants back will at best prevent them
  from flowering next season, and at worst result in their death.

- *Don't cut back any perennials that were planted this year. New*
  plants need the extra protection that snow provides, and leaving top-
  growth intact helps trap snow on them.

❀✍ Throw light snow over exposed perennials and flowerbeds in early spring. This adds moisture and keeps the ground cool enough to prevent plants from starting to grow actively too early in the season.

protective mulch, because they rot when wet. Compost and dry peat moss make good mulches, and the boughs of ever-green trees, such as spruce, are also effective.

- Sprinkling garden soil over peat moss prevents the moss from blowing away.

What to Do in Winter

- Remember that snow provides moisture and acts as insulation to prevent plant damage or death caused by freezing and thawing during and after winter warm spells.

- When clearing snow from walks and driveways over winter, pile some soft snow over tender plants and onto flowerbeds that are underneath house overhangs. During periods of thaw, pile additional snow around mulched plants for extra insulation. Do not do this if you use a lot of salt on your walkways.

- If there is an unusually warm, dry spell in late winter, water exposed flowerbeds, particularly those on the south or west side of the house.

What to Do in Spring

- As soon as the garden is dry enough to walk on, clear away any debris left from fall. Cut back dead growth from perennials to about 2 inches (5 cm) high. Leave new green growth intact.

- Do not cut back evergreen perennials or biennials at all. Honeysuckle, big-petal clematis and golden clematis should be cut back only to where the vines begin to leaf out.

- Water sheltered plants and dry areas underneath house overhangs.

Additional Care Required for Tender Perennials

- Watch the native trees. As soon as their buds start to swell, it is time to begin removing protective mulch coverings. Lift mulch off with your hands, rather than pulling it off with a rake, to avoid damaging tender new growth.

- Mulches must be removed sooner from garden 'hot spots' where snow melts early, such as flowerbeds against the south wall of your house. Check underneath these mulches fairly regularly. As soon as you see any signs of growth, remove the mulch. If mulches are not removed at this point, the plants will attempt to grow through them. The result is weak, spindly growth and, occasionally, plant death.

- If there is a risk of frost within two or three days of removing mulch, protect the newly exposed growth by covering it with an old sheet or blanket overnight. Don't panic if you miss covering before an unexpected frost; freezing temperatures will kill only newly exposed growth, not crowns or roots. The plants will survive, but will be set back a bit and take longer to grow to full size.

- Do not be premature in assuming that a plant has died over winter. Not all plants grow at the same rate. Some, such as bleeding hearts, poke new shoots through the earth in early spring, while others, such as hostas, do not begin to grow until several weeks later.

- Distraught gardeners often appear at our greenhouses in early spring with plants that they have dug out of the garden, thinking that the plants have died over winter. Usually, swelling white buds on the roots confirm that they have survived winter rather well. Most of us have done this at one time or another; just put the plants back in the soil and let them grow.

- With any plant that you suspect didn't make it over winter, wait until late spring. Before uprooting it, gently pull away the surrounding soil with your fingers. If you see any greenery or white buds, the plant is still alive and merely taking its time to begin actively growing.

Anemone

Anemone nemorosa
Woodland Anemone, European Wood Anemone

Anemone sylvestris
Snowdrop Anemone, Windflower

Anemone χ hybrida
Japanese Anemone

🌸 lavender, rose, pink, cream, white

Anemone's delicate-looking flowers are a welcome sight in my garden at either end of summer. In early spring, woodland anemones form low carpets of white, pink or lavender flowers. Snowdrop anemones bloom profusely in late spring, with masses of showy, scented, nodding, white flowers, each 2 inches (5 cm) across and marked with a yellow centre. The long-lasting, satiny flowers give way to attractive, woolly, white seedheads. In late summer, Japanese anemones begin their show and continue blooming until fall frosts.

Height • Woodland Anemone: 4–5 inches (10–12.5 cm)
Snowdrop Anemone: 12–15 inches (30–38 cm)
Japanese Anemone: 18–36 inches (45–90 cm)

🌸🌿 'Anemone' comes from the Greek word *anemos* meaning 'wind,' hence the name 'windflower.'

Spread • All: 12–18 inches (30–45 cm)

Blooms • Woodland Anemone: early spring
Snowdrop Anemone: late spring
Japanese Anemone: late summer to fall

PLANTING

Seeding: Sow woodland and snowdrop anemones indoors in February. Cover seed slightly with soil mix; germination is sporadic and slow, 3–4 weeks. Sow outdoors in late fall. Snowdrop anemones may bloom the first year from seed, and woodland will bloom in the second. Sowing Japanese anemones is not recommended, because cultivars do not come true from seed.

The rosy flowers of 'Bressingham Glow' Japanese anemone brighten gardens when summer flowers start to fade.

Transplanting: Space 18 inches (45 cm) apart.

GROWING
Partial shade to sun.

Snowdrop and Japanese anemones will grow in sites that receive a half to a full day of sun, provided they have moist soil. Woodland anemones only in partial shade.

Woodland areas, rock gardens, groundcovers, mass plantings under trees, wildflower gardens, slopes, with bulbs and ferns. Japanese also in mixed borders.

Anemones dislike dry soil. Keep well-watered.

Divide Japanese anemones every 5 years. Allow other types to spread, unless you want more plants. See page 54, method B.

RECOMMENDED VARIETIES
Japanese Anemone

Bressingham Glow • semi-double, rosy-red flowers.

Pamina • semi-double, rosy-pink flowers.

Queen Charlotte • semi-double, light pink flowers.

Snowdrop anemones dance in spring breezes, and summer winds carry their fluffy seeds to new sites. They are the hardiest type of anemone.

Snowdrop and woodland anemones are usually available only under one of the names listed above. If you can find it, try 'Flore Pleno,' a rare, double-flowered snowdrop anemone, which blooms with white, pom-pom flowers in early summer.

TIPS

Be sure to choose only early-blooming varieties of Japanese anemone, as some bloom too late in the season to be of much use in northern gardens.

Although snowdrop anemones grow in sunny areas, their flowers last longest in partial shade. They bloom most heavily in spring, sporadically throughout the summer, and occasionally again in fall.

For Japanese anemones, avoid low sites where puddles form in spring after snow melts, or where water pools after a rainfall.

Woodland anemones are one of the first flowers to bloom in spring.

All anemones do well in acidic soil.

When woodland anemones are finished flowering, the plants go dormant and may completely disappear from the garden by mid- to late summer. Take care not to disturb them with summer planting. Disguise bare spots with ferns or hostas.

For bouquets, cut flowers when they have just started to open. They last 7–10 days in a vase.

Aster

Aster alpinus
Alpine Aster

Aster amellus
Italian Aster

Aster novi-belgii
New York Aster

Aster χ dumosus
Bushy Aster

purple, red, pink, white

Asters are prized by gardeners because they bring colour to the garden late in the season, when most other flowers are finished. I love the look of their brilliant blooms among the fall leaves. These long-lived perennials are native to North America, but they were taken abroad over 300 years ago, and some of today's best varieties have been produced by Europeans. The flowers have brilliant hues that you won't find in wild meadows. Alpine aster is an exception to most, because it blooms in spring, with single stems of lavender-blue or white flowers.

Other types of asters look similar and bloom in a wider range of colours. The main difference is in height and shape. New York asters are tall, upright plants, while Italian and bushy asters are shorter and dome-shaped.

Height • Alpine Aster: 6 inches (15 cm)
Italian Aster: 15–24 inches (38–60 cm)
New York Aster: 18–36 inches (45–90 cm)
Bushy Aster: 18–48 inches (45–120 cm)

Asters bloom for a month or longer in fall, with brightly coloured flowers.

Spread • Alpine Aster: 12 inches (30 cm)
Italian Aster: 18–24 inches (45–60 cm)
New York Aster: 18 inches (45 cm)
Bushy Aster: 18–24 inches (45–60 cm)

Blooms • Alpine Aster: spring
Italian Aster: late summer to frost
New York Aster: late summer to frost
Bushy Aster: late summer to frost

PLANTING

Seeding: Only alpine asters are easy to raise from seed. Sow indoors in February or March; germination 2–3 weeks. Seed needs light to germinate; do not cover with soil. Sow outdoors in early spring. Seeding other types is not recommended as germination is slow and sporadic, and the hybrid cultivars do not come true from seed.

Transplanting: Space alpine asters 12–15 inches (30–38 cm) apart, and the other types 18–24 inches (45–60 cm) apart.

65

GROWING

Sun to partial shade.

Tall varieties middle to back of border; dwarfs in small beds, rock gardens or near front of border.

Provide support for tall varieties in windy locations.

Keep well-watered. Water from the base of plants rather than overhead. Wet foliage can lead to disease.

Divide every 3 years, or when clumps start to die out in centre. Discard the old, woody centres. See page 54, method A.

RECOMMENDED VARIETIES
Alpine Aster

Goliath • 6 inches (15 cm) tall; bright purple-blue, single flowers; bigger blooms and brighter colours than the species.

Offset the daisy-like flowers of 'Violet Queen' Italian aster with spiky-leaved perennials such as bearded irises, daylilies or ornamental grasses.

Unlike most asters, the alpine aster blooms in spring.

Italian Aster

Violet Queen • 15–18 inches (38–45 cm) tall; rich, blue-purple, single flowers, 1–1½ inches (2.5–3.5 cm) across; forms a tight mound covered from top to bottom in flowers.

New York Aster

Crimson Brocade • 24–36 inches (60–90 cm) tall; masses of vibrant crimson, 1½-inch (3.5 cm), semi-double flowers; resistant to powdery mildew.

Winston Churchill • 18–24 inches (45–60 cm) tall; tons of deep red, single flowers, 1–1½ inches (2.5–3.5 cm) across; resistant to powdery mildew.

Bushy Aster

Jenny • 18–30 inches (45–75 cm) tall; lots of deep rose-red, double flowers.

Professor Kippenberg • 18–30 inches (45–75 cm) tall; masses of semi-double flowers; the best clear-blue colour of this species; an excellent old variety that has remained popular through the years.

✿ *Aster* means 'star' in Greek, referring to the appearance of the flowers.

New York asters are one of the most popular species. There are hundreds of varieties, with new ones being added each year. 'Crimson Brocade' is one of the best, for its brilliant colour and profusion of flowers.

TIPS

Choose early-blooming varieties of asters or those that are recommended for northern gardens. Most asters are quite hardy but many bloom too late in the season to be of much use here.

Asters are not at all fussy. They will grow in poor soil and need little attention except for an occasional watering when soil is dry.

Never crowd asters. These plants are susceptible to powdery mildew, a disease which is thwarted by good air circulation.

New York asters sometimes self-sow. To prevent this, just pinch off the finished flowers before seeds form. Alternatively, wait to see where seedlings sprout and uproot any that are unwanted.

Grow asters if deer are a problem in your garden; they will not eat these plants.

Bushy asters are large plants, with lots of flowers for long-lasting fall bouquets.

Asters are splendid cutflowers, lasting up to 2 weeks in bouquets. Cut when the majority of flowers in a spray is open. Flowers cut too early will not open.

OTHER RECOMMENDED SPECIES

Aster novae-angliae (New England Aster, Michaelmas Daisy): 36–48 inches (90–120 cm) tall and 24–36 inches (60–90 cm) wide; available in a wide range of colours; clusters of showy flowers from late summer to frost. The variety 'Harrington's Pink' blooms in soft salmon-pink.

Aster sedifolius 'Nanus' (Dwarf Rhone Aster): 10–15 inches (25–38 cm) tall; compact plants with masses of small, starry, lavender-blue flowers from midsummer to fall.

Astilbe

Astilbe χ hybrida
False Spirea,
False Goatsbeard

red, coral, pink, lavender, white

Of all the shade-loving plants, astilbe is my favourite. Few other shade plants have such showy flowers. Astilbe's flowers are gorgeous, graceful plumes on tall stems above airy foliage. Grow these perennials with bold-leaved plants such as pulmonaria, hostas and elephant-ears, or with fine-textured plants like bleeding hearts and ostrich ferns. There are over 100 kinds in cultivation today. Choose a mixture of varieties to extend the blooming period.

Height • 12–36 inches (30–90 cm)

Spread • 12–24 inches (30–60 cm)

Blooms • all summer

PLANTING

Seeding: Not recommended. Germination is slow and seedlings are not true to type; plants will take 3 years to bloom.

Roots: Plant bare roots in early spring. The 'eyes' (sprouts, like a potato's) should be about half an inch (1 cm) below soil surface.

Transplanting: Space 12–18 inches (30–45 cm) apart.

GROWING

Light to partial shade. An area that receives only morning sun or a couple of hours of sun in the afternoon is ideal.

Shade and woodland gardens, as an accent plant, in small groups or massed as groundcover. Front to middle of border.

Water regularly. Plants will not tolerate dry soil.

Divide every 3–4 years to maintain vigour. Ensure each division has 3–4 eyes. See page 54, method B.

RECOMMENDED VARIETIES

Bressingham Beauty • 30–36 inches (75–90 cm) tall; lightly scented; early-blooming; the richest pure pink yet seen in astilbes.

Bronze Elegance • dark bronze, finely divided foliage; late bloomer.

Cattleya • 18 inches (45 cm) tall; orchid-pink flowers; late bloomer; longer blooming than many.

Astilbes thrive in a site with half-day sun as long as the soil is constantly moist. The less intense rays of morning sun are best.

Deutschland • 18–24 inches (45–60 cm) tall; short, compact plumes; the best white-flowered astilbe on the market; blooms early.

Fanal • 24 inches (60 cm) tall; full, narrow, dark red plumes; begins blooming slightly earlier than others.

Peach Blossom • 18–24 inches (45–60 cm) tall and 12–18 inches (30–45 cm) wide; soft peach-pink flowers; fragrant; blooms early.

Sprite • 15–18 inches (40–45 cm) tall; soft pink plumes over deeply cut, dark green foliage; plants more dainty than others; exceptional pest resistance; late bloomer; the Perennial Plant Association's 1994 Plant of the Year.

TIPS

Astilbes have a reputation for being 'fussy,' but we find they are easily satisfied, as long as you choose the right spot. Simply avoid dry

Astilbes blend nicely with annual flowers, which help fill in gaps until perennials reach mature size.

soils, windy locations and areas where the snow is last to melt in spring. Brown, curled leaf tips are a sign that plants are unhappy with their site.

Add peat moss or leaf mould when planting to enrich soil and improve water retention.

Astilbe does well in acidic soil.

Astilbes are what we call 'heavy feeders'— they use up a lot of nutrients. These plants really benefit from regular applications of fertilizer.

Deadheading will not extend the blooming period, but I remove the finished flowers anyway because I think they detract from the plants' appearance.

Allow flowers to open fully before cutting for bouquets. They generally last up to 2 weeks.

For dried flowers, cut when blooms are just beginning to open. Let a few leaves remain for added interest. Stand stems upright in a vase without water.

A mixture of colours in a mass planting of astilbe creates an arresting display. Grow several varieties to extend the blooming period.

Baby's Breath

Gypsophila paniculata
Chalk Plant, Common Baby's Breath

Gypsophila repens
Creeping Baby's Breath

white, pink

Common baby's breath blooms so profusely that a single plant will provide enough flowers for fresh bouquets and dried arrangements, as well as extras to share with friends or neighbours. In the garden, these lacy-stemmed plants form clouds of flowers throughout the summer. Creeping baby's breath is not as well known. It blooms in spring with masses of blooms on shorter stems, and spreads into a wide mat of foliage.

Height • Common Baby's Breath:
24–36 inches (60–90 cm)
Creeping Baby's Breath: 6–8 inches
(15–20 cm)

Spread • Common Baby's Breath:
36 inches (90 cm)
Creeping Baby's Breath: 12–15 inches
(30–38 cm)

Blooms • Common Baby's Breath:
all summer
Creeping Baby's Breath: late spring
to early summer

Baby's breath is one of the best flowers for fresh bouquets and dried arrangements.

Creeping baby's breath adds a frothy cloud of spring flowers to rock gardens. Add these short-stemmed flowers to miniature bouquets and dried arrangements.

PLANTING

Seeding: Indoors in February or March; germination 5–10 days. Seed needs light to germinate; do not cover with soil mix. Sow outdoors in early spring. Plants will bloom the first year. The varieties 'Perfecta,' 'Bristol Fairy' and 'Pink Fairy' cannot be grown from seed because they are sterile. Professional growers usually raise these plants from cuttings.

Transplanting: Space creeping baby's breath 18–24 inches (45–60 cm) apart, and common baby's breath 36 inches (90 cm) apart.

GROWING

Common baby's breath in sun; creeping baby's breath in sun to partial shade.

Common baby's breath in mixed flowerbeds, cutting gardens. Middle to back of border. Creeping baby's breath in rock gardens, trailing over the wall of a raised bed. Front of border.

Do not divide. These plants usually die if you attempt to divide or move them, because it is difficult to dig up enough of their roots. Baby's breath has a long, thick taproot (like that of a dandelion, but bigger).

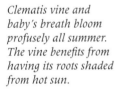

Baby's breath does well in hot, dry areas of the garden.

RECOMMENDED VARIETIES
Common Baby's Breath

Bristol Fairy • 24–36 inches (60–90 cm) tall; lots of large, pure white, double flowers; the largest and longest-blooming of the white, double-flowered plants, from early summer to fall; sterile, does not produce seed.

Pacifica • 30 inches (75 cm) tall; pink, single flowers.

Perfecta • 24 inches (60 cm) tall; white, double flowers twice the size of 'Bristol Fairy,' but fewer; sterile.

Pink Fairy • 24–36 inches (60–90 cm) tall; large, light pink, double flowers; similar and a great companion to 'Bristol Fairy'; sterile.

Creeping Baby's Breath

Usually available only under one of the names listed above. 'Alba' has pure white flowers, and 'Rosea' has light pink flowers.

Clematis vine and baby's breath bloom profusely all summer. The vine benefits from having its roots shaded from hot sun.

TIPS

The name *Gypsophila* means 'chalk-loving,' indicating this plant's preference for 'chalky' (alkaline) soil. Most garden soils are adequate.

Use common baby's breath as a 'filler' to hide the withering foliage of plants such as spring-flowering bulbs (tulips and daffodils, etc.) and Oriental poppies.

Remove the first flowering stalks as blossoms fade, and common baby's breath will continue to produce flowers occasionally until frost.

Common baby's breath is the type often found at florists. It is most often used in mixed bouquets and makes an outstanding 'filler,' usually lasting more than 2 weeks after cutting. Cut stems when two-thirds of the flowers have opened. Flowers cut when not in full bloom usually do not open at all.

For drying, pick when flowers are fully open. Hang stems upside-down in a shaded, airy place, or put them into a large basket or vase and allow them to dry upright.

Baby's breath, silver mound sage and dwarf spruce thrive in hot, sunny gardens.

Beardtongue

***Penstemon digitalis*
'Husker Red'**

Husker Red
Beardtongue,
White Penstemon

 white

The variety 'Husker Red' is so spectacular that we don't bother growing the plain, green-leafed beardtongue. 'Husker Red' has dark, burgundy-bronze leaves and stems, and creamy-white, speckle-throated, tubular flowers that look a little like miniature foxgloves. We grow this sturdy, upright perennial with variegated moor grass and yellow tickseed. Dwarf Shasta daisies or other white-flowered plants also provide a striking show.

Height • 18–24 inches (45–60 cm)

Spread • 18–24 inches (45–60 cm)

Blooms • late spring to early summer

PLANTING

Seeding: Indoors in February or March. Seed needs light to germinate; press seed lightly on top of soil. Sow outdoors in early spring or late fall. Plants will bloom the second year.

'Husker Red' beardtongue has striking and unusual foliage.

Transplanting: Space 12–18 inches (30–45 cm) apart.

GROWING

Sun to light shade; must have well-drained soil.

Mixed flowerbeds. Middle to back of border.

Divide every 2 years.
See page 54, method A.

Recommended Varieties

'**Husker Red**' is the only variety that we recommend.

Tips

Do not plant in areas where melting snow forms puddles in spring.

Beardtongue is drought-tolerant and grows well in gravelly, sandy or acidic soil. Deer will not bother these plants.

Cut these striking flowers to add to mixed bouquets.

Other Recommended Species

Penstemon pinifolius (Pineleaf Beardtongue): 10–15 inches (25–38 cm) tall and 12 inches (30 cm) wide; very fine leaves that resemble pine needles; bright scarlet flowers from early to late summer; plants resemble mounded, miniature evergreen shrubs; striking.

Penstemon χ hybrida (Hybrid Beardtongue): 24–30 inches (60–75 cm) tall and 18 inches (45 cm) wide; blooms all summer with 2-inch (5 cm) tubular flowers on long, thin spikes. The variety 'Prairie Dusk' has vivid, rose-purple flowers. 'Prairie Fire' is a good partner; it grows slightly taller and blooms in bright scarlet.

Have a close look at beardtongue (above) to see how it earns its name. Each flower appears to be sticking out its tongue. This is a stamen, which may be hairy or bearded. The flowers attract hummingbirds and the unusual foliage colour of 'Husker Red' (left) is an attractive contrast in gardens all season.

Beebalm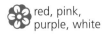

Monarda didyma
Oswego Tea,
Sweet Bergamot

red, pink,
purple, white

Gardeners love beebalm for its lemony-mint scent, and its showy, brightly coloured flowers are a traffic-stopper. In summer, when beebalm is blooming in the show garden outside the greenhouses, customers constantly ask: 'What is that big plant with the pink flowers?' The whole plant is fragrant and is loved by butterflies and hummingbirds.

Height • 36–48 inches (90–120 cm)

Spread • 24–36 inches (60–90 cm)

Blooms • summer through early fall

Beebalm's aromatic leaves are a source of flavouring for Earl Grey tea. This plant also goes by the name 'Oswego Tea.' During the time of the Boston Tea Party, when black tea was unavailable, people living near Oswego, New York used beebalm's leaves for tea.

PLANTING

Seeding: Not recommended, as the best varieties are not available in seed. Newer cultivars are so greatly improved over species plants that they are the only ones we recommend growing.

Transplanting: Space 36 inches (90 cm) apart. Do not crowd plants.

GROWING

Sun to light shade. Avoid partially shaded areas near buildings, where there is little air movement.

Mixed borders, cutting gardens, mass plantings, in clumps or centre of flowerbed. Middle to back of border.

Water beebalm in the morning, at the base of the plants. Try not to wet the foliage; keeping leaves dry helps to prevent powdery mildew.

Divide every 3–4 years to prevent overcrowding. See page 54, method A.

Recommended Varieties

Beauty of Cobham • light pink flowers and purple-tinted foliage; a striking colour combination; mildew-resistant.

Gardenview Scarlet • rich, crimson-scarlet flowers; mildew-resistant; the best red variety.

Marshall's Delight • large, hot-pink flowers on strong stems; highly rust- and mildew-resistant; a Canadian variety.

Twins • dark pink flowers; mildew-resistant.

'Gardenview Scarlet' is an improved, mildew-resistant variety.

Tips

Plant beebalm near a walkway so you will brush the plant on passing, and release its pungent fragrance.

Beebalm does best in rich, moist soil; add lots of compost or peat moss before planting to help retain moisture.

Deadhead regularly to prolong blooming period.

Beebalm is susceptible to attacks of powdery mildew. To prevent this disease, don't crowd the plants; good air circulation helps ward it off. Better still, grow only newer, mildew-resistant varieties.

Deer will not eat beebalm. Grow it if deer are a problem in your yard.

Cut beebalm's flowers often to mix in bouquets.

Oil of beebalm is sometimes used commercially in the perfume industry. Leaves have a strong, lemony-mint fragrance. Pick and dry them to use in potpourris. Dry the flowerheads for added colour.

Cut entire flowerstalks for dried arrangements. Pick when flowers are fully open but before they begin to lose central petals, and strip off the leaves. Hang in bunches upside-down to dry for about a week.

'Marshall's Delight' (left) is one of the best beebalm varieties. The bushy plants have large, hot-pink flowers and are highly resistant to mildew and rust. The variety was named for plant breeder Henry Marshall, who worked for Agriculture Canada for 40 years, mainly at the Morden, Manitoba research station.

Bellflower

Campanula carpatica
Carpathian Bellflower,
Carpathian Harebell

**Campanula
glomerata**
Clustered Bellflower,
Danesblood Bellflower

**Campanula
persicifolia**
Peachleaf Bellflower,
Persian Bellflower

**Campanula
cochlearifolia**
Fairy Thimble,
Spiral Bellflower

 blue, purple,
white

*Bellflowers are a wonderfully diverse group,
ranging from tall, upright plants to low, creeping
mats. Carpathian bellflowers form compact
mounds, with flowers so large they seem out of
character with the plants. Clustered bellflowers are
sturdy, upright plants that spread slowly into open
clumps, with flowers in tight clusters on tall stems.
Peachleaf bellflowers are stately, upright plants,
with large bells held high above leaves. Spiral
bellflowers spread into low mats, with masses of
flowers in early summer.*

Height • Carpathian Bellflower:
   12 inches (30 cm)
   Clustered Bellflower: 18–24 inches
      (45–60 cm)
   Peachleaf Bellflower: 24–36 inches
      (60–90 cm)
   Spiral Bellflower: 4 inches (10 cm)

Spread • Carpathian Bellflower:
   12 inches (30 cm)
   Clustered Bellflower: 24 inches (60 cm)
   Peachleaf Bellflower:
      15–18 inches (38–45 cm)
   Spiral Bellflower: 24 inches
      (60 cm) or more

Blooms • Carpathian Bellflower: all
      summer
   Clustered Bellflower: late spring to
      early summer
   Peachleaf Bellflower: late spring
      to midsummer
   Spiral Bellflower: early summer

PLANTING

Seeding: Sow indoors in February or
   March; germination 18–21 days. Sow
   outdoors in early spring. Carpathian
   bellflowers will bloom the first year.

Transplanting: Space Carpathian
   bellflowers 8 inches (20 cm) apart,
   clustered bellflowers 15 inches
   (38 cm) apart, and peachleaf bellflowers
   18 inches (30–45 cm) apart. These
   bellflowers look best planted in groups.

Spiral bellflowers spread into wide mats, so group planting is not necessary. Space 12 inches (30 cm) apart.

GROWING

Sun to partial shade.

Carpathian and spiral bellflowers in rock gardens, trailing over walls, edging beds. Front of border. Clustered and peachleaf bellflowers in mixed beds. Middle to back of border.

Keep bellflowers well-watered during periods of drought. These plants do not like to dry out.

Divide Carpathian bellflowers every 3 or 4 years to rejuvenate plants. See page 54, method C. Clustered bellflowers spread more rapidly than others and may need to be divided more often. Peachleaf bellflowers can be divided every 3–4 years, but you may find it easier just to replace plants that have lost vigour with new seedlings. Use method A for these two; see page 54. Spiral bellflowers do not need to be divided.

Bellflowers are among the longest-blooming perennials.

81

Clustered bellflowers bloom with masses of royal-purple or white flowers early to midsummer. These plants spread quickly, but are not aggressive. They are one of the hardiest bellflowers.

Gardeners often refer to Carpathian bellflowers (above) as 'Blue Clips' or 'White Clips.' These are actually variety names rather than common names for these plants. We prefer the varieties 'Jewel' and 'Karl Foerster' because they have larger and more flowers on more compact plants. Here, Carpathian bellflowers grow with creeping stonecrop.

RECOMMENDED VARIETIES
Carpathian Bellflower

Jewel • blue; very large flowers; more compact than the species.

Karl Foerster • deep violet-blue; more flowers than species; long-lasting blooms; smaller plants than 'Jewel.'

Spiral Bellflower

Elizabeth Oliver • powder-blue, double flowers; very unusual.

Peachleaf and **clustered** bellflowers are often available only under one of the names listed above.

TIPS

Clustered and peachleaf bellflowers self-sow readily. Transplant seedlings as desired; unwanted ones are easily uprooted.

Deadhead Carpathian and peachleaf bellflowers to prolong blooming period. Remember to leave some faded flowers on plants if you want seedlings.

Clustered bellflowers are more drought-tolerant than others.

Clustered bellflowers and peachleaf bellflowers are splendid cutflowers. For the longest-lasting bouquets, cut when the first buds on the stem are clearly showing colour but have not yet opened. They generally last 7–10 days after cutting.

OTHER RECOMMENDED SPECIES

Campanula dasyantha (Shaggy Bellflower): 3 inches (7.5 cm) tall and 12 inches (30 cm) wide; huge, sky-blue flowers on 3-inch (7.5 cm) stems; mat-forming plants; blooms early summer.

Campanula medium (Canterbury Bells): 24–36 inches (60–90 cm) tall and 15–18 inches (38–45 cm) wide; blue, white or rose flowers in summer; biennial, be sure to allow a few flowers to go to seed.

Campanula portenschlagiana (Dalmatian Bellflower): 4–6 inches (10–15 cm) tall and 12 inches (30 cm) wide; l-inch (2.5 cm) blue or purple flowers late spring to summer; kidney-shaped leaves; great for rock gardens or trailing over walls.

Campanula poscharskyana (Serbian Bellflower): 3–5 inches (7.5–12.5 cm) tall and 12–18 inches (30–45 cm) wide; lavender-blue, star-shaped flowers in summer; good spreader and trails more than Dalmatian; excellent for rock gardens, edging borders, trailing over walls; very drought-resistant.

The long-stemmed blooms of peachleaf bellflowers (above) are marvellous in bouquets. The name Campanulla *means 'bell-like' in Latin. Spiral bellflowers (below) provide masses of bell-shaped, white or blue flowers for rock gardens and border fronts.*

Bishop's Hat

**Epimedium χ
rubrum**
Red Barrenwort

red

*Stephen Raven, who works at our greenhouses,
has more than 300 perennials in his garden.
Bishop's hat is one of his favourite plants. He grows
it under two large trees, a shady and often dry spot
during summer months. There, bishop's hat
provides a splash of colour, with clusters of small,
starry flowers in early spring. The thick, upright
foliage remains attractive all season, and stays
fresh-looking even in conditions that cause nearby
plants to wilt.*

Height • 6–12 inches (15–30 cm)

Spread • 12 inches (30 cm)

Blooms • mid- to late spring

Bishop's hat is
one of the few plants
that does well in either
moist or dry soil.

PLANTING

Seeding: Not recommended. Germination is
sporadic and plants will grow slowly.

Transplanting: Space 12–15 inches
(30–38 cm) apart.

GROWING

Partial to full shade.

Woodland and rock
gardens, accent
plants,
groundcover.
Front to middle of
border.

Bishop's hat does
not need to be
divided. If you
want more plants,
however, divide
every 3 years.
See page 54,
method B.

RECOMMENDED
VARIETIES

Usually available
only under one of
the names listed
above.

Tips

Bishop's hat is an erect-growing plant that does well in either moist or dry soil. It grows well underneath trees, and in acidic soil near spruce or pine trees.

Gardeners often ask for 'deer-proof' plants. Bishop's hat is one.

For dried arrangements, cut flowers before they fully open. Hang upside-down in bunches to dry.

In late fall, cut foliage back almost to ground level. The following spring, the flowers will rise above the new foliage. If left unpruned, the flowers will be almost hidden beneath the leaves.

Other Recommended Species

Epimedium χ versicolour 'Sulphureum' (Bicolour Barrenwort): 6–9 inches (15–23 cm) tall and 15–18 inches (38–45 cm) wide; bright yellow flowers with pale yellow sepals; the best variety for dry, shaded areas; blooms middle to late spring.

Epimedium χ youngianum (Young's Barrenwort): 6–8 inches (15–20 cm) tall and 8 inches (20 cm) wide; more flowers per stem than other types; light pink or white flowers; the last of the epimediums to bloom in spring.

Most gardeners grow bishop's hat for its attractive foliage. In spring, the green, heart-shaped leaves are tinged in pink, and in fall they turn bronze-red. The name 'bishop's hat' refers to the flowers, which look like tiny replicas of their namesake. Each stem bears 15–20 flowers.

Bitterroot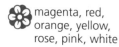

Lewisia columbiana
Columbia Bitterroot

Lewisia cotyledon
(has no common name)

Lewisia rediviva
Bitterroot Lewisia

86

magenta, red, orange, yellow, rose, pink, white

Bitterroot is a favourite of our perennials manager, Bob Stadnyk. Watching him unpack a new shipment of these plants, you'd have to smile—it's like watching a child on Christmas morning. Bitterroot arrives in 'bare-root' form, wrapped in newspaper without soil, with some plants still in full bloom. Bob exclaims over each one: 'Look at the colour! Isn't it beautiful!' Most gardeners share his delight after discovering these charming but relatively uncommon plants.

Height • Columbia Bitterroot: 6–8 inches (15–20 cm)
L. cotyledon: 4–5 inches (10–12.5 cm)
Bitterroot Lewisia: $1^1/_2$ inches (3.5 cm)

Spread • Columbia Bitterroot: 5–6 inches (12.5–15 cm)
L. cotyledon: 8–10 inches (20–25 cm)
Bitterroot Lewisia: 3–4 inches (7.5–10 cm)

Blooms • Columbia Bitterroot: spring
L. cotyledon: most of summer
Bitterroot Lewisia: spring

PLANTING

Seeding: Only *L. cotyledon*; the others are difficult to grow from seed. Sow indoors in February; germination is often slow and sporadic. Outdoors in early spring. Plants will bloom the second year.

The name 'bitterroot' refers to the bitter taste of this plant's roots. Native American Indians used to boil and eat the roots.

Transplanting: Space 6–8 inches (15–20 cm) apart. Mix very coarse sand into soil before planting and add more around the crowns, so that they are sitting on pure sand. This prevents the crowns from rotting.

L. cotyledon *brightens up summer gardens. 'Sunset Hybrids' (above) blooms in a great range of vivid colours.*

Growing

Sun.

Rock gardens, mixed flowerbeds, edging paths. Front of border.

Bitterroot should not be divided. If you want more plants, you can divide only *L. cotyledon*. Do so in early September. See page 54, method C.

Recommended Varieties

L. cotyledon

Regenbogen • extra-large flowers, and more of them than the species; more striping than other strains.

Sunset Hybrids • wide range of intense colours, including pink, yellow, orange, magenta, red and white.

Bitterroot lewisia and Columbia bitterroot are usually available only under one of the names listed above.

Lots of large flowers with marked stripes make L. cotyledon 'Regenbogen' an outstanding variety. Regularly pinching off the finished blooms results in even more flowers.

Bitterroot is the official state flower of Montana. It is illegal to dig plants from the wild in that state.

TIPS

These small plants are remarkable for their flowers. Foliage grows into tight rosettes only a few inches tall. Columbia bitterroot and *L. cotyledon* bloom with clusters of gorgeous flowers on slender stalks held high above the leaves. Bitterroot lewisia's huge flowers sit just on top of the leaves; each bloom is close to half the plant's width.

L. cotyledon makes a wonderful addition to rock gardens, because it begins to bloom when many other rockery plants have finished flowering.

Bitterroot grows well in rocky soil. In the wild, these plants are found on screes—mountain slopes covered with stones that slide when you walk on them. Bitterroot does best when not competing for nutrients, so keep beds well-weeded.

Bitterroot lewisia is considered a collector's plant. The species name *rediviva* means 'brought back to life.' Two-year-old herbarium specimens have been known to send up fresh leaves! (A herbarium is a systematically arranged collection of dried plants, often used for reference by students of botany.)

Bitterroot lewisia goes dormant after flowering, only to reappear and bloom gloriously the following spring. By early summer, these plants completely disappear from the garden, so mark their spot and be careful not to disturb them when working in the garden. To minimize the bare spots, grow hens & chicks, saxifrage, sea thrift or cheddar pinks nearby.

Bitterroot has a long blooming period and does well in hot, dry locations.

89

Columbia bitterroot blooms in spring with bright flowers that stand well above the leaves. Provide lots of moisture while plants are blooming and temperatures are hot, but hold back on watering in cooler weather.

Black-eyed Susan

Rudbeckia fulgida
Showy Coneflower

yellow

As a child, I used to pick bouquets of the black-eyed Susans that grew wild along roadsides in Saskatchewan. They were beautiful, but too spindly and weed-like for most gardens. The new hybrids are more vigorous, compact, branching plants with masses of bright flowers on strong stems. Black-eyed Susan blooms all summer and into fall, lasting through a couple of frosts.

Height • 18–30 inches (45–75 cm)

Spread • 24 inches (60 cm)

Blooms • summer to early fall

PLANTING

Seeding: Indoors in February or March; germination 10–15 days. Sow outdoors in early spring. Plants will bloom the first year.

Transplanting: Space 12–18 inches (30–45 cm) apart.

GROWING

Sun to partial shade.

Mixed flowerbeds, cutting gardens, mass plantings. Middle to back of border.

Divide every 3–4 years. See page 54, method A.

Black-eyed Susan blooms all summer.

Grow black-eyed Susan wherever you want a warm splash of summer colour.

RECOMMENDED VARIETIES

Goldsturm • 18–24 inches (45–60 cm) tall; masses of 3–4 inch daisy-like flowers, deep yellow with black centres; very compact plants.

TIPS

Black-eyed Susan is drought-tolerant and grows well in poor soil. These plants are rarely troubled by insects or disease, and deer will not eat them.

I love black-eyed Susans in mass plantings with blue or Russian sage. They look great in mixed flowerbeds with Shasta daisies, asters, blue fescue or blue oat grass. The silvery foliage of sages also provides a nice effect.

Cut flowers for bouquets when they begin to open. They last about 10 days in a vase.

'Goldsturm' is vigorous, compact and far superior to older varieties.

Blanketflower

**Gaillardia
grandiflorum**
Gaillardia

red, orange, yellow

I remember blanketflowers growing wild in meadows. Apparently, these plants once grew in such profusion that they created a brightly coloured blanket of flowers over North American plains and prairies. This led to the name 'blanketflower.' The blanketflowers that we grow in our gardens are sturdier plants, with slightly larger flowers that bloom over a longer period. These flowers also have more red in their petals than do their wild relatives.

Height • 6–36 inches (15–90 cm)

Spread • 18–24 inches (45–60 cm)

Blooms • early summer to frost

PLANTING

Seeding: Indoors in February; germination 7–14 days. Sow outdoors in early spring. Plants started indoors will usually bloom the first season.

Transplanting: Space 10–12 inches (25–30 cm) apart.

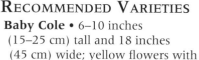 Blanketflower blooms all summer, with masses of vivid flowers.

GROWING

Sun.

Mixed flowerbeds, cutting gardens, mass plantings. Front to middle of border.

Divide every 3 years. See page 54, method B.

RECOMMENDED VARIETIES

Baby Cole • 6–10 inches (15–25 cm) tall and 18 inches (45 cm) wide; yellow flowers with red bands.

Goblin • 12 inches (30 cm) tall and 18 inches (45 cm) wide; red petals with yellow edges; commonly considered the best variety.

Monarch Strain • 24–36 inches (60–90 cm) tall and 24 inches (60 cm) wide; mixed shades of yellow, copper, rust and 2-toned flowers; larger flowers than most.

Blanketflower thrives in hot, dry and windy areas, full sun and poor soil; it needs little supplementary watering. This is one of the longest-blooming perennials.

TIPS

Do not plant in low-lying areas where puddles form in spring after snow melts. Overly wet soil can be fatal.

Deadhead regularly to prolong blooming period, but leave some faded flowers if you want plants to reseed. Dig up and transplant or discard seedlings as they appear.

Cut flowers for bouquets when they are fully open. They generally last 10–14 days after cutting.

For dried arrangements, harvest flowers before they fully open. Hang upside-down to dry.

The dwarf variety 'Baby Cole' (left) is great for rock gardens and edging. 'Goblin' (opposite) is slightly taller and is a versatile, outstanding plant for sunny spots.

Bleeding Heart

Dicentra formosa
Fernleaf Bleeding
Heart, Pacific Bleeding
Heart, Western
Bleeding Heart

Dicentra spectabilis
Common Bleeding
Heart, Valentine
Flower

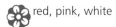 red, pink, white

 Bleeding hearts
are elegant, long-lived
perennials.

Bleeding hearts are lovely plants for shaded gardens. The common bleeding heart is the most familiar to many gardeners. It blooms in spring, with long, arching stems of deep pink or white-tipped flowers. The blue-green, cut-leaf foliage provides an attractive background for other flowers. Fernleaf bleeding hearts bloom all summer. Their flowers are smaller and rather square-shaped, in pink, white or red.

Height • Common Bleeding Heart:
24–36 inches (60–90 cm)
Fernleaf Bleeding Heart: 8–15 inches
(23–38 cm)

Spread • Common Bleeding Heart:
36 inches (90 cm)
Fernleaf Bleeding Heart: 8–24 inches
(20–60 cm) or more

Blooms • Common Bleeding Heart:
mid- to late spring
Fernleaf Bleeding Heart: midspring to
late summer

PLANTING

Seeding: Not recommended, because it takes too long for plants to reach maturity.

Roots: Plant in spring. Bleeding heart roots are brittle and must be handled carefully. Plants should bloom the first year.

Transplanting: Space fernleaf bleeding hearts 18 inches (45 cm) apart, and common bleeding hearts 18–24 inches (45–60 cm) apart.

A row of bleeding hearts along the driveway is attractive even when the plants are not blooming.

GROWING

Common bleeding hearts in partial shade. Fernleaf bleeding hearts in partial sun to shade. Morning sun is best; moist soil.

Common bleeding hearts as feature plants, in groups; middle to back of border. Fernleaf bleeding hearts in woodland, rock and shade gardens; front to middle of border.

Bleeding hearts are best left undisturbed. If you want more plants, divide after 3–4 years, in fall. See page 54, method A.

RECOMMENDED VARIETIES
Fernleaf Bleeding Heart

Bacchanal • 12–14 inches (30–35 cm) tall and 15–18 inches (38–45 cm) wide; dark cherry-red flowers.

Langtrees • 8–15 inches (20–38 cm) tall and 15–18 inches (38–45 cm) wide; white flowers and blue-green foliage; long-bloomer; late spring to fall.

Luxuriant • 10–15 inches (25–38 cm) tall and 18–24 inches (45–60 cm) wide; deep carmine-pink flowers; compact, mounded plants; long-bloomer; late spring to late fall.

Zestful • 12 inches (30 cm) tall and 8–15 inches (20–38 cm) wide; large, rose-red flowers with a light scent.

Common Bleeding Heart

Usually available only under one of the names listed above. 'Alba' has an impressive display of pure-white flowers, and is somewhat less vigorous.

Although these plants are commonly referred to as fernleaf bleeding hearts, technically that name is assigned to a different species: Dicentra exima. *The two species look very similar, but we prefer* Dicentra formosa *(below) because it has a longer blooming period.*

Tips

Do not plant bleeding hearts in hot or windy areas of the garden. These plants prefer moist soil. In extremely hot or dry conditions, common types go dormant by midsummer. With less sun and moist soil, however, the blue-green foliage remains attractive through most of the season.

Fernleaf bleeding hearts spread by underground rhizomes. Plant several in shade under trees, and they will quickly spread to fill the area with flowers and foliage.

Add sprigs of bleeding heart flowers and foliage to mixed bouquets.

Deer will not eat bleeding hearts.

One glance at bleeding heart's flowers will tell you how these plants got their name. The flowers resemble pink hearts with drops of blood at the tips. One gardener tells us he also knows these plants as 'naked-lady-in-a-bath.' Turn an individual flower upside-down and gently pull apart the two pink wings to expose the white lady in her bath. Another gardener says she remembers her mother peeling apart the flower in a different manner and telling her the love story of a prince and princess.

Blue Fescue

Festuca glauca
Blue Grass,
Sheep's Fescue

 blue

Gardeners often fight to keep grass out of the garden, but blue fescue is an exception. Ornamental grasses make wonderful additions to flowerbeds, and blue fescue is one of the best available. These handsome plants form tidy mounds of wiry, steel-blue foliage, with tan-coloured flowerheads on short stems in summer.

Height • 12–18 inches (30–45 cm)

Spread • 15–18 inches (38–45 cm)

Blooms • summer

PLANTING

Seeding: Indoors in February or March; germination 15–21 days. Sow outdoors in late fall. Keep in mind that seedlings may not have the same vivid blue colouring as parent plants.

Transplanting: Space 6–12 inches (15–30 cm) apart.

GROWING

Sun to light shade.

Rock gardens, accent plants, mass plantings, on slopes, in geometric patterns in small areas or as an edging for flower beds. Front of border.

Divide every 4–5 years. See page 54, method B.

Blue fescue is a tidy, clump-forming ornamental grass.

Recommended Varieties

Azurit • the bluest fescue; plants slightly more compact and do not produce seedheads as freely as others; long period of striking blue foliage.

Elijah Blue • good strong blue colour; variety named for the son of Greg Allman and Cher.

Tips

For best colour, shear plants back to about 2 inches (5 cm) tall in early spring. Plants in shaded areas will be less blue than those in sunny areas.

Blue fescue is drought-tolerant and grows well in hot, dry, windy locations.

One gardener told us he had planted 18 blue fescues together, arranged to resemble a stream running from his fountain through his rock garden.

I like to snip flowerheads to add to mixed bouquets. If you want to dry seedheads, harvest while still green and hang in bunches upside-down to dry.

If you don't like the look of the seedheads in the garden, just snip them off to tidy plants up.

Blue fescue mixes well with fernleaf bleeding hearts and Asiatic lilies (above).
Use blue fescue (left) as an alternative to silver mound sage for striking foliar accents in flowerbeds. This handsome grass is completely non-invasive.

Blue Himalayan Poppy

Meconopsis grandis
Large Himalayan
Poppy, Himalayan Blue
Poppy

blue

Blue poppies are absolutely stunning, but be careful which you choose. Meconopsis grandis, *the large blue Himalayan poppy, is the best one for the average gardener. It is longer-lived than others, and blooms in a more intense shade of sky-blue, with big flowers 3–5 inches (7.5–12.5 cm) across. Blue is the usual colour, but occasionally you can find some with white, purple or pinkish-purple flowers.*

Height • 24–36 inches (60–90 cm)

Spread • 12–15 inches (30–38 cm)

Blooms • early to midsummer

PLANTING

Seeding: Not recommended. Blue Himalayan poppies are notoriously difficult to germinate, and will take a long time to bloom.

Transplanting: Space 12–15 inches (30–38 cm) apart.

GROWING

Partial shade; rich, moist soil.

Woodland and shade gardens. Middle to back of border.

Blue Himalayan poppies bloom in a shade of sky-blue rarely seen in flowers.

Do not let plants dry out.

Divide every 5 years. See page 54, method B.

RECOMMENDED VARIETIES

Usually available only under one of the names listed above.

TIPS

Blue Himalayan poppies like rich, slightly acidic soil. Be sure to add lots of compost or peat moss when planting.

We grow blue Himalayan poppies in a shaded area on the north side of a large tree, along with hostas and primroses.

Blue Himalayan poppies are not true poppies, although the flowers look similar. The botanical name *Meconopsis* comes from the Greek word *mekon*, meaning 'poppy,' and the suffix *-opsis*, which indicates resemblance.

The intense, sky-blue colour of the petals is offset by bright yellow stamens.

Blue Himalayan poppies are irresistible in bloom; at first sight, almost everybody wants one for his or her own garden. We can always tell when a magazine or newspaper has run a feature article on them by the ensuing rash of phone calls from gardeners looking for these plants.

Blue Oat Grass

Helictotrichon sempervirens

 blue

Blue oat grass is beautiful in mixed borders. Its steel-blue leaves form tight, rounded clumps, and arching stems support graceful, tan flowerheads in summer. Combine blue oat grass with silvery sages and yellow, white or pink flowers for a stunning display. This undemanding plant is rarely troubled by pests.

Height • 18–24 inches (45–60 cm)

Spread • 24 inches (60 cm)

Blooms • summer

PLANTING

Seeding: Seed of blue oat grass is difficult to find, but you can save some from your plants. Sow indoors in February or March; germination 15–21 days. Sow outdoors in fall.

Transplanting: Space 12–18 inches (30–45 cm) apart.

GROWING

Sun to partial shade.

Feature plant, rock gardens, mixed flower beds. Accent plantings with evergreens, trees and shrubs. Middle to back of border.

Divide every 3 years to maintain vigour. See page 54, method B.

Blue oat grass is the best blue-leaved ornamental grass for general border use.

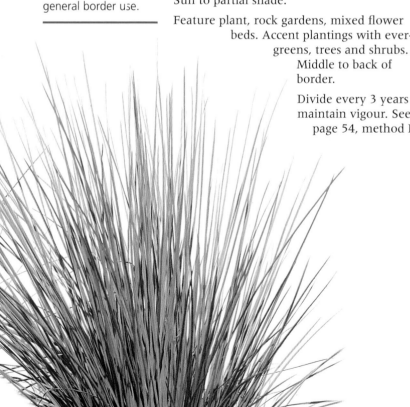

Recommended Varieties

Usually available only under one of the names listed above.

Tips

Many people think grasses do not bloom because their flowers don't look like the flowers of other plants. The showy, tan-coloured spikes that arch above the blue foliage throughout the summer are actually the flowers of oat grass.

Blue oat grass forms a tidy mound and does not outgrow its allotted space. It provides a wonderful alternative to silver mound sage.

Snip a few flowerheads and stems of foliage to add to bouquets. They last as long as, or longer than, many flowers.

Use the seedheads in dried arrangements. Cut seedheads when they're still green, and hang upside-down in bunches to dry.

We have added an ornamental grass section to the show garden at the greenhouses (above), to demonstrate how beautiful and useful these plants are in flowerbeds. Judging from the favourable comments, many people agree.

The steely blades of blue oat grass look attractive in a bouquet with sneezeweed and Joe Pye weed.

Blue Sage

Salvia nemorosa
Salvia χ sylvestris
Perennial Salvia

purple

Blue sage blooms throughout the summer, with masses of long, deep-violet flowerspikes and savory-scented, grey-green foliage. Each plant forms an upright, spiky clump. Grow blue sage with ornamental grasses and silver-leaved sages, or mix it with other flowers. I like strong colour contrasts, so I grow blue sage with yellow tickseed, cherry-red yarrow and black-eyed Susans.

Height • 15–24 inches (38–60 cm)

Spread • 18–24 inches (45–60 cm)

Blooms • all summer

The botanical name *Salvia* is derived from a Latin word meaning 'to save,' referring to this plant's early reputation as a cure-all.

PLANTING

Seeding: Sow indoors in February; seed needs light to germinate; do not cover. Germination often erratic. Sow outdoors in early spring. Plants will bloom the following season.

Transplanting: Space 12–18 inches (30–45 cm) apart.

GROWING

Sun to partial shade.

Mixed beds, mass plantings. Middle to front of border.

Division is not required, unless you want more plants. See page 54, method A.

Butterflies and hummingbirds like blue sage. The variety 'May Night' (left) has larger flowers than most. Blue sage blooms throughout the summer, and grows well in hot, dry areas with alkaline or poor soil (below).

RECOMMENDED VARIETIES

Blue Queen • 18–24 inches (45–60 cm) tall; rich, deep violet-blue flowers; excellent heat and drought tolerance; mildly scented foliage.

East Friesland • 15–18 inches (38–45 cm) tall; slender spikes of rich violet-purple flowers; sturdy, upright plants; long-bloomer; mildly scented foliage.

May Night • 18–24 inches (45–60 cm) tall; profusion of dark, rich violet-blue flowers, larger than most; long-bloomer; leaves very strongly scented.

TIPS

Blue sage looks stunning with yellow tickseed in front, and peonies and Oriental poppies behind.

Blue sage blooms all summer, and you can do one of two things to increase both the number of flowers and the blooming period. Deadhead regularly throughout the season, or, when the number of flowers begins to decline after the initial heavy flush, trim off all remaining flowerstalks. The plants respond by sending up new flower stalks from further down the stems.

Blue sage is related to culinary sage, and its leaves have a similar fragrance when crushed. Choose a spot in the garden where you are apt to brush the plant on passing. Add dried leaves to potpourris.

Cut flowers for bouquets when spikes are starting to open. They last 7–10 days in a vase.

Campion

Lychnis chalcedonica
Maltese Cross,
Jerusalem Cross,
Scarlet Lightning,
Soldier's Coat

Lychnis χ arkwrightii
Arkwright's Campion

Lychnis χ haageana
Haage's Campion

orange,
red

If you like red flowers, you will love campions. Maltese cross blooms in midsummer with the most brilliant, true red flowers available in perennials. They look stunning mixed with blue or lemon-yellow blooms. We always grew Maltese cross with delphiniums in the garden on the farm. Haage's campion blooms throughout the summer, with showy, 2-inch (5 cm) wide, orange-scarlet flowers. Arkwright's campion is equally showy, with slightly smaller, orange-red flowers and striking, bronze-green foliage.

Height • Maltese Cross: 24–36 inches
   (60–90 cm)
   Arkwright's Campion: 10–15 inches
   (25–38 cm)
   Haage's Campion: 10–18 inches
   (25–45 cm)

Spread • Maltese Cross: 24 inches (60 cm)
   Arkwright's Campion: 8–12 inches
   (20–30 cm)
   Haage's Campion: 12 inches (30 cm)

Blooms • summer

PLANTING

The botanical name *Lychnis* means 'lamp' in Greek, referring to the vivid flower colours.

Seeding: Indoors in February or March. Seed needs light to germinate; do not cover with soil mix. Sow outdoors in early spring. Plants seeded in spring will often produce blooms that year.

Transplanting: Space Arkwright's and Haage's campion 12–15 inches (30–40 cm) apart, and Maltese cross 24–36 inches (60–90 cm) apart.

GROWING

Sun to partial shade.

Mixed flowerbeds. Middle to back of border.

Divide every 4–5 years, or when centres start to die out. See page 54, method A.

RECOMMENDED VARIETIES
Arkwright's Campion

Orange Zwerg • 8–10 inches (20–25 cm) tall and 12–15 inches (30–38 cm) wide; a dwarf variety with large, bright orange flowers.

Vesuvius • 12 inches (30 cm) tall and 8–12 inches (20–30 cm) wide; large, vivid, deep vermilion flowers and dark bronze-green foliage; striking colour contrast.

The other two species are often found only under one of the names listed on the facing page. Maltese Cross is sometimes also available in white ('Alba') or pink ('Rosea'), but these plants are less showy.

TIPS

Hummingbirds love these flowers! Grow campion near a window so that you can watch the tiny birds visit.

Regular deadheading may prolong the blooming season, but leave a few spent flowers if you want seedlings to form. Maltese cross self-sows readily, but the other two types usually don't come true from seed.

Add the flowers of Maltese cross to bouquets. I particularly like these blooms mixed with Shasta daisies and yellow lilies.

Maltese cross (above) may have the most brilliant scarlet flowers of any perennial. Arkwright's campion (left) is shorter, with bigger, equally vivid flowers; here, 'Orange Zwerg' and 'Vesuvius' grow side by side. Haage's campion (opposite) has the largest flowers.

Candytuft

Iberis sempervirens
Evergreen Candytuft,
Perennial Candytuft

white

Candytuft is one of the most popular low-growing
perennials. In spring, brilliant white flowers
completely cover the narrow leaves. The plants
grow into low mats, with foliage that stays pretty
throughout the season. Candytuft often reblooms
in fall, although less profusely than in spring.
One of the most attractive plantings I have seen is
a mass of candytuft growing under a cherry tree.
In spring, with both in full blossom, the display
is breathtaking.

Height • 4–6 inches (10–15 cm)

Spread • 18–24 inches (45–60 cm)

Blooms • early to late spring

PLANTING

Seeding: Indoors in February or March;
germination 7–21 days. Seed needs light to
germinate; do not cover with soil. Outdoors in early spring. Plants will bloom the
following year.

Candytuft
brightens gardens in
spring with masses of
pure white flowers.

Transplanting: Space 12–15 inches
(30–40 cm) apart.

GROWING

Sun to partial shade.

Rock gardens, edging walks,
in mixed borders, mass
plantings, on slopes and
banks. Front of border.

Candytuft is an evergreen
perennial; do not cut back
foliage. Severe pruning
prevents next season's
blooms, and may harm
plants.

Divide every 3–4 years.
See page 54, method B.

RECOMMENDED
VARIETIES

Snowflake • dazzling
white flowers, even
brighter than
the species.

TIPS

Candytuft's leaves remain green in winter, but the plants need a good snow-cover for protection. Don't plant candytuft in exposed areas, where the wind whips away snow and leaves the ground bare, because top growth will brown off and die. The plants will survive and re-grow from the base, but they won't bloom that season. Pile extra snow on top for added protection.

Clusters of snow-white flowers make candytuft one of the showiest spring-blooming perennials. The stems are long enough to cut for bouquets.

After blooming has finished, shear off the top few inches (5–7.5 cm) of leaves. This keeps the plants from becoming leggy, and encourages the growth of fresh new stems.

OTHER RECOMMENDED SPECIES

Iberis saxatilis (Rock Candytuft): 3–5 inches (7.5–12.5 cm) tall and 6 inches (15 cm) wide; masses of white flowers that become tinged in pink as they age; a compact candytuft for rock gardens; spring-blooming. Care as above.

A mass planting of candytuft in full bloom provides an unmatched display.

Catmint

Nepeta mussinii

blue, white

Catmint is one of the longest-blooming perennials. In summer, small spikes of lavender-blue or white flowers almost completely mask the grey-green, heart-shaped leaves. The foliage of this bushy, spreading perennial has a pleasant, minty scent appealing to cats, but not as attractive to them as catmint's close relative, catnip.

Height • 12 inches (30 cm)

Spread • 12–15 inches (30–38 cm)

Blooms • summer to early fall

PLANTING

Seeding: Indoors in February or March. Outdoors in early spring. Plants will bloom the first year.

Transplanting: Space 12–18 inches (30–45 cm) apart.

GROWING

Sun to partial shade.

Rock gardens, edging, on slopes, trailing over front of raised beds. Front of border.

Divide every 3 years. See page 54, method B.

RECOMMENDED VARIETIES

Usually available only under one of the names listed above.

Catmint blooms all summer, is drought-tolerant and rarely bothered by pests.

Tips

My husband Ted and I saw a rock garden with catmint and orange California poppies growing together. The display was stunning. Both plants bloom all summer, and the annual poppies self-sow so well that you are sure to have them in your garden for years.

Deadhead catmint regularly to extend the blooming period. Alternatively, shear plants back to half their size when the number of flowers begins to decrease after the first flush of blooms. The plants will respond quickly with a second flush.

Catmint looks wonderful in hanging baskets and patio pots. We often grow it in a large pot, with a clematis vine supported by a trellis. Both plants bloom all summer. In northern gardens, they must be transplanted into the ground to survive the winter, but the splendid summer show is worth the extra effort.

A bushy mound of catmint (top) looks lovely along walks, edging beds or at the front of a border. The chartreuse flowers of lady's mantle (bottom) provide an outstanding contrast to catmint throughout the summer.

Checker Mallow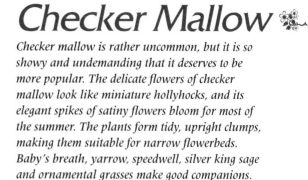

Sidalcea malviflora
Foothill Checker
Mallow, Mallow

purple, red,
pink, white

Checker mallow is rather uncommon, but it is so showy and undemanding that it deserves to be more popular. The delicate flowers of checker mallow look like miniature hollyhocks, and its elegant spikes of satiny flowers bloom for most of the summer. The plants form tidy, upright clumps, making them suitable for narrow flowerbeds. Baby's breath, yarrow, speedwell, silver king sage and ornamental grasses make good companions.

Height • 1½–4 feet (45–120 cm)

Spread • 2 feet (60 cm)

Blooms • summer

PLANTING

Seeding: Indoors in February. Outdoors in early spring. Plants will bloom the first year.

Transplanting: Space 12–18 inches (30–45 cm) apart.

Checker
mallow blooms
nearly all summer.

GROWING

Sun to partial shade.

Meadow gardens, middle to back of border.

Divide every 3–4 years, when plants become crowded or die out in the middle. See page 54, method A.

RECOMMENDED VARIETIES

Brilliant • 2–4 feet (60–120 cm) tall; carmine red flowers; brilliant colour.

Elsie Heugh • 1½–3 feet (45–90 cm) tall; satiny, soft pink, fringed flowers.

Mr. Lindbergh • 2–3 feet (60–90 cm) tall; purple-rose flowers.

TIPS

Checker mallow's flowers are outstanding against a background of shrubs.

After blooming, cut plants back to encourage a second flush of flowers. Trim foliage if it begins to look unsightly, and the plants will respond with fresh new growth.

Cut flowers for bouquets when they start to open. They last about a week in a vase.

OTHER RECOMMENDED SPECIES

Sidalcea candida (White Checker Mallow): 2–3 feet (60–90 cm) tall and 2 feet (60 cm) wide; pure white, cup-shaped flowers. Blooming period and care as above.

Grow checker mallow with daylilies, yarrow, baby's breath, purple coneflowers or ornamental grasses.

Checker mallow is the perfect plant for gardeners who love hollyhocks but do not have room to grow them.

Clematis

Clematis alpina
Alpine Clematis

Clematis integrifolia
Solitary Clematis, Bush Clematis

Clematis macropetala
Big-petal Clematis, Downy Clematis

Clematis tangutica
Golden Clematis

Clematis viticella
Viticella Clematis

Clematis χ hybrida
Hybrid Clematis

red, rose, pink, purple, blue, yellow, white

Everybody loves clematis. The vines are gorgeous, with showy flowers for most of the season. By growing a variety of them, you can have clematis in bloom from spring right through until frost. Solitary clematis is unusual; unlike most clematis, it grows into a large, rounded bush. Its flowers are porcelain-blue, white or rose, upturned and bell-shaped, with twisted, curled-back petals. Big-petal clematis is one of the tallest vines, with nodding, bell-shaped flowers 2–3 inches (5–7.5 cm) across, in blue, purple, white or pink. The flowers of alpine clematis are similar but slightly smaller, and bloom in the same colours except purple. Big-petal and alpine clematis are the only spring bloomers. Golden clematis is the largest, hardiest and most vigorous vine. Masses of bright yellow, bell-shaped flowers are followed by clouds of feathery seedheads that remain on the vine, and provide an interesting winter display. Viticella clematis has the familiar, open-faced shape to its flowers, which are 2–4 inches (5–10 cm) across. All of these are referred to as species clematis. They are hardier than hybrids, and undemanding to grow.

Hybrid clematis vines are the well-known, large-flowered clematis. There are hundreds of varieties with a wide array of flower colours. In northern gardens, hybrid vines are more specific in their growing requirements than are species types. Any type of clematis, however, makes a striking addition to gardens.

Height • Alpine Clematis: 6–8 feet (1.8–2.5 m)
  Solitary Clematis: 3 feet (1 m)
  Big-petal Clematis: 10–20 feet (3–7 m)
  Golden Clematis: 15–20 feet (4.5–7 m)
  Viticella Clematis: 8–10 feet (2.5–3 m)
  Hybrid Clematis: 8–10 feet (2.5–3 m)

 Clematis is the most popular perennial vine.

Spread • Alpine Clematis: 4 feet (1.2 m)
  Solitary Clematis: 3 feet (1 m)
  Big-petal Clematis: 4 feet (1.2 m)
  Golden Clematis: 10 feet (3 m)
  Viticella Clematis: 3 feet (1 m)
  Hybrid Clematis: 4 feet (1.2 m)

Blooms • Alpine Clematis: spring and sometimes again in fall
  Solitary Clematis: summer to early fall
  Big-petal Clematis: spring and sometimes again in fall
  Golden Clematis: most of summer to frost
  Viticella Clematis: midsummer through fall
  Hybrid Clematis: most of summer to frost

PLANTING

Seeding: Not recommended. Big-petal and golden clematis are easily grown from seed sown outdoors in fall, but take 2–3 years to reach flowering size.

Roots: Plant roots in spring. For species types, plant with crowns at soil surface. Plant hybrid clematis roots about 4 inches (10 cm) deep. Roots must be at least 3 years old to flower profusely.

Transplanting: Space 36 inches (90 cm) apart. Plant species clematis at the same level as in the pot, but hybrid clematis varieties about 4 inches (10 cm) deeper. The extra soil covering the crowns helps to protect plants in winter.

Solitary clematis is a rounded bush, covered with porcelain-blue bells in summer and fluffy seedheads in fall.

'Ville de Lyon' is an
outstanding hybrid
clematis. Gold stamens
offset the large, rosy
flowers.

Golden clematis (right)
is the largest, hardiest
and most vigorous
vine. It blooms from
midsummer to frost,
and the large
seedheads remain
attractive all winter.
The popular hybrid
'Jackmanii' (opposite)
was developed in
England almost 150
years ago. The annual
marigolds help the
vine by shading its
roots from hot sun.

GROWING

Full sun to partial shade.

Solitary clematis in mixed beds, as an accent plant. Species clematis varieties can be planted anywhere in the yard, but hybrid clematis varieties must be planted against the foundation of a heated building on the west or south side.

All clematis vines need something for their leaf tendrils to cling to, like a trellis or lattice. Species vines will clamber along fences or up trees. Solitary clematis needs a hoop or other type of support to keep it upright.

Do not cut back alpine, big-petal or golden clematis vines. These types are hardier than others, and the top growth will overwinter, so you can leave them on their trellises. Prune off only dead or broken branches. Treat solitary clematis the same as most perennials; cut it back in early spring.

Viticella and hybrid clematis vines die back over winter. You can cut them back in fall, from 6–12 inches (15–30 cm) above the ground. We prefer to leave pruning until spring, because these vines often won't die back entirely, and you can gain additional height by leaving them intact. To do this, in late fall gently remove the vines from their support and lay them stretched out on the ground. Do not cut the vines. Water heavily when the ground starts to freeze, and, when the ground has frozen solid, cover with 6–10 inches (15–25 cm) of dry peat moss. In spring, cut vines back to the new growth.

Dividing is not recommended; it is a difficult process with these plants.

Recommended Varieties

Alpine, solitary, big-petal and golden clematis are usually available only under one of the names listed above.

Viticella Clematis

Polish Spirit • dark purple, 4-petalled flowers; one of the largest of its type and the heaviest blooming; resembles 'Jackmanii' (the most popular hybrid) in size and colour, but it is much hardier.

Hybrid Clematis

There are hundreds of hybrid varieties. The following are a few of our favourites, and they provide a good colour selection.

Jackmanii Superba • masses of rich, violet-purple flowers; an improved form of 'Jackmanii' with larger flowers and better colour; mildew-resistant.

Nelly Moser • white flowers with deep pink bars; for best colour, do not plant in hot, sunny locations.

Ville de Lyon • rose-red flowers with deep crimson centres; showy gold stamens.

'Purpurea plena elegans' (right) is an unusual, double-flowered viticella clematis. Big-petal clematis (opposite) is one of the tallest vines, with a striking display of spring flowers.

TIPS

With proper care, clematis will reward you with larger flowers and more vigorous growth. For planting, use a 1:1 mix of soil and peat moss or compost, and work it in around the planting area at least 24 inches (60 cm) deep. The result for your extra effort will be flowers up to twice the size. Remember too that these vines live for about 15–20 years!

Paler flowers tend to bleach in bright sunlight. To retain the brightest colours, choose a site that is shaded for a couple of hours during the hottest part of the day.

Clematis like cool roots. Grow low, spreading plants at its base, place a large rock in front, or install a thick mulch. Any of these options helps enormously.

Try planting various colours of the same type of clematis together. A mix of white, pink, purple and rose-flowered varieties is absolutely breathtaking.

Clematis also looks splendid combined with climbing roses. Grow species vines with hardy climbers, such as 'Explorer' roses, which have the same winter protection requirements.

Clematis often blooms sparsely the first year after planting. Grow some vigorous, free-blooming annual vines on the same trellis, until the clematis settles in to its new location.

Species-type clematis make marvellous groundcovers. Simply allow the vines to sprawl rather than providing them with a trellis. They do well in sloped areas.

Surprisingly, clematis makes a good cutflower. Cut for bouquets when petals are starting to open, and place the vase away from direct sunlight, drafts and heat. The cutflowers last 7–10 days.

The flowers and seedheads of golden clematis air-dry beautifully. Harvest flowers for drying at different stages, from green buds to three-quarters open. Pick seedheads within a few days of petals dropping, while they are new and green. They will open and become woolly as they dry.

Coneflower

Echinacea purpurea
Purple Coneflower

purple, rose, white

Coneflowers are wonderful for sunny gardens. The large, daisy-like flowers have protruding centres, broad, reflexed petals and a light scent. They bloom abundantly all summer long, and thrive for years with little care. The botanical name Echinacea *comes from the Greek word* echinos, *meaning 'hedgehog,' and refers to the prickly scales at the base of the flowers.*

Height • 18–36 inches (45–90 cm)

Spread • 24 inches (60 cm)

Blooms • early summer to fall

Planting

Seeding: Indoors in February or March; erratic germination, 1 month. Sow outdoors in early spring. Plants will bloom the second year.

Roots: Plant in spring, with crowns at or slightly below soil surface.

Transplanting: Space 18–24 inches (45–60 cm) apart.

Growing

Sun to partial shade.

Coneflower is one of the longest-blooming perennials.

Flowerbeds, cutting gardens, in small clumps. Middle to back of border.

Divide every 3–4 years. See page 54, method A.

RECOMMENDED VARIETIES

Bravado • 18 inches (45 cm) tall; rose-pink flowers on sturdy stems; compact plants.

Bright Star • 24–36 inches (60–90 cm) tall; rose-red flowers; blooms more profusely than others.

Magnus • 24–36 inches (60–90 cm) tall; rose flowers with more upright petals than others.

White Swan • 18–24 inches (45–60 cm) tall; pure white flowers.

Coneflowers thrive in hot areas, such as this bed alongside a heat-reflecting wall.

TIPS

Coneflowers are drought-tolerant. They also grow well in poor soil and hot, dry or windy locations.

Add these bright flowers to bouquets. Cut when blooms have just opened. They last about a week.

Both the flowers and the spiky, conical seedheads make interesting additions to dried arrangements. To dry flowers, cut when blooms are fully open and hang them upside-down. For seedheads, wait for petals to drop, then cut stems to the desired length and allow to dry within the arrangement.

The name 'coneflower' refers to the raised centres of these large, daisy-like blooms.

Coralbell

Heuchera χ brizoides
(H. sanguinea)
Coralbell

Heuchera americana
American Alumroot

 white, pink,
red

Coralbells are perfect for edging flowerbeds and
borders. Create a cool, serene display by planting
them next to blue-flowering perennials, such as
delphiniums or monkshood. Use red-flowering
plants, such as beebalm or campion, for an
arresting show in sunny areas of the garden.
White-flowered plants, such as Shasta daisies,
produce a softer, more subtle effect.

Height • Coralbell: 18–24 inches (45–60 cm)
American Alumroot: 36–48 inches
(90–120 cm)

Spread • Coralbell: 12–18 inches (30–45 cm)
American Alumroot: 18–24 inches
(45–60 cm)

Blooms • Coralbell: late spring to
midsummer
American Alumroot: early to
late summer

Coralbell
blooms for most of the
summer, with clusters
of tiny bellflowers on
delicate stalks.

PLANTING

Seeding: Indoors in February or March;
germination 21–30 days. Seed needs light
to germinate; press on top of soil mix. Sow
outdoors in early spring. Plants will bloom
the following year. Variety selection in seed
is limited.

Transplanting: Space 12 inches (30 cm)
apart.

GROWING

Coralbells in sun to partial shade. American alumroot in partial shade.

Accent plants, in rock gardens, edging pathways. Front of border.

Keep soil moist; do not allow plants to dry out.

Divide every 4–5 years. See page 54, method B.

The purple-bronze leaves of 'Bressingham Bronze' hold their colour all season. Blue fescue and cottage pink are good partners.

RECOMMENDED VARIETIES
Coralbell

Brandon Pink • elegant sprays of light pink bellflowers in midsummer; dense, green foliage; developed by Agriculture Canada; one of the hardiest varieties.

'Brandon Pink' coralbells are a striking addition to almost any garden. The tiny bellflowers attract hummingbirds.

Bressingham Bronze • small white bellflowers in spring; crinkled, bronze-purple foliage; striking, unfading colour.

Frosty • known for its profusion of vibrant red bellflowers; attractive, mottled green-on-white foliage.

American Alumroot

Chocolate Ruffles • huge, ruffled leaves up to 9 inches (23 cm) wide, dark chocolate-brown on top and burgundy underneath; masses of tiny, white bellflowers on purple stems in summer.

Ruby Veil • greenish-white bellflowers midsummer; leaves up to 5 inches (12.5 cm) across; maple-leaf-shaped foliage with a metallic copper sheen, slate-grey veins and dark purple undersides; absolutely stunning.

Velvet Night • velvety, slate-black leaves overlaid with metallic purple, up to 7 inches (17.5 cm) across; white bellflowers midsummer.

TIPS

American alumroot's flowers are less colourful then those of coralbells, but flowerstalks are twice the height, rising up to 4 feet (120 cm) above the foliage.

Coralbells do not spread past their allotted space. Plant them in a narrow bed lining the driveway.

The bright flowers add splendid accents to mixed bouquets. Cut stems when at least half of the flowers are open. They last 7–10 days after cutting.

Many of the exotic American alumroots are propagated by a technique called tissue culture. Individual cells are extracted from the newest growing tip of a plant and grown inside a sterile test tube. In the laboratory, an environment about as far removed from a garden as one can get, thousands of identical plants are created from single cells.

125

Bright red coralbells put on an impressive display in summer. They can be grown at the front of flowerbeds and borders because their thin flowerspikes rise from low foliage, allowing plants behind to be easily seen.

Cornflower

Centaurea montana
Mountain Bluet,
Perennial Bachelor's
Button

blue, white

The annual bachelor's button, also known as cornflower, is one of my favourite flowers, so naturally I feel the same about the perennial cornflower, which has similar but larger flowers on sturdier stems, and green leaves outlined in silvery-white. This perennial blooms for a good part of the summer, with large, cobalt-blue or pure white flowers that can be added to either fresh or dried bouquets. The flowers have a gentle apricot scent.

Height • 24–36 inches (60–90 cm)

Spread • 24–36 inches (60–90 cm)

Blooms • late spring to midsummer

PLANTING

Seeding: Indoors in February or March; germination 14–21 days and often sporadic. Cover seed lightly. Sow outdoors in early spring. Plants will bloom the second year.

Transplanting: Space 24–30 inches (60–75 cm) apart.

GROWING

Sun to partial shade.

Feature plant, backgrounds in perennial or shrub beds, mass plantings, informal gardens.

Middle to back of border.

Plants in windy locations may require staking.

Divide every 3 years, when plants begin to bloom less than in previous years or if the centre of the plant dies out. See page 54, method A.

Cornflowers are tough perennials that need very little care. They grow well in poor soil, hot, dry locations and hard-to-plant areas such as slopes or parched beds near heat-radiating brick walls.

Recommended Varieties

Usually available only under one of the names recommended above. 'Alba' is a white-flowered variety with a coconut-like scent.

Tips

Most plants tend to grow taller and less compactly in shaded locations than in sunnier areas. Cornflowers grown in shade are looser and a bit floppy. Some gardeners like the informal effect this creates; if you prefer a neater look, use a support to hold plants in place.

Deadhead regularly to extend the blooming period.

For a second flush of blooms in late summer, cut plants back to about one-third of their height after the main flush of flowers has finished. This will also keep plants neat and compact.

Pick flowers for bouquets when they are half-open. They generally last 7–10 days after cutting.

Harvest flowers for drying when they are fully open, and hang small bunches upside-down for about a week. Stagger the flowerheads up the length of each bunch for best results.

Other Recommended Species

Centaurea dealbata (Persian Cornflower): 24–36 inches (60–90 cm) tall and wide; pink flowers from late spring to midsummer; cut-leaf foliage is white on undersides. Follow the care procedures listed above.

Cornflowers bloom for weeks in summer, and are exceptionally resistant to pests and disease.

Cranesbill

Geranium cinereum
Grey-leaf Cranesbill,
Grey-leaf Geranium

Geranium endressii
Endres Cranesbill

Geranium macrorrhizum
Bigroot Cranesbill,
Bigroot Geranium

Geranium psilostemon
Armenian Cranesbill

red, pink, lavender, white

Most gardeners are better acquainted with the annual geranium than with cranesbill, the perennial geranium. Recently, though, cranesbills have begun to catch on, as people discover their pretty, cup-shaped flowers, attractive foliage and undemanding growth habits. Grey-leaf cranesbill forms a low mound of silvery leaves, with large, white, lavender or pink flowers. Endres cranesbill grows into a dense mound of shiny green leaves, with light pink flowers that last for weeks, while bigroot cranesbill makes a dense groundcover with fragrant leaves and pale pink flowers. Armenian cranesbill is a big, bushy plant with wide, heart-shaped leaves and striking cherry-red flowers, each marked with a central black eye.

Height • Grey-leaf Cranesbill: 6–10 inches (15–25 cm)
Endres Cranesbill: 12–15 inches (30–38 cm)
Bigroot Cranesbill: 12–15 inches (30–38 cm)
Armenian Cranesbill: 24–36 inches (60–90 cm)

Armenian cranesbills have magnificent, 2-inch (5 cm) flowers.

Spread • Grey-leaf Cranesbill: 12 inches (30 cm)
Endres Cranesbill: 18 inches (45 cm) wide
Bigroot Cranesbill: 18–24 inches (45–60 cm)
Armenian Cranesbill: 18–30 inches (45–75 cm)

Blooms • Grey-leaf Cranesbill: late spring through summer
Endres Cranesbill: midspring to mid-summer
Bigroot Cranesbill: late spring to early summer
Armenian Cranesbill: most of summer

Aromatic foliage and clusters of flowers in late spring and early summer are outstanding features of bigroot cranesbills.

PLANTING

Seeding: Not recommended. Germination is sporadic and the best varieties are not available in seed.

Roots: Plant in spring with crowns at or slightly below soil level.

Transplanting: Space 12–24 inches (30–60 cm) apart.

GROWING

Sun to partial shade.

Mixed flowerbeds, accent plants, groundcovers, on slopes. Middle to back of border. Shorter types as edging, in rock gardens, front of border.

Divide every 4–5 years. See page 54, method A.

RECOMMENDED VARIETIES
Grey-leaf Cranesbill

Ballerina • 6 inches (15 cm) tall; large, lilac-pink flowers with purple veins and centres; unusual colouring; finely cut leaves; blooms far longer than most grey-leaf cranesbills, from midspring to late summer; award-winning variety.

Cranesbills are low-maintenance perennials with long blooming periods.

130

Endres Cranesbill
Wargrave Pink • deeply notched, pink flowers held high above the foliage; more vigorous than species.

Bigroot Cranesbill
Spessart • 12–15 inches (30–38 cm) tall; masses of soft pink flowers; extremely hardy.

Armenian Cranesbill
Usually available only under one of the names listed on page 128.

Tips

Cranesbills are fairly drought-tolerant and will grow in nooks or crannies with very little soil. These plants are rarely troubled by disease or insects.

Cut back Endres and Armenian cranesbills after the first flush of blooms has finished, to keep plants tidy. This should give you a greater number of flowers.

Deadhead other types regularly for more abundant blooms.

The leaves of bigroot cranesbills have a pungent scent, a bit like a combination of lemon, mint and sage. This plant is the commercial source of oil of geranium.

The aromatic foliage of bigroot cranesbill turns wine-red in fall.

Other Recommended Species

Geranium sanguineum (Blood-red Cranesbill): 6–8 inches (15–20 cm) tall and 18–24 inches (45–60 cm) wide; masses of bright purple-red or white flowers all summer; spreading plants that are great in rock gardens; will trail over walls; foliage turns orange-red in fall.

Geranium χ 'Ann Folkard' (Ann Folkard Cranesbill): 18 inches (45 cm) tall and 18–24 inches (45–60 cm) wide; abundance of electric-magenta flowers from late spring to late fall; blooms far longer than most cranesbills; very showy, semi-trailing plants; new growth is gold.

Blood-red cranesbill (below) is heat-tolerant and blooms all summer.

The flowers of grey-leaf cranesbill 'Ballerina' (above) have exquisite colouring, and put on a fine show all summer.

Creeping Jenny

Lysimachia
nummularia
Moneywort

 yellow

Before you give up on an area of the garden where nothing seems to grow, try creeping Jenny. This beautiful, low-growing plant spreads rapidly to form a ruffled mat of penny-sized leaves. Creeping Jenny grows well in moist or wet areas, on slopes, in poor soil, in sun or shade. But don't limit it to difficult areas. This versatile plant can also be used to brighten rock gardens and flowerbeds. Bright yellow flowers, about the same size as the leaves, cover the foliage throughout the summer.

Height • 2–4 inches (5–10 cm)

Spread • 24 inches (60 cm)

Blooms • late spring to early fall

PLANTING

Seeding: Indoors in February or March. Outdoors in early spring. Plants will flower the first year.

Transplanting: Space 12–18 inches (30–45 cm) apart.

GROWING

Sun to partial shade.

Groundcover, in rock gardens, on slopes, trailing over the edge of raised beds. Front of border.

Creeping Jenny is remarkably easy to grow, and blooms throughout the summer.

Keep soil moist; these plants do not like to dry out.

Does not need dividing to maintain vigour, but if you want more plants, use method C, page 54. Alternatively, just cut off a few trailing branches and poke them into the soil in a new location.

RECOMMENDED VARIETIES
Aurea • bright golden leaves; best in partial shade.

TIPS
Creeping Jenny makes an excellent groundcover and can withstand an occasional trampling. It spreads rapidly by creeping runners that form roots wherever they touch the ground. Any excess spread is easily checked; just pull out unwanted stems.

If you have a garden pond, grow creeping Jenny around the edge. These plants do well even in moist, boggy conditions.

The species name nummularia *means 'coin-shaped leaves.' Moneywort is another reference to the foliage; 'wort' simply means plant. Allow these plants to trail over raised walls (above) or spread into a showy groundcover (left).*

Daylily

**Hemerocallis χ
   hybrida**

black, purple,
mahogany, red,
orange, yellow,
pink, cream

Daylilies are so named because each of their lily-like flowers lasts only one day. A mature plant, however, produces fifty or more flowers, and blooms for a month or longer. Some varieties bloom for almost the entire summer. Daylilies are undemanding, as tough as they are beautiful. They are drought-tolerant, rarely troubled by pests and have an inviting array of flower colours, sizes and forms. Once established, these plants quickly form dense, broad clumps of bright green, strap-like leaves.

Daylilies are one of the most adaptable, low-maintenance and pest-free perennials. They thrive in virtually any type of soil, partially shady or hot, dry areas and are untroubled by pests and deer.

Height • 10–48 inches (25–120 cm)

Spread • 24–36 inches (60–90 cm)

Blooms • summer

PLANTING

Seeding: Not recommended. Plants take up to 3 years to bloom from seed.

Roots: Plant in spring, with the crown just barely below soil level.

Transplanting: Space 18–24 inches (45–60 cm) apart.

GROWING

Sun to partial shade. The sunnier the location, the more flowers are produced.

Mixed flowerbeds, mass plantings, accent plants, on slopes. Middle to back of border.

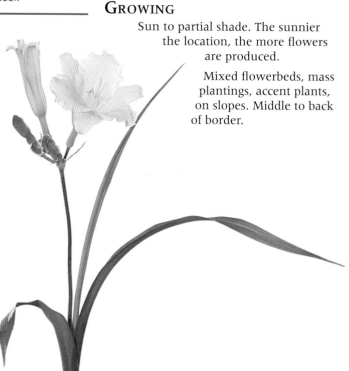

When older daylilies begin to bloom less or not at all (usually after 4–6 years), it's a sign that they need dividing. Early fall is the best time to divide. Use method A, page 54. Ensure that each division has a healthy fan of leaves.

RECOMMENDED VARIETIES

Hyperion • 24–30 inches; pure lemon-yellow flowers, highly fragrant; an old favourite; blooms early to midsummer.

Manilla Moon • 24–36 inches (60–90 cm) tall; 5-inch (12.5 cm), golden flowers with a touch of orange; blooms mid- to late summer.

Pandora's Box • 15–20 inches (38–50 cm) tall; scented, cream flowers with maroon centres; striking colour combination; blooms most of the summer.

Stella de Oro • 10–15 inches (25–38 cm) tall; bright golden-yellow flowers; the best dwarf variety; more flowers and longer-blooming than all others.

The flowers of most daylilies last only for a day, but are produced in such abundance that this goes almost unnoticed. The botanical name Hemerocallis *comes from the Greek words* hemera *(day) and* kallos *(beauty)— literally, 'beautiful for a day.' 'Hyperion' (opposite) is a popular, fragrant variety.*

TIPS

Daylilies hide the yellowing foliage of spring-flowering bulbs, such as tulips and daffodils.

The foliage of most daylilies stays tidy all season, but a few older cultivars have leaves that yellow. Remove these leaves as they appear by grasping them firmly and tugging quickly to snap them off at the base.

Some varieties require deadheading; others drop their spent flowers. Cut the entire flowerstalk off after the last blossom is finished. Don't allow seedpods to develop, because they deplete the plant's energy.

A recent breeding breakthrough has resulted in reblooming daylilies, which have flowers that last longer than a single day. They bloom twice in a single season: once in June and July, and again in mid-August to early fall. Reblooming daylilies produce more flowers than any other type of daylily, on plants that are about half the average height.

Different varieties bloom at different times, and by growing a mixture you can have daylilies in bloom from early summer to early fall. As a general rule, short varieties begin blooming early and tall varieties late. Some dwarf varieties, including 'Stella de Oro' (below), bloom throughout the summer.

Daylilies have been cultivated for more than 2,500 years and are familiar to most people. There are now over 12,000 varieties available, with 700–800 new ones added each year. The variety 'Starling' (above) is particularly striking combined with yellow daylilies.

Drought-tolerant daylilies and potentilla shrubs thrive in a sun-baked flowerbed.

Delphinium

Delphinium elatum
Bee Delphinium,
Candle Larkspur,
Garden Delphinium

light blue, dark blue, lavender, purple, pink, white

Delphiniums are tall, stately perennials with long wands of glorious flowers.

My grandmother always kept bouquets of delphiniums in her farmhouse. In those days, few people cut flowers from their gardens, but delphiniums were her favourite flower and she could not resist cutting the tall, beautiful stalks to bring them indoors. Blue was the most common colour for delphiniums then, but the newer hybrid varieties now bloom in a much greater range of hues.

Height • 3–9 feet (90–225 cm)

Spread • 3–4 feet (90–120 cm)

Blooms • late spring to midsummer

PLANTING

Seeding: Indoors in February or March; refrigerate moistened seeds for 1 week prior to sowing. Cover seeds lightly; germination 7–30 days. Sow outdoors in August or September. Plants will bloom the first year.

Transplanting: Space 24–36 inches (60–90 cm) apart.

GROWING

Sun for at least half the day. Avoid hot or windy areas of the garden.

Backgrounds, cottage gardens, back of border.

Keep soil evenly moist; these plants do not like to dry out.

Staking is usually required.

Divide every 3 years to rejuvenate plants. If you do not, these plants lose vigour rapidly and die out after a few years. See page 54, method A.

RECOMMENDED VARIETIES

Fountain Mix • 3–4 feet (60–90 cm) tall and 2–3 feet (60–90 cm) wide; compact plants; flowerstalks hold up well in adverse weather; often does not need staking.

Pacific Giant Hybrids • 5–7 feet
(150–215 cm) tall; large, well-formed
florets as large as 2 inches (5 cm) across;
individual colours include pastel-blue, deep
violet, lavender, indigo-blue and pure
white; often available separately as named
varieties, including 'Astolat' (lavender with
black centres) and 'King Arthur'
(dark blue).

139

Tips

Delphiniums prefer rich soil. For the best
show of flowers, work the soil deeply before
planting, and add lots of compost, well-rotted
manure or peat moss.

These plants are heavy feeders. Be sure to add
bone meal each spring, and fertilize plants
regularly until midsummer.

Deadheading keeps plants tidy and more
vigorous. Remove faded flowerheads before
they set seed; seed production uses up a lot of
the plant's energy. Deadheading will give you
sturdier plants with more flowers in following
years.

Unless divided regularly, delphiniums are
relatively short-lived, lasting about 3–4 years.
They self-sow readily, but seedlings are usually
inferior to the parent plants. Regular division
can extend their life to about 10 years.

Plant delphiniums where they will be sheltered from strong winds. Bright Shasta daisies are good companions.

If you do want seedlings, leave some faded flowers on the plant.

Gardeners who grow delphiniums for exhibition or garden shows often prune off some of the side-shoots as they appear in spring. The result is larger flowers on sturdier spikes, but they usually need to be staked.

For a second flush of blooms in fall, remove flowerspikes as soon as the blooms fade. Cut plants back to 12 inches (30 cm) above ground level and fertilize once or twice with 20–20–20. The new stalks will produce flowers of smaller size but equal intensity.

Delphiniums are often susceptible to powdery mildew, a disease which looks like powdery white patches on the leaves. To help prevent

Delphinium's majestic flowers are striking in bouquets with silver king sage.

Delphiniums bloom in tall spires, with tightly packed individual flowers from 2–3 inches (5–7.5 cm) across. Each flower has a double ring of petals, and many have contrasting centres called 'bees.'

it, water around the base of plants, rather than from overhead, to keep foliage dry. Watering in the morning is best. Don't crowd plants; good air circulation helps ward off the disease.

Watch plants in late spring for signs of the 'delphinium worm.' Leaves that appear to be tied together are the earliest sign that the worm is present. Remove and destroy the little green worms, cut off affected parts of the plant, or use an insecticide. If you do not get rid of the worms, your plants will fail to bloom, have distorted flowers, or only single blooms rather than tall flowerspikes. The key is to get rid of these worms as soon as possible, before flower buds are damaged.

Cut flowerstalks for bouquets when the majority of lower blooms are open. They will last 7–10 days. Delphiniums tend to drop their petals, but using flower food and frequently recutting stems helps to reduce that.

For dried flowers, cut when the lower two-thirds of the flowerspike is open. Strip off most of the leaves, tie a few stems in bunches and hang upside-down for about a week.

The tall flowerstalks of delphiniums are quite top-heavy and individual stalks often need to be staked. Newer hybrids bloom in a variety of colours.

Elephant-ears

Bergenia cordifolia
Bergenia, Giant Rockfoil, Heart-leaf Bergenia, Leather-leaf, Rockfoil, Saxifrage

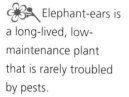 red, pink

Elephant-ears is a long-lived, low-maintenance plant that is rarely troubled by pests.

As soon as snow begins to melt in spring, the green leaves of elephant-ears become visible. Soon after, nodding stems rise up to a foot (30 cm) above foliage, bearing clusters of delicate flowers in hues ranging from deep magenta to pale pink. Large leaves 8–10 inches (20–25 cm) across remain attractive throughout the season. In autumn, the foliage turns a handsome reddish-bronze.

Height • 15–18 inches (38–45 cm)

Spread • 24–36 inches (60–90 cm) or more

Blooms • spring

PLANTING

Seeding: Not recommended. Plants will take 3–4 years to flower.

Roots: Plant in spring, with crowns at soil surface.

Transplanting: Space 12–24 inches (30–60 cm) apart.

GROWING

Shade or sun, in a site that is shaded from hot, late-afternoon rays.

Elegant clusters of red or pink flowers rise on sturdy stalks in spring.

The species name cordifolia *means 'heart-shaped leaves.' In the fall, the foliage of elephant-ears turns a rich mahogany colour (below).*

Along paths, in mixed borders, rock gardens. Splendid groundcover. Front of border.

Never cut elephant-ears back. This plant is an evergreen perennial, and cutting it back will prevent it from flowering, or harm the plant.

Divide every 3 years or when centre of plant weakens or dies. Use method A, page 54. Divide after flowering.

RECOMMENDED VARIETIES

Morning Red • large bronze-green leaves with dark purplish-red flowers; very showy.

Perfect • rose-pink flowers; slightly taller plants than 'Morning Red.'

TIPS

Elephant-ears is one of the most versatile perennials. It grows well in sun or shade, wet or dry areas, acidic, alkaline, average or poor soil. Plant it in flowerbeds under shrubs and trees, or next to a garden pond or stream. We grow it along the east side of the house, where it flourishes with very little care.

Elephant-ears grows faster in moist areas.

Evening Primrose

Oenothera tetragona
Sundrops

 yellow

The genus Oenothera *includes various similar-looking plants noted for opening their flowers at a particular time of the day. Those that bloom late in the day and close the following morning are called 'evening primroses,' while those that open fresh each morning and close the same evening are called 'sundrops.' Although O. tetragona falls into the second group, it is still better known as an 'evening primrose,' and that's how we refer to it. In spring, its dark green leaves are tinted purple, and showy red buds open to bright yellow flowers through most of the summer.*

Height • 18–24 inches (45–60 cm)

Spread • 12–18 inches (30–45 cm)

Blooms • summer

PLANTING

Seeding: Indoors in February; germination 2–3 weeks. Seed needs light to germinate; do not cover with soil mix. Outdoors in early spring. Plants started indoors will bloom the first season.

Transplanting: Space 10–15 inches (25–38 cm) apart.

Evening primrose is a cheerful-looking plant, with bright, sunny-yellow flowers that last all summer long.

Tickseed and evening primrose make a cheery bouquet. The flowers last more than a week.

Growing

Sun.

Mixed flowerbeds, on slopes. Front to middle of border.

Divide every 3 years. See page 54, method B.

Recommended Varieties

Illumination • masses of 1-inch (2.5 cm) flowers; the best, brightest yellow of all varieties; forms a nice, compact mound.

Tips

Since evening primrose is not wide-spreading, it is a good choice for narrow flowerbeds. A long row of these plants along the driveway looks absolutely stunning.

These plants are the source of what it said to be the world's richest natural, unsaturated fatty acids. Capsules of evening primrose oil are commonly sold in health food stores.

Evening primrose does well in hot areas of the garden, as long as the soil is not too dry.

Evening primrose will brighten sunny spots with satiny, shimmering little flowers.

False-sunflower

**Heliopsis
helianthoides**
Sunflower Heliopsis

yellow

*'Super-impressive' is the rating assigned to
false-sunflower by our perennials manager, Bob
Stadnyk. He cites its long blooming period,
exceptional resistance to pests and disease and
ability to withstand 'whatever nature throws at it'
as outstanding features. False-sunflowers produce
lots of brassy, golden-yellow, single or double
flowers throughout the summer. These flowers are
excellent for cutting.*

Height • 24–36 inches (60–90 cm)

Spread • 36 inches (90 cm)

Blooms • early summer to fall

PLANTING

Seeding: Indoors in February or March;
germination irregular, 14–21 days. Sow
outdoors in early spring. Plants will bloom
the second year.

Transplanting: Space 24 inches
(60 cm) apart.

GROWING

Sun to partial shade; in hot areas, choose a
spot with afternoon shade.

False-sunflower
is one of the longest-
blooming perennials.

Mixed flowerbeds, shrub beds, cutting
gardens. Middle to back of border.

Divide every 3–4 years, when plants become
overcrowded. See page 54, method A.

Recommended Varieties

Summer Sun • 36 inches (90 cm)
tall; large, 3-inch (7.5 cm) flowers
on sturdy stems; stands up well to
winds and heavy rain without
being staked.

Tips

False-sunflower tolerates poor soil
and drought, but produces more
flowers in good soil with ample
moisture.

Like their namesake, false-sunflowers
are marvellous in bouquets. Cut these
flowers often to bring 'sunshine'
indoors.

False-sunflowers are also wonderful
in dried arrangements. Harvest when
blooms are three-quarters open and
hang bunches upside-down.

*False-sunflowers thrive
in a sunny garden with
spirea shrubs (above).*

Heliopsis
means 'like the sun,'
and the species name
helianthoides means
'like a sunflower.'

*False-sunflowers attract
butterflies to the garden.*

Flax

Linum flavum
Yellow Flax,
Golden Flax

Linum perenne
Blue Flax,
Perennial Flax

148

blue, yellow,
white

Flax looks pretty in almost any flowerbed. Blue flax has dainty, sky-blue flowers and needle-like, blue-green leaves; the effect is an airy mass of flowers. Yellow flax has larger flowers on shorter plants and is less common. It looks wonderful in a sunny rock garden or at the front of a border. Both types of flax are good for long, narrow beds, such as those along a driveway, where wider-spreading plants won't fit.

Height • Blue Flax: 18 inches (30 cm)
Yellow Flax: 10 inches (25 cm)

Spread • Blue Flax: 12–18 inches (30–45 cm)
Yellow Flax: 10 inches (25 cm)

Blooms • Both: late spring to late summer

PLANTING

Seeding: Indoors in February or March; germination 8–12 days. Outdoors in spring. Plants will bloom the second year.

Transplanting: Space 12–18 inches (30–45 cm) apart.

GROWING

Sun to partial shade.

Rock gardens, flowerbeds, in small groups. Front to middle of border.

Do not divide flax. These plants have long taproots and cannot easily be divided or moved.

Flax blooms for many weeks, with an abundance of dainty flowers.

Recommended Varieties

Usually available only under one of the names listed above. 'Alba' is a white-flowered form of blue flax.

Tips

Blue flax is a short-lived perennial. It lasts only 2–3 years, but it self-sows readily. If you allow some seedheads to form you will have blue flax growing in your garden for years. Yellow flax lives longer, but self-sows reluctantly.

Flax grows well in poor soil, but blooms longest when soil is moist.

Cut yellow flax for bouquets, but leave blue flax to bloom only in the garden, because it does not make a good cutflower.

The round seedpods of blue flax make interesting additions to dried arrangements. Cut when individual pods are still tightly closed. Hang upside-down in bunches to dry.

Offset yellow flax's cheerful flowers with moor grass, beebalm and blue sage.

Each of blue flax's flowers (above) lasts only a day or two, but they are produced generously throughout the summer. The flowers remain closed at night, in dense shade and on cloudy days. In a partially shaded location, such as a flowerbed under sunlight dappled by overhead trees, the flowers will be bluest, but sunnier locations will generate more flowers.

Fleabane

Erigeron speciosus
Daisy Fleabane,
Oregon Fleabane

purple, pink,
white

If you like asters, you will also enjoy fleabane. The flowers of these two plants look remarkably similar, but fleabane blooms in summer and finishes just as asters begin to bloom in fall. Fleabane puts on a spectacular show all summer long, with masses of flowers that hide most of its foliage. They are marvellous in bouquets. Grow fleabane with evening primroses, garden phlox and ornamental grasses.

Height • 15–24 inches (38–60 cm)

Spread • 18–24 inches (45–60 cm)

Blooms • early to late summer

PLANTING

Seeding: Indoors in February or March; germination 10–21 days. Press seed firmly into mix. Sow outdoors in fall or early spring. Plants will bloom the first year.

Transplanting: Space 12–18 inches (30–45 cm) apart.

GROWING

Sun to partial shade.

Mixed borders, cutting gardens. Front to middle of border.

Fleabane is a long-lived perennial that blooms for two months in summer.

The dried flowers of these plants were once used as a flea repellent, hence the name 'fleabane.'

Water at the base of plants rather than from overhead. This prevents the wet foliage that can lead to powdery mildew disease.

Divide every 4–5 years. See page 54, method A.

Recommended Varieties

Darkest of All • 24 inches (60 cm) tall; violet-blue flowers; the best blue available.

Pink Jewel • 18–24 inches (45–60 cm) tall; soft-pink flowers; one of the prettiest pinks available.

Tips

Fertilize fleabane sparsely, because too many nutrients can result in floppy plants. When these plants need support, we've found that a wide-mouthed tomato cage works nicely.

Do not crowd plants. Fleabane can be prone to powdery mildew, which is warded off by good air circulation.

Cut for bouquets when flowers are starting to open. They last 7–10 days after cutting.

Plant fleabane with bearded irises and sea holly. Black-eyed Susans and Shasta daisies are also good partners.

Fleeceflower

**Persicaria affinis
(Polygonum affine)**
Knotweed, Himalayan
Fleeceflower

pink

*The ideal groundcover plant is beautiful, fast-
growing and requires very little maintenance.
Fleeceflower meets those requirements. It has low
tufts of small, leathery leaves and abundant
flowerspikes that look like pink bottle brushes. This
is a great plant for hot, dry areas of the garden.*

Height • 6–12 inches (15–30 cm)

Spread • 24 inches (60 cm) or more

Blooms • early summer through fall

PLANTING

Seeding: Not recommended. Germination is
slow and sporadic.

Transplanting: Space 12–18 inches (30–45
cm) apart.

GROWING

Sun to partial shade.

Excellent groundcover for difficult areas.

Fleeceflower can remain undisturbed
indefinitely. If you want more plants, divide
using method A, page 54.

RECOMMENDED VARIETIES

Border Jewel • 12 inches (30 cm) tall; light
pink flowers later turn red; foliage turns
bright red in fall.

Fleeceflower is
one of the longest-
blooming perennials.

The flowerstalks remain bright red after the pink petals drop, making it appear that the plant is blooming in two different colours. The attractive 'redheads' last until freeze-up, creating the illusion that this plant blooms for nearly four months. Often, the leaves will turn red in fall.

Darjeeling Red • 9–12 inches (23–30 cm) tall; long-lasting, rose-pink flowers that deepen to russet-red; one of the best varieties for brilliant flower colour; foliage turns red in fall.

Tips

Fleeceflowers thrive in dry soil, but they also do well in any garden soil. With more moisture, they spread more quickly. Our fleeceflower grows in a low, moist area at the end of a large flowerbed. In 3 years, it has spread to 4 feet (120 cm) wide.

Fleeceflowers grow well in poor soil and are good for growing on slopes.

Add these upright flowerspikes to fresh bouquets.

Both the flowers and 'red' seedheads dry so perfectly that they appear to be fresh. Snip some of each for a combination of colours. Let leaves remain on stems, as they dry nicely too. Hang stems in bunches upside-down to dry.

Fleeceflower puts on a show stopping display with cheddar pink, tickseed, blue fescue, lady's mantle, delphiniums and Russian sage.

Foxglove

Digitalis purpurea
Common Foxglove

 purple, rusty-red, rose, pink, yellow, bronze, pearly grey, white

154

Foxglove attracts humming-birds.

Foxglove's botanical name Digitalis *comes from the Latin* digitus, *meaning 'finger.' Each tubular flower is shaped a little like the finger of a glove. Purple is the original colour of these flowers (hence the species name* purpurea), *but newer hybrids bloom in a far wider range of colours, with and without speckled throats. The flowers are not very fragrant, but curiously, the leaves smell somewhat like peanut butter.*

Height • 3–6 feet (90–180 cm)

Spread • 3 feet (90 cm)

Blooms • early to midsummer

PLANTING

Seeding: Indoors in February or March; germination 7–10 days. Seed needs light to germinate; press on top of soil mix and do not cover. Sow outdoors in fall or spring. Plants will form an attractive clump of foliage the first year, and bloom the second.

Transplanting: Space 15–18 inches (40–45 cm) apart.

GROWING

Sun to light shade.

English, cottage and woodland gardens; against a wall or fence. Back of border.

Plants may require staking.

Do not cut back plants; that will prevent them from flowering.

Division is not required since these plants are biennial.

RECOMMENDED VARIETIES

Excelsior Hybrids • 4–6 feet (120–180 cm) tall; large, more upward-facing blooms than other varieties; flowers circle the stem, unlike others which bear flowers on one side only.

Tips

Foxgloves like moist soil, but do not plant them in areas where water sits after snow melts in spring.

These plants bloom mainly in early summer, but if you cut off the first flowering stalks before seeds form, the plants often rebloom in midsummer. Remember though, that foxgloves are biennials; if you want them in your garden for more than 2 years, you must allow plants to set seed. Foxgloves do not always self-seed successfully; you may want to add new seeds to the garden each year to ensure their survival.

Foxgloves are rarely troubled by pests and deer.

Foxgloves make superb, long-lasting cutflowers. Cut when only the lower flowers on the stalk are starting to open. The rest of the flowers will slowly open in the vase; pinch off lower flowers as they wilt. Cut stems last well over 2 weeks; frequent recutting extends vase-life.

Combine foxgloves with false-sunflowers, delphiniums, clustered bellflowers and St. John's wort.

After their first flowering, cut off foxgloves' main spikes. Sideshoots then develop, and plants continue to bloom for a few more weeks.

Foxtail Lily

**Eremurus
stenophyllus**
Narrow-leaf Foxtail
Lily, Desert Candle

**Eremurus χ
isabellinus**
Shelford Foxtail Lily

yellow, copper,
pink, white

Foxtail lilies are
one of the tallest
flowers in the early
summer garden.

*Foxtail lilies are stunning perennials, with tall,
narrow flowerspikes that rise up to 3 feet (90 cm)
above yucca-like leaves. Each spike bears masses of
small flowers. Narrow-leaf foxtail lilies have yellow
blooms that turn burnt-orange as they age.
Shelford foxtail lilies have the most flowers, in
yellow, copper, pink or white. We grow these plants
near a blue, big-petal clematis vine. The vine's
trellis protects the foxtail lilies from wind, and
helps trap snow over plants for winter protection.*

Height • Narrow-leaf Foxtail Lily:
3–4 feet (90–120 cm)
Shelford Foxtail Lily: 4–6 feet
(120–180 cm)

Spread • Narrow-leaf Foxtail Lily:
2 feet (60 cm)
Shelford Foxtail Lily: 4 feet (120 cm)

Blooms • early summer

PLANTING

Seeding: Not recommended.
Germination may take
6–12 months.

Roots: Plant tuberous roots
4–6 inches (10–15 cm) deep in
spring or fall. Handle with care; the
octopus-shaped roots are brittle and
break easily. Be sure to mix coarse
sand into soil before planting, as
well as around the plant's crowns.
Plants will bloom the first year.

Transplanting: Space plants
24 inches (60 cm) apart.

GROWING

Sun.

Accent plants, mixed flowerbeds,
shrub beds. Middle to back
of border.

Do not divide. Successful division
is difficult because these plants
have hard crowns and brittle, spreading roots.

Recommended Varieties

Narrow-leaf foxtail lilies are usually available only under one of the names listed above.

Shelford Foxtail Lily

Ruiter Hybrids • brighter flower colours and more compact plants than species.

Tips

Do not plant in areas where puddles linger. Wet soil, especially in spring, can kill these plants.

Yarrow, delphiniums and painted daisies mix well with foxtail lilies.

By late summer, these plants go dormant. Allow foliage to yellow and die before cutting it off, and be sure to mark the spot so you don't disturb the roots. Grow airy plants like baby's breath or statice nearby to hide the gap.

Cut for bouquets when only flowers on the bottom half of flowerspikes are open. Foxtail lilies last 7–10 days.

The botanical name Eremurus *comes from Greek words meaning 'a desert' and 'a tail,' describing this plant's natural habitat and the shape of its flowers.*

The foxtail lily is a tough, drought-tolerant perennial that thrives in hot, dry locations.

Garden Mum

Dendranthema χ **morifolium (Chrysanthemum** χ **morifolium)**

Morden Mum, Hardy Garden Mum, Hardy Chrysanthemum, Cushion Mum

purple, lavender, pink, red, orange, bronze, yellow, white

I like mums because they round off the year with masses of cheerful flowers. Mums bloom through late summer and fall, undeterred by light frosts. They are often one of the last flowers blooming in the garden. Morden mums are the hardiest type available, with large flowers that cover plants in an array of colours. It is rather unfortunate that these plants were recently reclassified as **Dendranthema**, *as* **Chrysanthemum** *is one of the few well-known botanical names.*

Height • 18–24 inches (45–60 cm)

Spread • 15–24 inches (38–60 cm)

Blooms • late summer to late fall

PLANTING

Seeding: Not recommended. Morden mums are hybrids and do not come true from seed.

Transplanting: Space 12–18 inches (30–45 cm) apart.

Garden mums bloom from late summer until late fall.

GROWING

Sun to partial shade.

Mixed flowerbeds. Front to middle of border.

Garden mums have aromatic foliage and masses of flowers from late summer through to fall (left). For rosy-purple, double blooms, choose 'Morden Fiesta' (opposite).

Keep well-watered during dry periods; mums have shallow roots and need constant moisture.

Soak plants heavily just before freeze-up. In exposed sites, apply a mulch around the base of plants after the ground is frozen. Try to keep mums covered with snow during winter. Leave top-growth standing to help trap snow on the plants.

Divide every 2 years for best flowering. Centres of these plants tend to die out at this point; discard them and replant other pieces. See page 54, method B.

Recommended Varieties

Morden Aztec • 18–24 inches (45–60 cm) tall; bronze, double flowers.

Morden Cameo • 18–24 inches (45–60 cm) tall; large, creamy-white, double flowers.

Morden Canary • 24 inches (60 cm) tall; brilliant yellow, double flowers; great for cutting.

Morden Candy • 18–24 inches (45–60 cm) tall; soft pink, double flowers.

Morden Delight • 18–24 inches (45–60 cm) tall; large, bronze, fully double flowers.

Morden Eldorado • 18–24 inches (45–60 cm) tall; bright yellow, double flowers; mound-forming plants.

'Morden Everest' (right) has white flowers like big powderpuffs.

Morden Everest • 24 inches (60 cm) tall; beautiful, pure snow-white, fully double flowers.

Morden Fiesta • 18–24 inches (45–60 cm) tall; rosy-purple, double flowers.

Morden Garnet • 18 inches (45 cm) tall; intense cardinal-red, double flowers.

Tips

Be sure to choose varieties that begin blooming no later than mid-September. Later-bloomers are unlikely to flower before hard frosts arrive. Any of the Morden cultivars are fine.

You can plant florist mums into the garden, but treat them as annuals. These types are unlikely to survive the winter in northern gardens.

Some gardeners pinch their mums back to obtain bushier plants. Morden mums are naturally bushy, so this step is unnecessary.

Mums have shallow roots that dry out quickly. Using a mulch around plants reduces the need to water.

For the longest-lasting cutflowers, cut just as flowers open. Mums last about 2 weeks in a vase.

Because garden mums need to be divided regularly, you'll end up with a lot of plants. Choose colours that you love in both the garden (below) and bouquets. 'Morden Canary' blooms in bright yellow (left); 'Morden Delight' is an attractive bronze (bottom).

Gasplant

Dictamnus albus
(D. fraxinella)
Burning Bush, Dittany

 white, pink,
purple

Gasplants are so named because their flowers emit a flammable oil. On a still, muggy evening, a lit match held just below a blossom will ignite this volatile oil, with a soft 'pop'! Gasplants bloom abundantly in early summer, with heavily scented, very showy flowerspikes in white, pink or purplish-pink. All parts of this hardy, long-lived perennial are strongly lemon-scented when bruised.

Height • 3–4 feet (90–120 cm)

Spread • 3 feet (90 cm)

Blooms • early summer

PLANTING

Seeding: Not recommended. Plants take 3–4 years to bloom from seed.

Transplanting: Space 30 inches (75 cm) apart.

Gasplants do well in hot, dry areas of the garden.

GROWING

Sun to light shade.

Mixed flowerbeds. Back of border.

Do not divide. Gasplants have a long taproot and usually cannot be moved without injury. They remain vigorous and healthy in the same site for 20 years or more.

Recommended Varieties
Usually available only under one of the names listed above.

Tips
Often in the first year after planting, these plants do not appear to grow at all. Don't worry—the gasplants are just taking their time settling in, and will show obvious growth in following years.

Combine gasplants with peonies, Oriental poppies and lupins, all of which bloom at the same time. Yarrow, fleabane and asters make good, later-blooming partners, as do cranesbills, baby's breath and statice.

Although the blooming period is rather short, flowers produce starry, bronze seed-capsules, and the glossy, dark green foliage remains pretty all season.

Gasplants are one of the longest-lived perennials, lasting for 20 or more years; they grow into sturdy bushes.

Grow gasplant along a walkway, so that you can enjoy its fragrance on passing.

Gentian

Gentiana acaulis
Stemless Gentian,
Spring Gentian

Gentiana septemfida
Crested Gentian,
Seven-Lobed Gentian

**Gentiana sino-
ornata**
Chinese Gentian

 blue, white

 Gentians have
the truest-blue flowers
of all perennials.

One of our customers is from Switzerland, and
shares with us stories of springtime in her home-
land, when the gentians bloom and turn
mountainsides into carpets of blue. Stemless
gentians are the gentians of the Swiss Alps,
and are easiest of all to grow. These plants form
thick mats of foliage with 2-inch (5 cm), bright
blue flowers in spring.

Crested gentians are one of the hardiest types. They
bloom throughout summer with clusters of deep
blue, tubular flowers. Chinese gentians bloom last,
with rich cobalt-blue, upturned flowers that persist
through several hard frosts. Stems grow outward
from the plant's centre, a little like the spokes of a
wheel. For the best likelihood of success in your
garden, stick to the types of gentians listed on these
pages, as they are far easier to grow than most.
Adventurous gardeners, however, may enjoy
experimenting with other species.

Height • Stemless Gentian: 4 inches (10 cm)
Crested Gentian: 8–10 inches (20–25 cm)
Chinese Gentian: 2–4 inches (5–10 cm)

Spread • Stemless Gentian: 12 inches (30 cm)
Crested Gentian: 15–18 inches (38–45 cm)
Chinese Gentian: 12–18 inches (30–45 cm)

Blooms • Stemless Gentian: late spring
Crested Gentian: most of summer
Chinese Gentian: late summer
to frost

PLANTING

Seeding: Not recommended.
Gentians are difficult to grow
from seed.

*Crested gentians bloom
in summer, brightening
rock gardens and
flowerbeds.*

Transplanting: Space stemless and Chinese
gentians 8–10 inches (20–25 cm)
apart, and crested gentians 12–15 inches
(30–38 cm) apart. Gentians look best
in groups.

GROWING

Partial shade to sun; do not plant in areas
with hot afternoon sun. Moist soil.

Rock and woodland gardens, as edging.
Front of border.

Water during dry spells; do not allow plants
to dry out.

Division is seldom required, as gentians will continue to spread and
thrive for years in ideal locations. If you want more plants, however,
divide stemless gentians after blooming and the others in spring. See
page 54, method C.

RECOMMENDED VARIETIES

Usually available only under one of the names listed above.

TIPS

Not all gentians have the same growing requirements. Most prefer
slightly alkaline soils, but Chinese gentians are an exception. These
plants must have acidic soil, so add lots of peat moss to soil when
planting. Average garden conditions are usually fine for others.

Gentians need cool, moist soil, so they should be shaded from hot
afternoon sun. With stemless gentians in particular, regular watering
with ice-cold water seems to help initiate blooming.

OTHER RECOMMENDED SPECIES

Gentiana cachemirica (Himalayan Gentian): 3–6 inches (7.5–15 cm) tall
and 12–15 inches (30–38 cm) wide; lots of violet-blue flowers;
blooms late summer to early fall.

*Chinese gentians
(above) bloom
throughout the fall,
undeterred by several
killing frosts. We have
had these plants
blooming in our garden
until late November,
when snow finally
covered the flowers.
Spring-blooming
stemless gentians (left)
are the famed gentians
of the Swiss Alps.*

Globe Thistle

Echinops ritro
Small Globe Thistle

blue

Globe thistle is an unusual and striking plant. It blooms throughout the summer, with an abundance of spiky, steel-blue, spherical flowers that are marvellous in both fresh and dried bouquets. Globe thistle does well in hot, dry areas, and looks splendid with other drought-tolerant plants, such as ornamental grasses, yarrow and Oriental poppies.

Height • 36–48 inches (90–120 cm)

Spread • 18–24 inches (45–60 cm)

Blooms • early summer to early fall

PLANTING

Seeding: Indoors in February or March; germination 7–10 days. Seed needs light to germinate; do not cover. Sow outdoors in early spring. Plants will bloom the second year.

Roots: Plant in spring, with crown at or slightly below soil level.

Transplanting: Space 18–24 inches (45–60 cm) apart.

Globe thistles are stately, long-lived plants with unusual flowers.

GROWING

Sun to light shade; good in hot, dry locations.

Accent plants. Middle to back of border.

Globe thistle seldom needs to be divided and will thrive for years in the same spot. If you want more plants, remove a side-shoot rosette of leaves without disturbing the main plant. Do not try to split the main plant—its long taproot makes it difficult to divide without killing the plant. See page 54, method A.

Recommended Varieties

Usually available only under one of the names listed above.

Tips

Globe thistle grows into a sturdy, upright plant. Offset its bold foliage with fine-textured plants such as baby's breath, Russian sage and statice. The yellow flowers of black-eyed Susans provide a striking colour contrast.

Once established, globe thistles are quite drought-tolerant. They particularly dislike wet soil in spring, so do not plant where snow melts last.

Add these unusual flowers to mixed bouquets. Cut bouquets when a quarter of the blooms on each stem are open. The flowers last up to 2 weeks after cutting.

For dried flowers, cut stems before flowers fully open. Hang single stems upside-down. They dry into perfect, spiky spheres, providing an uncommon shape for dried arrangements.

Globe thistles are rarely troubled by pests.

The botanical name Echinops *is derived from a Greek word meaning 'hedgehog.' Globe thistle is a spiny plant, with spiky, rounded flowers and prickly stems.*

Globe thistle's flowers change from thistle-like globes to starry spheres.

Globeflower

Trollius europaeus
Common Globeflower

Trollius χ cultorum
Hybrid Globeflower

 orange, yellow,
white

*Globeflowers are among my favourite perennials.
These flowers look like huge buttercups, and
provide bright spots of colour in spring.
Globeflowers like moist soil and partial shade.
They mix well with hostas, rayflowers, ferns and
meadowsweet. If you have a garden pond, grow
globeflowers along the edge; they do well even in
boggy conditions.*

Height • Common Globeflower:
18–24 inches (45–60 cm)
Hybrid Globeflower: 15–24 inches
(38–60 cm)

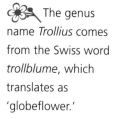 The genus
name *Trollius* comes
from the Swiss word
trollblume, which
translates as
'globeflower.'

Spread • Common Globeflower:
12–24 inches (30–60 cm)
Hybrid Globeflower: 12–24 inches
(30–60 cm)

Blooms • Common Globeflower: midspring
Hybrid Globeflower: late spring

PLANTING

Seeding: Not recommended. Seed may take
up to a year to break dormancy.

Roots: Plant in spring, with
crowns at or slightly below
soil surface.

Transplanting: Space
10–12 inches
(25–30 cm) apart.

GROWING

Partial shade; rich,
moist soil.

Shade gardens, mixed
flowerbeds. Middle of
border.

Keep well-watered at all
times; these plants do not
like to dry out.

Divide every 5 years, after
blooming has finished.
See page 54, method A.

RECOMMENDED VARIETIES
Common Globeflower
Superbus • similar to the species but has more flowers.

Hybrid Globeflower
Goldquelle • 15–18 inches (38–45 cm) tall and 12–15 inches (30–38 cm) wide; more compact than most; masses of 2-inch (5 cm), yellow, buttercup flowers; often reblooms in fall.

TIPS

Globeflowers thrive in low-lying, moist areas of the garden.

Globeflowers need moist soil. Add lots of compost or peat moss when planting to help retain water.

In dry soil, globeflowers may die back by midsummer. Remove dead foliage to improve appearance.

Cut flowers for bouquets when petals begin to separate from the centre. They last 7–10 days in a vase.

Common globeflowers (opposite) have rounded blooms, while hybrid ones have more open flowers (below). Lady's mantle, meadowsweet and hostas are good companions.

Goatsbeard

Aruncus dioicus
(A. sylvester)

 white

This lovely perennial looks like a giant, shrub-sized astilbe; the two plants resemble each other so closely that astilbe is sometimes called 'false goatsbeard.' Due to its size, the true goatsbeard is best planted at the back of your garden, where it provides a canvas of lush, green leaves to offset the flowers of other plants. For about a month in early summer, showy, smoke-like plumes of creamy-ivory flowers wave above goatsbeards' leaves. The foliage turns a rich bronze in fall.

Height • 2–5 feet (60–150 cm)

Spread • 4 feet (120 cm)

Blooms • early to midsummer

Goatsbeard is one of the largest perennials.

PLANTING

Seeding: Not recommended, as it is generally difficult to raise plants from seed.

Transplanting: Space 18–24 inches (45–60 cm) apart.

GROWING

Partial shade.

Mass plantings, woodland gardens, feature plant, centre of island beds, on slopes. Back of border.

Does not need dividing, but if you want more plants, divide after 3–5 years using method A, page 54. Do so only if necessary, because goatsbeard resents being moved.

170

RECOMMENDED VARIETIES

Kneiffii • 24–36 inches (60–90 cm) tall; similar to the species except in its leaves, which are very attractive, finely divided and saw-edged.

TIPS

Plant a single goatsbeard near a patio or deck, or line a few in a row along a fence. Grow hosta or elephant-ears in front for a contrast in foliage texture, or align it with snakeroot, which grows about the same height but blooms later in the season.

Goatsbeard will grow in densely shaded areas, but it will bloom only sparsely. For the best show of flowers, choose a site that receives dappled shade all day, or a half-day of full sun.

Snip a few of goatsbeard's flowers to add to bouquets. These showy plumes may be as much as 4 feet (120 cm) tall, adding dramatic height to floral arrangements. They last a week or more after cutting.

Goatsbeard is one of the most versatile perennials. It does well in almost any garden soil, including areas of dry shade and those that remain wet for extended periods. Magnificent, feathery, creamy-white flowers appear in early summer and its foliage remains attractive throughout the season.

The species name dioicus *literally means 'of two houses.' This refers to the fact that goatsbeard bears male and female flowers on separate plants. Male flowers are more feathery and upright, while female flowers are drooping plumes. Nurseries do not sell the sexes separately.*

Goldenrod

Solidago χ hybrida

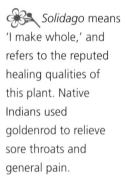
yellow

Goldenrod blooms with delicate spires of tiny, individual flowers in almost every shade of yellow, from pale primrose and lemon-yellow to dark gold. These large flower clusters make a wonderful display in the garden, and, contrary to popular belief, they won't make you sneeze! The real culprit for hay fever is ragweed, not goldenrod. Both bloom at the same time, but goldenrod's pollen is heavy and insect-borne, while ragweed's pollen is light and wind-borne.

Height • 15–36 inches (38–90 cm)

Spread • 18–36 inches (45–90 cm)

Blooms • late summer to fall

PLANTING

Seeding: Indoors in February or March. Outdoors in early spring. Plants will likely bloom the first year.

Transplanting: Space 18 inches (45 cm) apart.

GROWING

Sun to light shade.

Cutflower gardens, mixed beds, meadow gardens. Middle to back of border.

Tall goldenrod may require staking.

Divide every 3–4 years to prevent over-crowding. See page 54, method A.

Solidago means 'I make whole,' and refers to the reputed healing qualities of this plant. Native Indians used goldenrod to relieve sore throats and general pain.

RECOMMENDED VARIETIES

Crown of Rays • 15–20 inches (38–50 cm) tall; large, flat-headed plumes of bright yellow flowers; colour more intense than most other varieties; sturdy, compact plants that don't need staking.

TIPS

Goldenrod looks stunning with blue flowers such as asters, Russian sage and speedwell.

Don't fertilize goldenrod; one application of bone meal in spring is enough. This prevents the plants from spreading too quickly.

Goldenrod self-sows readily. Uproot and transplant or discard the seedlings as they appear. To prevent seedlings, simply remove faded flowers before seedheads form.

I can't resist cutting goldenrod to add to bouquets. Cut blooms when just a few of the tiny florets in each cluster are open. They last about 2 weeks in a vase.

Cut flowers for drying before they fully open. Hang about 5 stems in a bunch upside-down for about a week. For best results, stagger the flowerheads up the length of each bunch.

When I was a child, I used to pick bouquets of wild goldenrod. The hybrid plants we now grow in gardens are far more showy and compact, with sturdier stems than the wildflowers. 'Crown of Rays' (below) is one of the best hybrid varieties.

Goutweed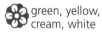

Aegopodium podagraria 'Variegatum'
Bishop's Weed, Goat's Foot, Snow-on-the-Mountain

174 green, yellow, cream, white

If you have a problem area of the garden, this plant is your dream come true. Goutweed will grow absolutely anywhere, which also means that it can become a nightmare if left uncontrolled. Properly planted, goutweed spreads rapidly into a lush carpet of pretty, ivy-shaped leaves, bright green and edged in yellow, white and cream. It brightens even the darkest corners of the garden, chokes out weeds, and needs very little care.

Height (without flowers) • 10–12 inches (25–30 cm)

Spread • 24 inches (60 cm) after 2 years; potentially unlimited

Blooms • midsummer

PLANTING

Seeding: Why bother? Like quackgrass, even the tiniest bit of goutweed's root will quickly grow into a new plant.

Transplanting: Space 12 inches (30 cm) apart. Goutweed will quickly spread to form a solid carpet of leaves.

GROWING

Sun or shade, in almost any soil.

Fast-growing groundcover.

Never needs dividing. If you want new plants, simply dig up a clump and transfer it to a new location. See page 54, method A.

RECOMMENDED VARIETIES

'Variegatum' is usually the only one available, because the type with solid green leaves is far less attractive.

TIPS

The key to success with goutweed is control. Plant it hemmed in along a driveway or sidewalk, or install an underground barrier to a minimum depth of 18 inches (45 cm). Goutweed spreads rampantly by creeping roots. If left unchecked, goutweed will

quickly take over less aggressive plants and even grow into lawn areas. It is extremely difficult to get rid of; most weed-killers have little effect.

Shrubs and large perennials that rarely need dividing, such as peonies or clematis vines, grow well with goutweed. They appear to be floating in a sea of variegated leaves, and are not threatened by their aggressive partner. (The reason you won't want to move or divide any perennials growing with goutweed is it is difficult to avoid taking goutweed with them.)

Occasionally, goutweed's leaves revert to green. Simply remove these shoots so that only the variegated leaves remain. If some leaves turn brown and unsightly, cut plants back as far as necessary. New foliage will grow quickly.

Goutweed produces pretty white flowers that resemble Queen Anne's lace, rising on long, slender stems above the leaves. I like to snip the delicate blooms to add to bouquets. If you dislike their look in the garden, just cut the blooms off as they appear.

Pests rarely, if ever, bother this plant. Goutweed crowds out weeds, and leaves fallen from trees drop through to the ground and act as a natural mulch.

Goutweed is the answer to almost any plant-defeating area of the garden. It is one of the few plants that does equally well in sun or shade, wet or dry spots, rich or poor soil and even in acidic areas around spruce trees.

Hens & Chicks

Sempervivum spp.
Houseleek

 pink, yellow, white

One look at these plants will tell you how they got their name: the central rosette looks like a hen with chicks peeping out from under her. Hens & chicks are fascinating plants. There are over 100 species of them, all of which form low, succulent rosettes of leaves. Some grow only a couple of inches wide, while others spread into mats a few feet across. There are little ones that look as if a spider has spun its web overtop of the plant, and others with leaf edges tipped in bright red, pink, purple, blue and even black.

Height (without flowers) • 1–3 inches (2.5–7.5 cm)

Spread • 2–36 inches (5–90 cm)

Blooms • summer

PLANTING

Seeding: Not recommended. These plants are very slow-growing and seed is not readily available.

Transplanting: Because of the range of spreading in mature plants, it is hard to provide exact advice on spacing. Generally, large rosettes require more room and small ones less. If you misjudge and your plants quickly become too crowded, don't worry! They are easy to divide.

The name *Sempervivum* means 'live forever.' These plants continually self-perpetuate. As the mother 'hen' dies out, young 'chicks' take its place, and new ones then grow into their place.

GROWING

Hot, dry, sunny location.

Rock gardens, edging borders, walls.

Divide whenever plants become too crowded. Unlike most perennials, hens & chicks can be divided at any time during the growing season. Simply break off the small rosettes, or 'chicks,' around the base of the old plants (they have their own roots), or the offshoots attached by an above-ground root to the central plant. With either type, just press them into the soil in a new location.

RECOMMENDED VARIETIES

As well as 100-plus species, there are over 300 varieties, ranging from sturdy, copper-coloured ones to tiny, green ones covered with silken cobwebs. I don't like to recommend particular varieties, because these plants are usually available as an assorted collection rather than as individual varieties.

Hens & chicks thrive in a hot, sunny site alongside annual gazanias.

Hens & chicks are low-maintenance plants, rarely troubled by pests and at their best in poor soil.

TIPS

Hens & chicks need little soil and will even grow in the cracks of a rock wall. In fact, the Romans used to grow them on their roofs in the belief that these plants would protect their houses from lightning! Even today, you may still see entire roof-tops of European houses covered with a tight mat of these tiny plants.

Do not fertilize hens & chicks. The foliage colours are most vivid when these plants are starved for nutrients. They also grow well in alkaline soil.

In summer, rather strange-looking flowers appear, rising from 6–12 inches (15–30 cm) above the foliage. The central rosette will die after blooming, but small ones quickly spread to fill the empty space.

LOOK-ALIKE COUSINS

Two other perennials so closely resemble hens & chicks in both appearance and growing needs that you will probably notice the difference only when they are in bloom. While the similarities between these three perennials may cause confusion, you will probably be equally happy with any of them.

1. False houseleeks
(*Jovibarbas* spp.) are most easily distinguished by their fringed petals. Only some of these plants produce side-shoot offspring; with others, the rosettes divide themselves but remain attached to a central root-stalk. These plants are known as 'rollers,' because during a hailstorm or heavy rain, small rosettes break away from the mother plant and go rolling off to another part of the garden. Wherever they stop, they will grow into another plant.

The central rosette of hens & chicks is called the hen, and the smaller ones are the chicks.

2. Orostachys (*Orostachys* spp.) bears bizarre, pale yellow, elongated flowers, from 2–12 inches (5–30 cm) tall, that rise like curved horns above the rosettes. These plants are often called false hens & chicks.

Bright, starry flowers rise on long stalks in summer. The central rosette of hens & chicks dies after blooming, but small ones quickly replace it.

Hollyhock

**Alcea rosea
(Althea rosea)**

black, red, lavender, yellow, salmon, rose, pink, white

Hollyhocks are one of the tallest perennials. Their long-lasting, satiny flowers attract hummingbirds to the garden.

Hollyhocks are old-fashioned flowers that bring memories of childhood summers to the minds of many gardeners. I remember these tall wands flowering along the wall of my mother's house, with their huge leaves, and fat seedheads tempting little fingers to peel them apart and pick out the seeds. Happily, this practice is helpful, as long as a few of the seeds fall to the ground. Hollyhocks are short-lived plants, but allowing them to drop seeds into surrounding soil ensures that you will have hollyhocks in your garden for years.

Height • 4–7 feet (120–215 cm)

Spread • 3–4 feet (90–120 cm)

Blooms • all summer

PLANTING

Seeding: Indoors in February or early March. Cover seed lightly; germinates in 7–14 days. Sow outdoors in late fall for blooms the following summer.

Transplanting: Space 24–36 inches (60–90 cm) apart.

GROWING

Sun.

English and cottage gardens, in rows against a fence, shed or wall. Back of border.

Stake in windy locations.

Water heavily. These plants do not like to dry out.

Hollyhocks never need dividing.

RECOMMENDED VARIETIES

Chater's Doubles • 4–7 feet (120–215 cm) tall; large, ruffled, double flowers; great mix of colours.

'Nigra' (opposite) looks particularly stunning when offset by pink or yellow hollyhocks. Although hollyhocks are short-lived plants, they self-sow readily and new seedlings quickly take the place of older plants. On summer drives along country roads, one often sees these tall, beautiful flowers in the hottest locations around farmhouses.

Negrita • 5–7 feet (150–215 cm) tall; huge, double, black-red flowers; stunning.

Nigra • 5–7 feet (150–215 cm) tall; huge, deep black-red, single flowers with extremely silky petals; unusual.

TIPS

Pinch out the central growing tip when seedlings are about 4 inches (10 cm) tall, or immediately after transplanting. This will give you multiple flowers on shorter, stocky plants that stand up well to wind.

Hollyhocks look best planted against a fence or wall or at the back of a border. A sheltered location eliminates the need for staking.

Cut these flowers for dramatic bouquets. Florists recommend filling the hollow stems to maximize the life of the cut blooms. If you want to try this, simply turn each one upside-down, pour water into the hollow stem until it is full and plug the end with a cotton ball. Hollyhocks usually last 7–10 days in a vase.

Single-flowered hollyhocks generally live longer than double-flowered hollyhocks, which die after two years. With either type, leave flowerstalks on after blossoms fade to permit self-seeding, and you will have a perennial show of hollyhocks in your garden.

Honeysuckle

Lonicera χ **Dropmore Scarlet**

Climbing Honeysuckle, Scarlet Honeysuckle Vine, Scarlet Trumpet Honeysuckle

 red, orange

Honeysuckle is the longest-blooming perennial vine.

Honeysuckles are one of the longest-blooming perennial vines; they flower from midspring right through to autumn frosts. In some years, we've had blooms on our vines right up until early November. These woody-stemmed vines are undemanding, have no special soil requirements and withstand periods of drought. I grow honeysuckle on a lattice attached to the side of a deck. The vines create a wall of dark green leaves and bright, 2-inch-long (5 cm), tubular flowers, providing both beauty and privacy.

Height • 10–15 feet (3–4.5 m)

Spread • 4 feet (120 cm)

Blooms • spring to frost

PLANTING

Seeding: Not recommended. Seeds need stratifying and take 7 or more months to germinate.

Transplanting: Space 36–48 inches (90–120 cm) apart.

GROWING

Sun to partial shade; south or west exposure is best.

Climbing on a fence, arbour or trellis.

Honeysuckle is a twining vine and needs a wire or lattice to climb.

Leave vines standing over winter.

Do not divide these woody-stemmed plants; it is difficult to do successfully.

RECOMMENDED VARIETIES

Usually available only under one of the names listed above.

TIPS

If possible, plant honeysuckle near a window of your home, so that you can watch hummingbirds visit the flowers.

Honeysuckle vines bloom on new wood. Wait until leaves begin to unfold in spring before pruning, and cut vines back just above the uppermost buds.

OTHER RECOMMENDED SPECIES

Lonicera japonica 'Halliana' (Hall's Honeysuckle): 8–12 feet (2.5–3.75 m) tall; sun to partial shade; white to cream flowers in summer.

Honeysuckle's tubular flowers attract hummingbirds.

Honeysuckle is more shade-tolerant than most vines. Few vines bloom in shady sites, but honeysuckle flowers from spring to fall frosts.

Hops

Humulus lupulus
Bear Hops, Common
Hops, Hop Vine

green, gold

Hops is an incredibly fast-growing, thick vine with large, heart-shaped leaves. The vine dies to the ground in winter, but quickly shoots up the next season to a height of about 20 feet (6 m). This plant is ideal if you want an attractive, thick mass of leaves to provide privacy, shade a front porch or hide unattractive areas. I particularly love hops vine in the fall, when attractive cones hang in clusters among the leaves.

Height • 12–20 feet (3.75–6 m)

Spread • 4–5 feet (120–150 cm)

Blooms • summer

PLANTING

Seeding: Not worth the bother, since plants grow easily and quickly from cuttings. Hops grow roots wherever their stems touch soil; simply chop the stems off behind the rooted area, and poke the pieces into the soil in a new location. Packaged seed is hard to come by.

Hops is probably the fastest-growing perennial vine and the best vine for creating screens.

Transplanting: Space 4 feet (120 cm) apart.

GROWING

Sun or partial shade.

Climbing vine, as a screen or groundcover.

Needs a trellis, fence or other support to climb.

Cut back in fall or spring. Blooms on new wood.

Don't bother trying to divide hops, as mature vines have long roots and numerous suckers that make successful division difficult. Most growers start their plants from root cuttings.

RECOMMENDED VARIETIES

Aureus • 12–15 feet (3.75–4.5 m) tall; showy, golden-green leaves.

TIPS

Although hops does well in either sun or partial shade, it will grow most quickly in a sunny location with a constant supply of moisture.

For a stunning display, grow the golden- and green-leafed hops vines together. The 2 colours enhance each other as the bristly stems intertwine.

Snip off the cones to add to wreaths and dried arrangements. Use the woody stems as a base for wreaths. Hang cones to dry, and allow fresh stems to dry after weaving them into a wreath.

The cone-like fruits are also called hops, and were used commercially in beer-making as a flavouring and preservative during the 9th and 10th centuries. Today, brewers use dried hops chiefly to give a bitter taste to malt liquors.

Hops grows quickly, but major growth does not begin until the second year. We planted two small golden hops next to an 8-foot (2.5 m) arbour. By the end of the next season, these plants had bushed out and clambered up to completely cover their support in an impressive arch of golden leaves.

Hops vines produce male and female flowers on separate plants. Male plants produce small, greenish flowers in clusters (above), and female plants produce the hops (below) when the vines are a couple of years old. The plants look the same until they bloom, so you won't know which one you have until it blooms in your garden. Lupulus means 'like a wolf,' an apparent reference to this vine's vigour. Hops is reputed to have a calming effect on the human body; as an old time cure for insomnia, people used to put hops inside pillowcases.

Hosta

Hosta spp.
Funkia, Plantain Lily

white, purple

Hostas are one of the most popular shade plants in North America, and deservedly so. These handsome perennials grace gardens with decorative foliage from spring to fall frost. The leaves vary enormously in size, pattern and colour. Some are huge and round; others are tiny and narrow. There are varieties with shiny or dull leaves, wavy edges, quilted markings or strong veins. Choose from solid colours, or leaves with contrasting margins, in combinations of green, gold, yellow, blue and white. In summer, exotic, lily-like flowers on slender, leafless stems rise above the foliage. These rich-looking plants are one of my favourite perennials.

Hostas are one of the best foliage plants, and offer an unmatched range of leaf patterns, colours and sizes.

Height (without flowers) • 6–24 inches (15–60 cm)

Spread • 15–30 inches (33–75 cm)

Blooms • summer

PLANTING

Seeding: Not recommended. Plants take several years to reach an acceptable size.

Roots: Plant in spring, so that buds are 1 inch (2.5 cm) below soil.

Transplanting: Space 12–24 inches (30–60 cm) apart.

'Frances Williams' is a showy hosta with large, blue-green leaves. Its elegant, pale mauve flowers bloom in midsummer.

GROWING

Full to partial shade.

Accent plants, groundcovers, rock gardens, edgings. Front of border.

Hostas grow slowly and can be allowed to spread indefinitely. They seem to get better with age! If you want more plants, divide using method B, page 54.

RECOMMENDED VARIETIES

Francee • 12–15 inches (30–38 cm) tall and 18–24 inches (45–60 cm) wide; dark green leaves with white edges; lilac flowers in late summer; relatively sun-tolerant; excellent groundcover; an elegant, award-winning variety.

Frances Williams • 12–18 inches (30–34 cm) tall and 22 inches (55 cm) wide; pale lavender flowers in midsummer; large, round, blue-green leaves with wide yellow margins; spectacular when mature; nice feature plant.

A row of hostas puts on a impressive show in a frontyard flowerbed.

Ginko Craig • 6 inches (15 cm) tall and 15–18 inches (38–45 cm) wide; narrow, dark green leaves outlined with a crisp white border; vivid mauve flowers in summer; takes more sun than most hostas; an especially good variety for the Prairies; great for rock gardens.

Gold Standard • 12–18 inches (30–45 cm) tall and 20 inches (50 cm) wide; large leaves with dark green margins; centre of leaf is light green in spring, changes to burnt-gold by summer; prefers morning sun to bring out the golden colour; lavender flowers; great groundcover.

Sum and Substance • 18–24 inches (45–60 cm) tall and wide; huge, round, golden leaves, up to 9 inches (22.5 cm) across; lavender flowers in summer; some built-in resistance to slugs; needs some sun for the best gold colour.

A groundcover of lamium offsets the large leaves of 'Gold Standard' hosta (below). 'Francee' (opposite), is an award winning hosta variety. The large leaves of rayflowers provide a nice textural contrast.

Wide Brim • 12–18 inches (30–45 cm) tall and 24 inches (60 cm) wide; blue-green leaves with wide, creamy-white to gold margins; lots of lavender flowers in mid-summer; great feature plant.

Elegans • 12–18 inches (30–45 cm) tall and 24–30 inches (60–75 cm) wide; round, blue-green, quilted leaves; short-stemmed white flowers in midsummer; sun or shade; lovely background plant.

TIPS

When shopping for roots, choose top-grade ones with 3 or more eyes. Lower-grade roots are younger, with fewer eyes, and take longer to grow into full-sized plants.

Have patience in spring. Hostas are one of the last perennials to poke through the earth, especially in deeply shaded areas.

Hostas thrive in rich, moist soil and do best in light shade. They can be grown in deep shade or in sun, but full-day sun usually causes foliage colours to fade.

Mulch prevents foliage from being splashed with mud during rainy weather.

Add hosta's flowers to mixed bouquets. Cut when only a few flowers on a spike are open, and the majority are still in bud but showing colour. The blooms last up to 2 weeks. Also experiment by adding hosta leaves to your arrangements: they look stunning!

OTHER RECOMMENDED SPECIES

Hosta plantaginea (Fragrant Hosta): 12 inches (30 cm) tall and 18 inches (45 cm) wide; the only hosta with fragrant flowers. Blooms late summer to early fall with large, white flowers that open in the evening and have a tuberose-like scent; 24 inches (60 cm) tall when blooming. Big, oval, shiny green leaves. Takes more sun than most hostas; a great feature plant. The variety 'Royal Standard' is vigorous and spreads rapidly; it has apple-green leaves.

Iris

Iris germanica
Bearded Iris, German
Iris, Poor Man's Orchid

Iris sibirica
Siberian Iris,
Fleur-de-Lis

190

black, brown,
purple, lavender,
blue, red, pink,
orange, yellow,
white

Irises have a
brief but glorious
blooming period.

*I believe irises are one of the most beautiful
flowers in the garden. Although their spectacular
flowers last only a few weeks, the attractive foliage
enhances other flowers when irises are not in
bloom. Bearded irises are familiar to most people;
they have large flowers, a wide colour range
and flat, fan-like leaves. Siberian irises have
delicate-looking flowers on tall stems and grassy
foliage; they are among the hardiest of all irises.*

Height • Bearded Iris: 5–40 inches
(12.5–100 cm) including dwarfs
Siberian Iris: 15–36 inches (38–90 cm)

Spread • Bearded Iris: 10–24 inches
(25–60 cm)
Siberian Iris: 20–30 inches (50–75 cm)

Blooms • Bearded Iris: late spring
Siberian Iris: early summer

PLANTING

Seeding: Not recommended. Bearded iris
seed is notoriously difficult to germinate,
and all irises take 3–4 years to bloom from
seed.

Rhizomes: Plant bearded iris
rhizomes in either spring or
fall. If you have light soil,
plant so that the top of
the rhizome is just
barely covered.

If you have heavy soil, leave rhizomes just barely exposed. Deep planting may retard blooming and result in rot. A good-sized rhizome will produce some flowers the first year.

Plant Siberian iris roots in spring, with crowns at soil level. Plants will bloom the first year.

Transplanting: Space bearded irises 12–15 inches (30–40 cm) apart, and Siberian irises 18–24 inches (45–60 cm) apart.

GROWING

Bearded irises in sun. Siberian irises in sun to partial shade.

Mixed flowerbeds. Middle to back of border.

Divide bearded irises every 3–4 years, or when you notice centres dying out. Divide just after they have finished blooming; see page 54, method C. Cut fans of leaves back by one-half. Siberian irises may not need dividing for up to 10 years.

In the 1100s, King Louis VII of France named the iris his 'fleur-de-Louis.' It is now known as the fleur-de-lis and is featured on Quebec's provincial flag.

Iris comes from the Greek word for rainbow. In mythology, the goddess Iris, who was Juno's personal messenger, travelled over the rainbow to reach Earth. Brightly coloured flowers sprang up from her footsteps.

Recommended Varieties

There are hundreds of wonderful iris varieties, in a rainbow of colours. Here are a few of our favourites.

Bearded Iris

Beverly Sills • ruffled, pink flowers.

Blue Staccato • bicolour; blue and white flowers.

Edith Wolford • huge, heavily-ruffled, blue and yellow flowers; winner of all major iris awards in Europe and North America in 1993; very showy.

Siberian Iris

Butter and Sugar • white and butter-yellow flowers; nice balance of colour.

Caesar's Brother • dark velvety-purple flowers; upright foliage.

Tips

With bearded irises, biggest isn't always best. Plants of short to medium height tend to be hardier than taller varieties, although there are some exceptions to this rule. Feel free to experiment, but if you want to play it safe, stick to recommended varieties or those that have been tested for your area.

For the best show of flowers, plant bearded irises so that the flat side of the leaves faces the direction from which you want to view the flowers.

Do not plant bearded irises in spots where puddles form when snow melts in spring. They often rot and die in those conditions. Siberian irises, on the other hand, tolerate wet conditions very well.

The ideal spot for bearded irises is a sheltered flowerbed against the west or south side of the house.

Choose plants with contrasting foliage to offset irises. Russian sage and sea holly look great with bearded irises. Shasta daisies, peonies and coneflowers are good companions to Siberian irises.

Remove faded flowers to extend the blooming season.

Cut flowers for bouquets when the buds are showing colour but have not yet opened. Irises generally last about a week after cutting.

The nut-like seed capsules of the iris make interesting additions to dried arrangements. Cut stems to desired length, place them in the arrangement and allow them to dry in place. The open seed capsules have a star-like form.

OTHER RECOMMENDED SPECIES

Iris cristata (Crested Iris): 4–6 inches (10–15 cm) tall and 12–15 inches (30–38 cm) wide; fragrant, blue-mauve flowers with a deep yellow crest; blooms in spring. Plant in rich soil and add lots of peat moss; spreads by creeping and rooting along soil surface. Good for rock and woodland gardens. The only iris that does well in shade. 'Alba' has white flowers.

Catalogues often describe bearded irises in terms of standards, falls and beards. Falls are the three drooping petals; standards are the three upright petals; beards are the fuzzy portions on the centre of the falls.

Jacob's Ladder

**Polemonium
caeruleum**
Charity, Greek-
Valerian, Polemonium

 blue, white

Gardeners often ask for blue flowers, and Jacob's ladder is one of the best. It blooms with soft clusters of dainty, cup-shaped flowers a gorgeous shade of bright sky-blue. The lush, ferny foliage remains attractive all season.

Height • 24–36 inches (60–90 cm)

Spread • 18 inches (45 cm)

Blooms • early to midsummer

Planting

Seeding: Indoors in February or March; germination 14–21 days. Seed needs light to germinate; press lightly on top of soil mix. Sow outdoors in early spring. Plants will bloom the second year.

Transplanting: Space 18 inches (45 cm) apart.

Jacob's ladder is one of the most beautiful blue-flowering perennials.

Growing

Sun to partial shade.

Flowerbeds, woodland gardens, in small clumps. Middle to back of border.

Divide every 3–4 years.
See page 54, method A.

Jacob's ladder is one of the first perennials to poke shoots through the earth in early spring.

Recommended Varieties
Usually available only under one of the names listed above.

Tips
While Jacob's ladder grows well in either sun or partial shade, plants in full sun wilt quickly if allowed to dry out.

Remove faded blooms to prolong flowering.

Jacob's ladder self-sows readily. If you want seedlings, be sure to leave some faded flowers on plants, so that seeds can form. Uproot and transplant seedlings as desired.

These blooms make lovely, long-lasting cutflowers.

The leaves give Jacob's ladder its name. Individual leaflets are offset along the leaf stalk, apparently resembling the ladder to Heaven of which Jacob dreamed in the biblical story.

Joe Pye Weed

Eupatorium purpureum

Boneset, Feverweed, Mistflower, Sweet Joe Pye Weed

 pink

We've always called this plant Joe Pye weed, but when one of our staff members referred to it by that name at a recent Perennial Plant Association conference in Philadelphia, he met with the horrified response: 'Good heavens, no, it's just Joe Pye!' Whether or not the word 'weed' is included in its name, we certainly do not assign 'weed' status to this plant in the garden. Joe Pye (weed) is one of the showiest perennials, with huge, fluffy flowerheads that tower above most other plants. Its flowers have a sweet vanilla scent.

Height • 3–6 feet (90–180 cm)

Spread • 3–5 feet (90–150 cm)

Blooms • late summer until freeze-up

Joe Pye weed has huge, fragrant flowerheads.

PLANTING

Seeding: Not recommended. Plants started from seed are slow-growing and take at least 2 years to reach full size.

Transplanting: Space 48 inches (120 cm) apart.

GROWING

Sun to light shade; moist soil.

Accent plant, formal borders, meadow gardens. Back of border.

Divide every 5 years or so. See page 54, method A.

RECOMMENDED VARIETIES

Usually available only under one of the names listed above.

TIPS

Joe Pye weed grows into a large, stately bush. Asters, daylilies, garden phlox, ornamental grasses and coneflowers are good companions.

Add these flat-headed flower clusters to mixed bouquets.

OTHER RECOMMENDED SPECIES

Eupatorium maculatum 'Atropurpureum' (Spotted Joe Pye Weed): similar in height and form; differs in its leaves, stalks and upper stems, which are more purple; more cold-hardy than other species.

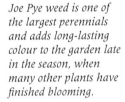

Joe Pye weed is one of the largest perennials and adds long-lasting colour to the garden late in the season, when many other plants have finished blooming.

This stately perennial is named after a native shaman who believed that it had special healing powers. This belief probably also led to the other common names of 'boneset' and 'feverweed.'

Lady's Mantle

Alchemilla mollis

 yellow-green

Lady's mantle, with its large clumps of rounded, downy leaves, is a charming addition to gardens. Huge, spreading heads of tiny, star-like flowers surround the greyish-green foliage through most of the summer, forming the loose cloak that gives the plant its common name. After a rainfall, water droplets linger on the leaves like glittering jewels. Lady's mantle is an undemanding plant that provides a bountiful source of flowers for fresh and dried bouquets.

Height • 12–15 inches (30–45 cm)

Spread • 24 inches (60 cm)

Blooms • spring to late summer

PLANTING

Seeding: Indoors in February. Outdoors in early spring. Plants will bloom the second year.

Transplanting: Space 18–24 inches (45–60 cm) apart.

GROWING

Partial shade. Can be planted in sunny beds if shaded for part of the day by other plants.

Edgings, woodland plantings, along pathways, as a groundcover. Front of border.

Rarely, if ever, needs dividing. If you want more plants, divide using method A (see page 54).

Alchemilla comes from the word 'alchemy,' because when used as an herb, these plants are believed to bring about miraculous cures. In Arab countries, for example, a tea made from the leaves is reputed to restore youth and beauty.

Recommended Varieties

Often available only under one of the names listed above. You may be able to find the variety 'Robusta,' which is slightly larger and taller than the species.

Tips

Although some books list lady's mantle as equally suited to sun or shade, we found that our plant wilted and looked terrible in a sunny part of the garden. We moved it to a site which receives only about 2 hours of sun each day, and it has thrived there for the past 9 years.

Lady's mantle can become somewhat ratty-looking late in the season. Just trim off finished flowers and unattractive leaves, and the plants will respond by sending up fresh foliage.

Cut for bouquets when flowers have just opened. They last 7–10 days after cutting. I also like to use the leaves as greenery in bouquets.

The flowers dry splendidly. Cut stems off close to the ground, strip off the leaves and hang upside-down in bunches for a couple of weeks.

Lady's mantle will grow in dry, shaded areas of the garden, where few other plants survive. In sunnier areas, it needs moist soil.

The species name *mollis* means 'soft hairs,' and refers to the light, downy covering on the leaves.

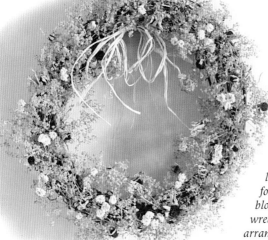

The chartreuse shade of lady's mantle is rarely found in flowers. The starry blooms are wonderful for wreaths and other dried arrangements.

Lamium

Lamium maculatum
Deadnettle,
Spotted Deadnettle,
White Archangel

 purple, pink, white

Lamium makes a beautiful ground-cover and grows in alkaline soil.

A friend of mine has a lovely garden, with stone steps leading down from the raised lawn to the patio below. The steeply sloped lawn beside the steps was a problem because it was shaded for most of the day by a large tree and a high fence, and it was terribly difficult to mow. The solution was to remove the grass and plant lamium as a groundcover. These plants quickly spread into thick mats of beautiful foliage, with tiny, snapdragon-like flowers throughout the summer.

Height • 6–8 inches (15–20 cm)

Spread • 24–36 inches (60–90 cm) or more

Blooms • spring to late summer

PLANTING

Seeding: Indoors in February or March. Outdoors in early spring. Plants will bloom the first year.

Transplanting: Space 12–15 inches (30–38 cm) apart.

GROWING

Sun to shade.

Groundcover, edging, on slopes. Front of border.

Do not allow to dry out; keep well-watered during dry spells.

Lamium rarely needs to be divided and can be allowed to spread indefinitely. If you want more plants, divide using method C (see page 54).

RECOMMENDED VARIETIES

Beacon Silver • very attractive foliage; pink flowers; silvery-white leaves with thin, green edges; compact grower.

Chequers • dark green leaves with a central silvery-white stripe; pink to pale purple flowers; vigorous, compact plants.

Pink Pewter • dark green and white leaves; soft pink flowers; vigorous, but more compact than others.

White Nancy • silvery, heart-shaped leaves; white flowers; spreads more than others.

Tips

Use lamium's colourful, showy foliage to brighten quiet corners of the garden, or to highlight shaded areas under trees.

Lamium is a tough groundcover. If you want to thicken the plants up, prune them back with shears, or even cut them once with the lawnmower.

Gardeners often ask for deer-proof perennials; lamium is a good choice.

Lamium is also commonly known as 'deadnettle.' This name was likely chosen because its leaves resemble those of nettles, with the prefix 'dead' because they do not sting. The species name maculatum *means 'spotted,' and refers to the leaf markings. Lamium makes a versatile groundcover and grows well in sun or with shade-loving plants like ferns (left). The silvery foliage of 'White Nancy' (above) is particularly striking.*

Liatris

Liatris spicata
Blazing Star,
Spiked Gayfeather,
Kansas Gayfeather,
Button Snakeroot

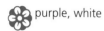 purple, white

Liatris is loved by florists for being one of the longest-lasting cutflowers. These tall, spiky blooms look as showy in the garden as they do in bouquets. Liatris is unique in that its flowerspikes bloom from the top down; flowers open at the top first, and buds gradually open down the spike. Most flowers that grow in spikes bloom the other way around, from bottom to top.

Height • 24–36 inches (60–90 cm)

Spread • 36 inches (90 cm)

Blooms • late summer to midfall

Liatris produces armloads of flowers for bouquets.

PLANTING
Seeding: Not recommended. Germination is very slow and erratic.

Bulbs: Plant bulbs in spring, about 4 inches (10 cm) deep. Plants will bloom the first season.

Transplanting: Space 12 inches (30 cm) apart.

GROWING
Light shade to sun.

Flowerbeds, cutting gardens. Back of border.

Divide every 3–4 years. See page 54, method C.

RECOMMENDED VARIETIES
Kobold • 24 inches (60 cm) tall; strong spikes of rosy-purple flowers; more compact with deeper flower colour than species; heavy bloomer.

TIPS
Unlike many plants, liatris looks best as a single plant rather than in groups. If you really like this plant, space several at regular intervals through your flowerbed.

Liatris is drought-tolerant. These plants dislike wet soil in spring, so do not plant them in areas where snow melts late.

Use liatris as a substitute for purple loosestrife (*Lythrum salicaria*), a perennial that bears similar tall spires of purple flowers, but which has been designated as a noxious weed in many parts of Canada.

Liatris sometimes self-seeds. Uproot and transplant seedlings as they appear, and discard unwanted ones.

Cut flowers for bouquets when only those on the top of the spike are open. They last 2 weeks or longer after cutting. Change vase water frequently; liatris pollutes water rapidly, and obstructs the flow of water into the stem.

For dried flowers, at least half of the flowers on the spike should be open. Strip off most of the leaves, but allow the top ones to remain for added interest. Hang stems upside-down.

Plant liatris in groups to act as 'exclamation marks' in the landscape (above). White liatris is showy (left) but is less common than purple. These flowers attract butterflies to the garden.

Lily

Lilium χ hybrida
Asiatic Lily

Lilium martagon
Martagon Lily,
Turk's Cap Lily

black, brown,
orange, yellow,
red, burgundy,
purple, rose,
pink, white

Lilies are one of the longest-lasting cutflowers.

Lilies bloom in an impressive rainbow of colours that few other flowers can match, from vibrant, bold and brassy hues to soft pastels. Asiatic lilies are the most common, with large flowers 4–6 inches (10–15 cm) across. Some flowers are spotted, most face outwards but a few varieties have nodding flowers. Martagon lilies are less well-known; their nodding flowers are smaller, from 1–2 inches (2.5–5 cm) long, but borne in great profusion. These tall plants bloom earlier and add delicate grace to shaded gardens.

Height • Asiatic lily: $1\frac{1}{4}$–5 feet (38–150 cm)
Martagon lily: 2–4 feet (75–120 cm)

Spread • Both: 12 inches (30 cm)

Blooms • Asiatic lily: early to late summer
Martagon lily: late spring to early summer

Asiatic lilies bloom in a rainbow of colours. Left to right: 'Gardenia,' 'Summer Night,' 'Avignon,' 'Sorbet,' 'Melissa Jaime.'

PLANTING

Seeding: Not recommended. Lilies take several years to reach flowering size from seed.

Bulbs: Lily bulbs can be planted in fall or very early spring, but a spring-planted bulb will not grow as tall or carry as many blooms the first season as one of the same size and variety planted the previous fall. Unlike most other bulbs, lilies can be planted throughout the fall, right up until the ground freezes.

Plant at a depth 3 times the length of the bulb. A 2-inch-long (5 cm) bulb, for example, should be planted 6 inches (15 cm) deep. The pointed end must be up or the bulb will not grow properly. Most will bloom the first year.

Martagons are very slow-growing until maturity. Bulbs are not usually available, as they may take over a year just to sprout, and longer still to flower.

Transplanting: All container-grown lilies can be planted at any time during the growing season. Space 9–18 inches (23–45 cm) apart. Plant lilies in groups rather than singly for the best show.

Many lilies are fragrant.

205

Lilies are long-lived, easy-to-grow perennials. They are rarely troubled by insects and many of the newer hybrids are disease-resistant.

GROWING

Asiatics do best in south or west exposures, with sun to light shade. Martagons do best in partial shade.

Mixed flowerbeds, in groups for focal point in borders, mass plantings in their own bed, growing among shrubs. Martagons also in woodland areas and gardens under trees. Middle to back of border.

Tall varieties may need staking, especially in windy locations.

Keep soil moist; do not allow lilies to dry out. Try to avoid wetting foliage when watering.

Lilies are one of the few perennials that actually benefit from being cut back in fall, rather than in spring. Before cutting plants back, allow stems to die down naturally at the end of the season; you'll have a better show of flowers the following year. Once the foliage is brown, cut off at ground level. This helps prevent disease.

The name 'martagon' comes from a Turkish word for a type of turban, and refers to the look of the flowers; hence the alternate name 'Turk's cap lily.'

A single, mature martagon lily can produce up to 200 flowers!

Lilies and pinks bloom abundantly in a sunny flowerbed.

Unless lilies are divided every 4–6 years, they will produce many thin, nonflowering stalks. Divide lilies in the fall. Use method C, page 54. Dig up the plant and gently separate bulblets (small bulbs) from the main bulb. Replant them immediately; the roots will die if they dry out. Discard any tiny bulblets. Divisions may take 2–3 years to flower.

RECOMMENDED VARIETIES

There are thousands of wonderful lily varieties, but if I could have only 2 of each type in my garden, these are the ones I would choose:

Asiatic Lilies

Connecticut King • 48 inches (120 cm) tall; large, bright coppery-yellow, upward-facing flowers; favoured by florists; an exceptional traditional variety.

Sorbet • 48 inches (120 cm) tall; magenta-rose, outward-facing flowers fading to paler rose-pink in centres; a newer variety with an unusual colour combination.

Martagon Lilies

Dalhansonii • 36–48 inches (90–120 cm) tall; chestnut-brown petals with gold spots; each tall stem bears 20–30 nodding flowers; lightly fragrant.

Mrs. R. O. Backhouse • 48 inches (120 cm) tall; very soft yellow, spotted, nodding flowers; long stems; vigorous.

Cut lilies often for long-lasting bouquets. Remove the orange, pollen-coated stamens to prevent staining.

TIPS

Lily bulbs, unlike other bulbs, should be planted with some of their live roots attached. They must be kept moist; the roots die if dried out. When shopping, buy only large bulbs with healthy roots. Do not buy any with dried-out roots or those showing any blue mould.

Different varieties of Asiatic lilies bloom at different times. By planting a mixture, you can extend the blooming period by as much as 6 weeks.

Try to choose a spot where lilies have not been grown before. This helps prevent infection by soil-borne disease.

Avoid areas where puddles form either from rainfall or snow melting in spring, as roots will rot in wet soil.

Unlike most bulbs, lilies do not go dormant after blooming, but the foliage has little impact after flowers fade. To improve the look, grow them against shrubs, between filler plants like baby's breath or with bushy-based perennials such as masterwort. Alternatively, mass lilies together in their own bed.

Don't move or divide lilies in spring, and delay working soil until after new stems have poked through the ground. New growth is tender and breaks easily. If shoots or sprouts are broken off, the bulb will not grow again until the next season.

Lilies are heavy feeders, and produce more flowers when fertilized regularly. We've had our best results by lightly working bone meal into soil in spring, and feeding with 20–20–20 once a month until August 1.

Lilies love 'warm hands and cool feet.' In other words, this sun-loving plant likes to have its roots cool. Use a mulch around lily plants, or plant a low-growing groundcover, such as creeping Jenny, thyme or lamium.

Lilies should always be deadheaded. Seed production robs the bulb of strength, and by nipping off faded flowers before seeds form, your plants will live longer. Cut stems just below the lowest flowers on the stalk.

When deadheading or cutting flowers for bouquets, always leave at least one-third of the stalk and leaves. The top growth sends energy to the bulb.

Cut lilies for bouquets when all flowers on the stem are in bud stage and the majority are showing good colour. Green buds usually will not open once cut. The flowers last well over 2 weeks. Use flower food sparingly.

The pollen of lilies stains clothing, and also (temporarily) noses that come too close when smelling flowers. Prevent stains by snipping off the orange stamens with scissors. The cutflowers look just as pretty, and usually last longer in a vase.

A sunny garden with lilies, delphiniums, bellflowers and lupins provides plentiful flowers for summer bouquets.

Lily-of-the-Valley

Convallaria majalis

white

Lily-of-the-valley is the sweetest-smelling spring flower.

My mother grew lily-of-the-valley in a shaded area beside the house. Each spring, almost every room in our home was perfumed by tiny bouquets of these flowers. Its sweet-smelling, spring flowers are reason enough to grow these plants, but lily-of-the-valley also provides a solution to problem areas of the garden. Lily-of-the-valley grows in dense shade and moist or dry areas, in rich or poor soil. These plants quickly spread into a thick mat of lush green leaves.

Height • 6–10 inches (15–25 cm)

Spread • 15 inches (38 cm) or more

Blooms • early spring

PLANTING

Seeding: Not recommended; plants take too long to reach mature size.

Roots: Lily-of-the-valley are grown from 'pips,' single rhizomes with growth buds. Plant these in early spring, about 1 inch (2.5 cm) deep. It may take 1–2 years for plants to produce flowers.

Transplanting: Space 6–8 inches (15–20 cm) apart. Lily-of-the-valley looks best in groups.

GROWING

Partial to full shade.

In beds around the bases of trees, as a groundcover under trees or shrubs. Effective in shaded areas where few other plants survive.

Lily-of-the-valley does not need to be divided and can be allowed to spread indefinitely. If you want more plants, divide in late summer. See page 54, method C.

RECOMMENDED VARIETIES

Usually available only under one of the names listed above. There is a pale pink-flowered variety ('Rosea') with less fragrant flowers. I prefer the white ones.

TIPS

Don't plant lily-of-the-valley in rock gardens, as it spreads quickly and soon crowds out less vigorous plants.

In shaded areas, lily-of-the-valley provides a dense carpet of green leaves that remain attractive until frost. The spring flowers are followed by attractive, glossy-orange berries.

Since lily-of-the-valley prefers moist soil, it helps to add liberal amounts of compost or other organic matter before planting.

These plants will grow in drier soil but the leaves will be smaller and paler, and there will be fewer flowers. Lily-of-the-valley was the solution for a friend of mine with a large raised bed on the shady side of her house. Adjacent large trees and the house overhang prevented rain from reaching that bed, and it seemed that nothing would grow there. Lily-of-the-valley did extremely well and quickly spread to fill the area. Even in those dry conditions, the plants produced an acceptable number of flowers each spring.

One gardener told us she grows lily-of-the-valley around the base of monkshood, and also in combination with snow-in-summer and rockcress. The effect was particularly lovely in spring, with lily-of-the-valley poking through an underlying carpet of flowers.

Lily-of-the-valley makes a delicate, perfumed bouquet. Cut when bells are well developed. The flowers usually last just over a week.

Lily-of-the-valley is one of the best groundcovers for shady areas.

Lupin

Lupinus χ hybrida

blue, purple, red, pink, yellow, white

The oldest seeds in the world to have been successfully germinated were carbon-dated to be about 10,000 years old. They were from an Arctic lupin (*Lupinus arcticus*) and were found in frozen soil in the Yukon in 1966. The soil's low oxygen content apparently contributed to their viability.

When lupins are blooming, they are virtually unmatched in splendour. Long, stiff stems, tightly packed with flowers, are produced generously in a rainbow of colours, both solid and bicolour. The leaves are deep green and palmate, like the spread fingers of a hand, and remain attractive right through until frost. These plants are rather short-lived and a bit fussier than most perennials, but the beauty of their flowers more than makes up for these shortcomings.

Height • 15–36 inches (38–90 cm)

Spread • 24 inches (60 cm)

Blooms • late spring to midsummer

PLANTING

Seeding: Lupin seed needs to be scarified (scratched or scraped) because it has a hard coat that inhibits germination; these seeds will not sprout until moisture can penetrate the seed coat.

Before seeding indoors, first gently scrape the seeds between a folded sheet of medium-grade sandpaper. Sow in February or March; germination 4–5 days.

Outdoors, sow as late as possible in fall, even in mid-November. The action of frost on the fall-sown seed will break down the hard seed coat.

Transplanting: Space 12–18 inches (30–45 cm) apart. Plant in groups for the best show.

GROWING

Sun to partial shade.

Mixed flowerbeds, mass plantings. Middle to back of border.

Tall plants may need staking.

Lupins (left) grow well in poor or alkaline soil, and withstand periods of drought. The densely packed flowerstalks of lupins (below) are as striking in bouquets as they are in the garden.

Do not divide. Lupins have a long taproot and hate being moved. They are short-lived perennials that lose their vigour after 3–4 years; replace them with new plants.

RECOMMENDED VARIETIES

Gallery Series • 15–18 inches (38–45 cm) tall; compact plants; available in pink, red, blue, yellow and white.

Russell Hybrids • 24–36 inches (60–90 cm) tall; classic tall spikes with profuse, brightly coloured flowers; usually available as a mix and in separate colours.

TIPS

Lupins dislike acidic soil. If you have trouble growing this plant, have your soil tested. Dolomitic lime is terrific for sweetening acidic soil.

Lupins also dislike waterlogged soil. Avoid planting in areas where puddles form from rainfall or melting snow in spring.

Deadhead to extend flowering. Towards the end of the blooming period, especially with older plants, you may want to allow some plants to go to seed. Lupins self-seed readily, but the seedlings often revert to blue or white. Transplant seedlings as desired.

Lupins are short-lived perennials. For a continuous show of flowers, add a few new plants every other year.

Deer will not eat these plants. Grow lupins if deer are a problem in your garden.

Cut lupins for bouquets when most flowers on the spike have begun to open. They usually last 7–10 days after cutting.

Masterwort

Astrantia carniolica
Lesser Masterwort

 red, pink,
white

I grow masterwort in a shaded bed against the north side of the house. It provides a nice background for other plants, and blooms with clusters of starry flowers through most of the summer. Masterwort looks somewhat like a coarse Queen Anne's lace, and is most showy in groups.

Height • 12–18 inches (30–45 cm)

Spread • 18–24 inches (45–60 cm)

Blooms • early to late summer

PLANTING

Seeding: Indoors in February or March; germination 7–21 days. Sow outdoors in early spring. Plants will bloom the following year.

Transplanting: Space 18 inches (45 cm) apart.

GROWING

Sun or shade.

Mixed flowerbeds, in small groups, woodland gardens. Middle to back of border.

Keep plants well-watered; they dislike dry soil.

Masterwort is a low-maintenance perennial that blooms throughout the summer.

'Rosea' is a pink-flowered variety of great masterwort. Plant it at the back of the border.

Masterwort rarely needs dividing. If you want more plants, divide using method A, page 54.

RECOMMENDED VARIETIES

Rubra • dark crimson flowers, of a deeper colour than the species; very showy.

TIPS

A few masterwort plants in a row look great growing in front of a fence or behind a row of hostas.

Masterwort is rarely troubled by pests.

These plants sometimes self-seed. Unwanted seedlings are easy to uproot.

Cut for bouquets when most flowers in a cluster are open. They usually last a little more than a week after cutting.

For dried flowers, cut blooms just after they open. Hang in bunches upside-down for about a week.

OTHER RECOMMENDED SPECIES

Astrantia major (Great Masterwort): 24–36 inches (60–90 cm) tall and 24 inches (60 cm) wide; green foliage and white flowers with touches of pink and green; blooms in summer. Care as above.

Versatile masterwort grows well in sun or shade and mixes well in any garden. Spiky flowers such as speedwell, blue sage and monkshood make good partners, as do daisy-like flowers such as black-eyed Susans, Shasta daisies and coneflowers.

Meadow Rue

Thalictrum delavayi
(T. dipterocarpum)
Yunnan Meadow Rue

lavender

Meadow rue
has airy foliage and
fluffy clouds of flowers
throughout the
summer.

I grow maidenhair ferns as houseplants, and I like baby's breath in bouquets, so I love meadow rue, which resembles both these plants. Meadow rue's lacy foliage looks like that of the fern, and its flowers look like purple baby's breath. These features alone would be enough to satisfy me, but meadow rue also blooms throughout the summer, looks attractive when not blooming and needs little care.

Height • 3–4 feet (90–120 cm)

Spread • 3 feet (90 cm)

Blooms • midsummer to midfall

PLANTING

Seeding: Sow outdoors in spring. Plants will bloom the second year.

Transplanting: Space 24 inches (60 cm) apart.

GROWING

Sun to partial shade.

Mixed flowerbeds. Middle to back of borders.

Keep plants well-watered; they dislike drying out.

Divide every 5 or more years. See page 54, method A.

RECOMMENDED VARIETIES

Hewitt's Double • clouds of rich lavender, double flowers that resemble baby's breath; the showiest variety.

Tips

To prevent unwanted seedlings, snip off finished blooms before they go to seed. Seedlings of meadow rue are rather difficult to uproot.

Unlike many tall perennials, meadow rue does not need to be staked.

Meadow rue's flowers transform an ordinary bouquet into a showy display. Cut stems when most flowers are open. They usually last 7–10 days.

Other Recommended Species

Thalictrum aquilegifolium (Columbine Meadow Rue): 2–3 feet (60–90 cm) tall; plumes of white, rose or violet flowers in early summer; blue-green foliage that resembles the leaves of columbines. The variety 'Thundercloud' has deep rosy-purple flowers.

Columbine meadow rue blooms in early summer.

Thalictrum rochebrunianum (Mistflower): 3–4 feet (90–120 cm) tall; large, rounded masses of fluffy, pink flowers; highly ornamental plants with long leaves and stout stems; blooms most of the summer to early fall.

Meadow rue's flowers are interesting. Some plants may have flowers with only pistils (female), some may have flowers with only stamens (male), and some have both. One gardener told us that in eight years his meadow rue plant had never produced seedlings, but it did so after he added a second plant to his garden.

Meadowsweet

Filipendula rubra
Queen-of-the-Prairie

Filipendula ulmaria
Queen-of-the-Meadow

pink, white

These stately plants provide a regal presence in gardens, with showy, fluffy flowerheads in early summer. It is said that Queen Elizabeth favours these flowers for their sweet scent. Queen-of-the-prairie is medium-sized, and has creamy-white or pink flowers and bold leaves. Queen-of-the-meadow is larger, with creamy-white flowers and broad leaves; it blooms slightly later than its counterpart.

Height • Queen-of-the-Prairie: 3–4 feet (90–120 cm)
Queen-of-the-Meadow: 2–5 feet (60–150 cm)

Spread • Queen-of-the-Prairie: 3 feet (90 cm)
Queen-of-the-Meadow: 2–3 feet (60–90 cm)

Blooms • early to midsummer

Meadowsweet is one of the showiest perennials.

PLANTING

Seeding: Outdoors in fall. Plants will bloom the second year.

Transplanting: Space 18–24 inches (45–60 cm) apart.

GROWING

Partial shade; moist soil.

Accent plant, woodland gardens. Back of border.

Division is seldom required, but if you want more plants, use method A, page 54.

RECOMMENDED VARIETIES

Queen-of-the-Prairie
Venusta • 3–4 feet (90–120 cm) tall; deeper pink flowers than the species.

Queen-of-the-Meadow
Aurea • 3–5 feet (90–150 cm) tall; golden-green foliage.

Flore-Pleno • 3–5 feet (90–150 cm) tall; long-lasting, creamy-white, double flowers; a very showy plant.

Variegata • 2–3 feet (60–90 cm) tall; green leaves variegated or edged in yellow.

TIPS

Meadowsweet does well in moist, acidic and even boggy soil. Grow these plants in a low-lying, wet area of the garden, or near a garden pond or stream.

Queen-of-the-prairie towers over spirea shrubs.

Gardeners sometimes ask for recommendations on plants that deer will not eat. Meadowsweet is one of them.

Cut these frothy flowers to add to bouquets. They look absolutely stunning with garden roses.

OTHER RECOMMENDED SPECIES

Filipendula vulgaris (Dropwort): 18–24 inches (45–60 cm) tall and 24 inches (60 cm) wide; creamy-white flowers; white, ferny leaves; great groundcover; more tolerant of sun than others. The variety 'Flore-pleno' is the best, with showy, double flowers.

'Variegata' is extremely attractive even when not blooming.

Monkshood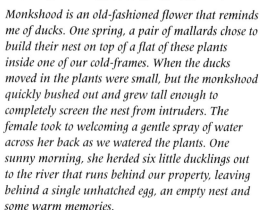

Aconitum napellus
Aconite Monkshood,
Helmet Flower,
Wolfsbane

 purple, blue,
white

220

*Monkshood is an old-fashioned flower that reminds
me of ducks. One spring, a pair of mallards chose to
build their nest on top of a flat of these plants
inside one of our cold-frames. When the ducks
moved in the plants were small, but the monkshood
quickly bushed out and grew tall enough to
completely screen the nest from intruders. The
female took to welcoming a gentle spray of water
across her back as we watered the plants. One
sunny morning, she herded six little ducklings out
to the river that runs behind our property, leaving
behind a single unhatched egg, an empty nest and
some warm memories.*

The name
'monkshood' origi-
nated in the Middle
Ages; the flowers
resemble tiny hoods
similar to those worn
by monks.

Height • 4–5 feet (120–150 cm)

Spread • 3 feet (90 cm)

Blooms • midsummer to frost

PLANTING

Seeding: Difficult and not recommended.
Germination is very slow and irregular;
plants take 2–3 years to bloom from seed.

Transplanting: Space 18–24 inches
(45–60 cm) apart. Set the plants at the
same depth as they were growing
in their pot, so that the crowns
are at the soil surface.

GROWING

Partial shade to sun. Requires
moist soil in sunny areas.

Mixed borders, cutting
gardens, back of border.
Good blue vertical accent.

The standard advice is
never to divide
monkshood. This seems to
be true for plants in shady,
moist locations, which
thrive for 10 or more
years with no signs of
decline. In our experi-
ence, however, plants in
sunny areas and drier
soil need to be divided
after 4 or 5 years, because

the centres become weak. Although monkshood is reputed to dislike being moved, we've never had a problem. Divide using method A, page 54.

RECOMMENDED VARIETIES

Usually available only under one of the names listed above.

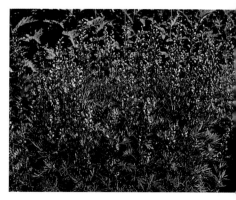

TIPS

Grow monkshood in shady gardens as a substitute for delphinium, which needs more sun. One gardener tells us his plants thrive in a bed on the north side of his garage, where they have bloomed abundantly for 10 years. Another gardener grows monkshood in an east-facing bed between 2 houses, which receives as little as an hour and a half of sun each day.

Monkshood is an excellent cutflower. Cut for bouquets when the bottom half of flowerspikes have begun to open. They last up to 2 weeks in a vase when placed out of direct sunlight.

As a precaution, wash hands well after handling tuberous roots because they are poisonous.

Deer will not eat monkshood. Grow them if deer are a problem in your garden.

OTHER RECOMMENDED SPECIES

Aconitum henryi (Autumn Monkshood): 4–5 feet (120–150 cm) tall; purple flowers in summer. Blooms later than aconite monkshood. 'Spark's Variety' has stunning, deep purplish-blue flowers.

Aconitum χ cammarum (Hybrid Monkshood): 3–4 feet (90–120 cm) tall; blooms in summer, earlier than aconite monkshood, and spreads only about 2 feet (60 cm) wide. The variety 'Bicolour' has pale blue hoods streaked with white, and lower petals of an intense blue.

Monkshood (above) is a long-lived, hardy perennial that blooms for two or more months in summer. The hybrid 'Bicolour' (left) has striking, two-toned flowers.

Moor Grass

Molinia caerulea
Variegata
Purple Moor Grass,
Striped Moor Grass,
Variegated Moor Grass

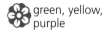 green, yellow, purple

Variegated moor grass is one of the most beautiful ornamental grasses. It forms a compact clump of pale green leaves striped in pale yellow, with creamy-yellow stems and purplish flowerspikes. Plant it in flowerbeds to enhance other flowers, or against a background of shrubs with blue-grey foliage, such as junipers or spruce. We grow it in a sunny garden alongside yellow flax, with blue sage and lilies behind, and low-growing pinks in front.

Height • 18–24 inches (45–60 cm)

Spread • 18–24 inches (45–60 cm)

Blooms • summer

Moor grass is virtually maintenance-free, and does well in poor soil as long as it is not too dry.

PLANTING

Seeding: Not recommended; seed is slow-growing.

Transplanting: Space 12–18 inches (30–45 cm) apart.

GROWING

Sun to partial shade.

Feature plant, mixed flowerbeds. Middle to back of border.

Divide every 3 years. See page 54, method B.

 Moor grass forms a tidy, colourful clump that does not spread from its allotted spot.

RECOMMENDED VARIETIES

Variegated moor grass is far more showy than the plain-leaved one, and is the only type that we recommend growing.

TIPS

Contrary to what most people think, grasses do bloom. The flowers are the feathery spikes that rise above the leaves in summer, and later turn to seedheads.

I often cut both the flowerheads and foliage to add to bouquets.

Use the seedheads in dried arrangements. Harvest stems while still green, and hang in bunches upside-down to dry.

'Marshall's Delight' beebalm provides a perfect backdrop for moor grass.

Plant moor grass where it will catch breezes, to show off its arching foliage and flowers to their best advantage.

Obedient Plant

***Physostegia
virginiana***
False Dragonhead,
False Lion's-heart

 rose-pink,
lavender, white

*Obedient plant is a lesser-known flower that people
fall in love with at first sight. This perennial forms
a tidy, upright clump of dark green, willowy leaves
and tall spires of flowers in jewel-like colours.
The flowers resemble miniature snapdragons, and
are aligned in four tidy, vertical rows along each
flowerstalk. If one of these tiny blooms moves out of
its row, you can simply push it back into place with
your finger, hence the name 'obedient plant.'*

Height • 18–36 inches (45–90 cm)

Spread • 24–36 inches (60–90 cm)

Blooms • midsummer to fall

PLANTING

Seeding: Not recommended. Hybrid varieties
are best, and they do not come true from
seed.

Obedient plant
is a showy, late-
blooming perennial.

Transplanting: Space 18–24 inches
(45–60 cm) apart.

GROWING

Sun to partial shade.

Mixed flowerbeds. Middle
to back of border.

Divide every 2–3 years to
prevent overcrowding.
See page 54, method A.

RECOMMENDED VARIETIES

Red Beauty •
24–36 inches
(60–90 cm) tall; deep
rose-pink flowers.

Vivid • 18–24 inches
(45–60 cm) tall; large
orchid-pink flowers;
compact plants;
blooms later than
others, adds fall
colour.

Tips

Obedient plants prefer moist soil in sun, and drier soil in shade.

These sturdy perennials stand up well to wind. They are rarely troubled by insects or disease.

Obedient plants are excellent for planting in narrow beds along driveways or sidewalks.

Add flowers to bouquets. Cut when flowers on the lower half of flowerspikes are open. They last 7–10 days after cutting.

The seedheads of obedient plant look a little like stalks of wheat and make interesting additions to dried arrangements. Harvest while still tightly closed and hang upside-down.

Obedient plant thrives in a hot, sunny flowerbed with annual lavatera, petunias and snapdragons. 'Vivid' (above) is one of the latest-blooming varieties.

The tiny flowers of obedient plant are held in neat rows.

Ornamental Onion

Allium christophii
(A. albopilosum)
Star-of-Persia

Allium giganteum
Globe Allium, Giant
Ornamental Onion

Allium karataviense
Turkestan
Ornamental Onion

Allium stipitatum
(A. aflatunense)
Persian Flowering
Onion, Persian
Ornamental Onion

purple, pink,
white

Ornamental
onions have striking,
spherical flowerheads
that can be added
to fresh or dried
bouquets.

Ornamental onions are marvellous in sunny gardens. Their distinctive flowerheads provide a striking contrast to other blooms. Giant ornamental onions, as you might guess by their name, are the tallest, and are absolutely stunning in the early summer garden. Huge, tight balls of purple flowers from 5–6 inches (12.5–15 cm) across rise on tall, leafless stalks, like giant drumsticks. Persian ornamental onions look similar, but are shorter and have lavender, pink or red-violet flowers.

Star-of-Persia is one of the most spectacular ornamental onions, with open clusters of star-like, silvery-lavender flowers on stout stems. Its flowerheads are immense, from 8–12 inches (20–30 cm) across. Shortest of all is the Turkestan ornamental onion. Its large, whitish flowerheads sit just above purple-grey, tulip-like leaves.

Height • Star-of-Persia: 12–15 inches (30–38 cm)
Giant Ornamental Onion: 48 inches (120 cm)
Turkestan Ornamental Onion: 10 inches (25 cm)
Persian Ornamental Onion: 24 inches (60 cm) or more

Spread • Star-of-Persia: 8–12 inches (20–30 cm)
Giant Ornamental Onion: 12–18 inches (30–45 cm)
Turkestan Ornamental Onion: 12 inches (30 cm)
Persian Ornamental Onion: 12 inches (30 cm)

Giant ornamental onions (above) have huge flowers in summer. Persian ornamental onions (opposite) look similar but are smaller and bloom in spring.

Blooms • Star-of-Persia: late spring to early summer
Giant Ornamental Onion: early to midsummer
Turkestan Ornamental Onion: mid- to late spring
Persian Ornamental Onion: mid- to late spring

Planting

Seeding: Not recommended. Although some ornamental onions are easily grown from seed, they take 3–5 years to bloom. Persian and Turkestan ornamental onions may take 2 years just to germinate in the garden!

Bulbs: Plant in fall, at the same time as tulips. Plant small bulbs 3–4 inches (7.5–10 cm) deep, larger bulbs 5–6 inches (12.5–15 cm) deep, and giant ornamental onions 8 inches (20 cm) deep.

Transplanting: Space 8–12 inches (20–30 cm) apart.

Growing

Sun.

Mixed flowerbeds. Tall ones at back of border, others from middle to front. Turkestan ornamental onions in rock gardens.

Ornamental onions generally do not need to be divided. If there are fewer flowers than in previous years, or you want more plants, divide using method C (see page 54), after flowering. Gently separate the bulblets from the main bulb. I usually replant these in a row, in an out-of-the-way site such as the vegetable garden, because they take a couple of years to reach flowering size. In the fall of the second year, transplant them into a permanent location.

Giant ornamental onions put on an impressive display, towering over other flowers.

RECOMMENDED VARIETIES
Persian Ornamental Onion

Purple Sensation • 24–36 inches (60–90 cm) tall; very showy, purple-red flowers in a perfect, rounded ball; vibrant colour.

All other listed species are usually available only under one of the names listed above.

TIPS

Plant ornamental onions in odd-numbered groups of 3–5 or more, rather than singly, for the most spectacular display.

Use ornamental onions to fill in gaps between blooming periods. These flowers bloom after spring-flowering bulbs such as tulips and daffodils have finished, and before many summer flowers begin their show.

Water regularly while ornamental onions are actively growing, but cut back on watering once they become dormant.

Like tulips and most other bulbs, ornamental onions become dormant after blooming. When the last flowers are finished, lightly work some bone meal into surrounding soil. Don't cut off the yellowing leaves, because as they wither and die back, nutrients are transported to bulbs and stored for next season's growth.

Combine ornamental onions with bushy plants like false-sunflowers, blue flax and tickseed to hide the yellowing foliage.

When adding fresh soil or compost to replenish garden soil, it may be necessary to lift the bulbs and replant them at the recommended depth. Do this in the fall. Bulbs planted too deep will not bloom properly.

Even the so-called 'experts' sometimes forget! We did not mark the site of our ornamental onions, and forgot they were there when we were working the garden one fall. As a result, our patch of Turkestan ornamental onions is now about 6–8 feet (1.8–2.5 m) wide. The following summer, we were amazed to discover that these 5-year-old plants had produced between 200 and 300 tiny plants from seed and bulblets! They didn't bloom that year, but next year's show should be absolutely spectacular.

Like other members of the onion family, ornamental onions are reputed to aid the growth of roses. They are also said to repel moles and aphids.

Cut ornamental onions for bouquets when one-third of the blooms on the cluster have opened. They last 2–3 weeks after cutting. I particularly like the globes of the giant ornamental onion in bouquets.

Both the flowers and seedheads can be dried. Cut flowers for drying when they are fully open and leave them standing in a vase with an inch (2.5 cm) of water until it evaporates. Turkestan onions and star-of-Persia result in lovely, spiky spheres.

Cut seedheads for drying when they are still tightly closed. Hang stems to dry upside-down in a warm, dry, dark place for about a week. Persian onions and star-of-Persia have the nicest seedheads for drying.

Star-of-Persia's flowerheads are impressive not only for their form, but also for their size. Their width can equal up to half the height of the plant!

Ostrich Fern

Matteuccia struthiopteris

 green

The name *struthiopteris* comes from Greek words meaning 'ostrich' and 'frond,' referring to the fronds that resemble ostrich plumes.

Ferns are becoming more popular as gardeners discover how easy and rewarding they are to grow. Ostrich ferns are the hardiest type for the Prairies; they form a spreading patch of upright, vase-shaped plants. The arching, green fronds are finely cut, and add grace to shaded gardens. A friend of mine has had a large patch of ferns growing in a moist corner on the north side of her house, where they have thrived with almost no care and little supplementary watering for over 20 years.

Height • 36–48 inches (90–120 cm)

Spread • 36 inches (90 cm)

Blooms • insignificant

PLANTING

Seeding: Not recommended. Ferns grow from spores and take years to reach an acceptable size.

Roots: Plant in spring with the crown slightly below soil surface.

Transplanting: Space 30–36 inches (75–90 cm) apart.

GROWING

Full to partial shade; rich, moist soil.

Shade, woodland and semi-wild gardens, as a groundcover.

Water during dry spells. Ferns do not like to dry out.

Ferns can be allowed to spread indefinitely, but the original plant can't be divided. Ferns spread by underground roots, so if you want more plants, carefully dig up and separate the young plants from the mother plant.

RECOMMENDED VARIETIES

Usually available only under one of the names listed above.

TIPS

Rayflowers, hostas and primroses are good companions for ferns.

Do not disturb soil too deeply in fern beds because the rhizomes are tender and grow at the soil surface.

Unlike most plants, ferns should not be fertilized because most commercial fertilizers are too strong and can damage rather than enhance the plants.

If you have a garden pond or woodland stream on your property, grow ostrich ferns in those areas.

Occasionally you may notice a shorter, darker, more erect frond on your fern. This is a 'fertile frond' that bears the spores ferns need to reproduce. If you find these fertile fronds unattractive, simply remove them.

The ostrich fern is one of the hardiest ferns, native to Newfoundland and Alaska. It is the largest fern native to North America.

Fern fronds can be snipped to use as greenery to accent bouquets, and last nearly 2 weeks after cutting. Frequently changing the water, recutting stem ends and misting with water helps extend vase life.

Ostrich ferns are grown commercially for their delicious, tender young shoots or 'fiddleheads.'

Ostrich ferns grow in acidic soil under spruce trees where few other plants survive. These perennials are long-lived and rarely troubled by insects or disease.

Ferns have been around for millions of years; after algae and mosses, they were the first plants on Earth!

Painted Daisy

Tanacetum coccineum (Chrysanthemum coccineum)
Pyrethrum Daisy

red, rose, pink, white

Daisies have an appealing charm, and the painted daisy especially so for its bright, rosy hues and lush, ferny foliage. These 3-inch (7.5 cm) daisies stand atop tall, slender stems above a mound of dark green leaves only about 8–12 inches (20–30 cm) high. The flowers have either a single or double row of petals, and remain in perfect condition for a long time. For a charming display, grow painted daisies with summer flowers such as poppies, yarrow and long-blooming varieties of daylily.

Height • 18–24 inches (45–60 cm)

Spread • 12–18 inches (30–45 cm)

Blooms • late spring to early summer

PLANTING

Seeding: Indoors in February; germination 14–21 days. Cover seed lightly. Sow outdoors in early spring. Plants started indoors will bloom the first year.

Roots: Plant roots in spring, with the crown at soil surface.

Transplanting: Space 12 inches (30 cm) apart.

The painted daisy contains pyrethrum, which is used in many organic insecticides. To make your own, crumble fresh or dried flowers into water. Use the spray to control aphids and other soft-bodied insects.

GROWING

Sun to partial shade.

Massed in odd-numbered groups of 3 or more. Middle of border.

Divide every 3 years, or when the centre of the plant begins to die out. See page 54, method A.

RECOMMENDED VARIETIES

James Kelway • bright vermilion-red flowers with golden-yellow centres; very showy.

Robinson Rose • bright rose-pink flowers with golden-yellow centres; large flowers with unfading colour.

TIPS

After blooming, foliage dies down and turns black. To improve appearance, cut away up to the top half of leaves. This sometimes results in a second flush of flowers. It helps to grow other plants in front to screen these unsightly leaves. Peachleaf bellflowers and asters are good companions.

Cut flowers for bouquets often or deadhead regularly to extend blooming period.

The painted daisy was once the mainstay of the European florist industry. Cut flowers for bouquets when they are starting to open. They last 7–10 days after cutting.

'James Kelway' is one of the showiest painted daisy varieties.

The large flowers of 'Robinson Rose' are wonderful in bouquets.

Pasqueflower

Pulsatilla vulgaris
(Anemone
pulsatilla)
Prairie Crocus,
Windflower, European
Pasqueflower

234

purple, red,
white

When I was a little girl, I loved to visit my grand-parents' farm. My grandfather would hold my hand, and as we walked to the cow pasture, we could see prairie crocuses blooming in early spring. Nearby hillsides appeared to have been painted purple. These flowers are more commonly known as pasqueflowers. Pasque means Easter, which is about the time they bloom in some places, but in northern gardens they bloom later in the spring.

Height • 8–12 inches (20–30 cm)

Spread • 10–15 inches (25–38 cm)

Blooms • early spring

PLANTING

Seeding: Indoor seeding is not recom-mended, as seed requires several months of cold treatment. Sow outdoors in late fall. Plants will bloom the second year.

Transplanting: Space 12–18 inches (30–45 cm) apart.

GROWING

Sun to partial shade.

Rock gardens, mixed flowerbeds, as edging. Front of border.

Divide every 3–5 years.
See page 54, method B.

Pasqueflower is one of the first perennials to bloom in spring.

The bright blooms of pasqueflower (above) are a welcome sign of spring. The variety 'Rubra' (left) has striking, burgundy-red flowers.

RECOMMENDED VARIETIES

Röde Klokke • deep red flowers.

Rubra • burgundy flowers.

TIPS

Pasqueflowers do best in slightly dry soil that has been supplemented with peat moss.

Pasqueflowers, like dandelions, produce silky, fluffy seedheads that disperse on the wind, but only the odd seedling has popped up in our garden over the years. Seedlings are easily uprooted and transplanted.

You can add the fluffy seedheads to dried arrangements. Cut stems while seeds are still tightly attached, and coat thickly with hair spray to keep them from releasing inside your home.

Cut flowers for bouquets. They last 7–10 days after cutting.

Some people use the purple petals of these flowers to create (oddly enough) a green dye, used to colour Easter eggs.

OTHER RECOMMENDED SPECIES

Pulsatilla patens (Anemone patens) (Spreading Pasqueflower, Prairie Crocus): 3–6 inches (7.5–15 cm) tall and 10–12 inches (25–30 cm) wide; blue, purple or white flowers bloom in early spring before leaves appear; fern-like foliage; native to many parts of Canada.

Peony

Paeonia lactiflora
Chinese Peony, June-
Flowering Peony,
Double Peony, Garden
Peony, Japanese Peony

Paeonia officinalis
Early Hybrid Peony,
Common Peony, May-
Flowering Peony

Paeonia tenuifolia
Fernleaf Peony

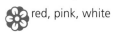 red, pink, white

Peonies are
one of the longest-
lived perennials,
easily lasting 20
or more years.

Peonies may just be the showiest, longest-lived and hardiest of all perennials. As well as having magnificent flowers, these plants are tough. My sons used to play football in a park where there was a huge bed of peonies. The boys used to crash into the plants during their games, and the peonies bounced right back. Neighbourhood kids (my daughter-in-law among them) would often sneak over and pick the huge blooms. Almost 20 years later, despite the abuse and with only rainfall for moisture, these same peonies still bloom in abundance every spring. For the best show in your garden, treat your plants a little more kindly.

Double or Chinese peonies are the most popular type, with massive flowers that resemble huge roses and smell as sweet. Each flower sits atop a long stem, above deep green, glossy leaves that remain attractive all season. These shrubby plants bloom between late spring and early summer, in shades of pink, red and white. Japanese peonies are of the same species, but have single flowers with prominent centres; the flowers look distinctly different. Plant these if you want more unusual flowers; almost everyone who sees these majestic blooms is smitten by them.

Early hybrid peonies have huge flowers up to 8 inches (20 cm) across, in pink, red and white. They bloom a week or two earlier than the Chinese peonies. Fernleaf peonies are rare, and so different-looking that people are often surprised to discover they are peonies! Deep crimson flowers float atop lovely, finely cut, ferny foliage. By planting a mixture of peony varieties and types, you can extend the blooming period by two or three weeks.

Height • Most: 30–48 inches (75–120 cm)
Fernleaf: 15–24 inches (38–60 cm)

Spread • All: 36 inches (90 cm)

Blooms • late spring and early summer

PLANTING

Seeding: Not recommended. Plants take 5–7 years to bloom from
seed.

Roots: Plant peony roots in spring, with the crown 1½–2 inches
(3.5–5 cm) deep. Don't plant any deeper, or the plant will not
bloom. Fall is the best time to plant, but strangely, roots are not
usually available until spring. Plant roots as soon as you can.

Transplanting: Space 36 inches (90 cm) apart. Be sure to plant so
that the crown is at recommended depth.

GROWING

Sun to light shade; peonies need at least 6 hours of sunlight each day
in order to bloom well.

Borders, flowerbeds, backgrounds, isolated groups, hedges.

Plants usually need staking while in bloom because of the weight and
size of the flowers, especially double peonies. Wire hoops with at least
3 legs are the most effective. Put supports in place before the leaves
unfold.

*Early hybrid peonies
have immense flowers
and bloom slightly
earlier than other types.*

Almost all peonies emit a pleasant perfume. Double peonies (above) are the most common type.

Water well during periods of drought, especially after flowering because this is when the next year's flowerbuds are formed. Water at the base of plant rather than overhead to avoid wetting foliage; this helps prevent disease.

In late fall, after a hard frost has turned peony leaves brown or black, cut the stems to the ground. This also helps prevent disease.

Peonies can be left undisturbed indefinitely, since they never outgrow their allotted spot. If you wish to divide your plants, however, do so in September. See page 54, method A. Throw out central part of the plant and replant divisions. Each division should have at least 2 or 3 buds or eyes, for a better chance of flowers the next season. Keep in mind, though, that it can take at least 4 years for divided plants to bloom profusely.

Japanese peonies (opposite) are stunningly beautiful. They are easily recognized for their single row of large petals and their prominent centres.

RECOMMENDED VARIETIES

There are literally thousands of excellent peony varieties, but if I could have only one of each type in my garden, these are the ones I would choose:

Double Peony
Sarah Bernhardt • 36–48 inches (90–120 cm) tall; soft apple-blossom pink; very large, double flowers up to 8 inches (20 cm) across; highly fragrant; non-fading colour; blooms early- to midseason.

Early Hybrid Peony
Red Charm • 30–36 inches (75–90 cm) tall; pure-red, double flowers; round ball of central petals with surrounding collar of broad guard petals; has won numerous awards for the purity of its colour; strong stems; heavy bloomer.

Fernleaf Peony
Flore Pleno • 15–24 inches (38–60 cm) tall; bright red, double flowers; even slower-growing than single fernleaf types, but worth the wait; very showy.

TIPS
Peonies take about 4–5 years to reach full size. Buy a 2-year-old root with 3–5 plump buds or eyes and you will likely get blooms the first year.

Have patience with fernleaf peonies. They are slow-growing and often do not seem to grow at all the first year of planting. In the years following, however, these plants produce a splendid show that is worth the wait.

Don't plant peonies near trees, where they will have intense competition for nutrients and moisture. Also avoid low spots, where puddles form after a rainfall. Peonies will rot in wet soil.

Never add manure to the planting hole, as this results in weak, spindly growth.

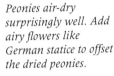

Peonies air-dry surprisingly well. Add airy flowers like German statice to offset the dried peonies.

As a general rule, early hybrid peonies have stronger stems than other peonies and are less likely to need support.

For the largest flowers, prune out some of the side-shoots in early spring. Gardeners who are planning to enter a garden show or exhibition often do this, but keep in mind that you will have fewer flowers.

Peonies are heavy feeders and really benefit from added nutrients. Twice a year, once in early spring and once in fall, sprinkle a handful of bone meal around each plant and lightly rake it into the soil. This usually results in more and larger flowers.

Don't worry about the ants! They are often found on peonies, and are simply feeding on the syrup exuded from the flowerbuds. They do not harm the plants.

Remove the finished flowers to keep plants tidy and prevent seeds from forming. Seed production depletes plant energy.

Peonies make excellent cutflowers. Blooms cut at the loose bud stage will open and last twice as long as those cut when they are fully open. Cut stems so that you take off only 2 or 3 leaves, because removing too much foliage weakens the plants. The best time to cut peony flowers is in the morning. They last about 2 weeks in a vase.

Snip a bit of foliage from fernleaf peonies to use as greenery in bouquets.

Cut flowers for drying before the centre is fully open. Hang single stems upside-down for about a week.

WHY PEONIES FAIL TO BLOOM

1. Recent transplanting, especially in small divisions.

Have patience. Root pieces that are too small will take a year or two to flower.

2. Planting too deep.

Lift plants in fall and replant to proper depth.

3. Insufficient moisture.

Water more often and add a mulch to help retain moisture.

4. Poor drainage or excessive shade.

Lift plants in fall and move to a more suitable location.

5. Botrytis blight, one of the most serious peony diseases.

Botrytis blight, or grey mould, is easily recognized, and is most prevalent in cool, wet weather. In spring, new shoots appear burnt. Infected flowerbuds turn black and often fail to develop beyond the size of a pea. Leaf spots may also develop, and stem bases usually look mushy and rotten.

As a preventive measure, some gardeners apply a protective fungicide before the disease strikes. Otherwise, ensure the plants are not crowded; good air circulation helps prevent botrytis. Water from the base of plants rather than overhead to avoid wetting foliage. Keep the area clean, and cut peony plants to the ground in late fall, after a hard frost. If botrytis persists, move your plants to another location in September, and don't replant peonies in that spot for at least 2–3 years.

6. Late spring frosts.

Frosts will kill flowerbuds. If there is a risk of frost in spring, throw old sheets or blankets on top of plants overnight.

Peonies (*Paeonia*) were named after Paeon, physician to the gods of Olympus, and were a source of potent medicines for early cultures.

241

Phlox

Phlox douglasii
Douglas Phlox,
Creeping Phlox

Phlox paniculata
Garden Phlox, Tall
Phlox, Summer Phlox

purple, red,
orange, pink,
white

Garden phlox is
one of the longest-
blooming perennials.

Phlox is another of my favourite perennials. I like its brightly coloured flowers and verstaility in the garden. In spring, Douglas phlox provides low mats of colour in rock gardens, and in summer, garden phlox opens its lovely flowers. Because of its popularity, we recently added a garden phlox section to our show garden at the greenhouses. The flowers of garden phlox have a lovely scent.

Height • Douglas Phlox: 2–4 inches
(5–10 cm)
Garden Phlox: 3–4 feet (90–120 cm)

Spread • Douglas Phlox: 12–15 inches
(30–38 cm)
Garden Phlox: 18–24 inches (45–60 cm)

Blooms • Douglas Phlox: early spring
Garden Phlox: all summer

PLANTING

Seeding: Not recommended. Germination is slow and sporadic.

Roots: Plant roots of garden phlox in spring, with crowns at soil level.

Transplanting: Space garden phlox 18 inches (45 cm) apart, and Douglas phlox 12 inches (30 cm) apart.

GROWING

Douglas phlox in sun to partial shade, and garden phlox in sun to light shade.

Douglas phlox on banks, in rock gardens, front of border. Garden phlox in mixed beds, cutting gardens. Middle to back of border.

Garden phlox may require staking.

Water garden phlox from the base of plants rather than overhead to help prevent powdery mildew disease.

Divide garden phlox every 3 years, or when centres begin to die out. See page 54, method A. Douglas phlox usually does not need dividing. Occasionally, centres of plants will die out; if this happens, divide using method B and discard central portions of plants.

RECOMMENDED VARIETIES
Douglas Phlox

Crackerjack • 3 inches (7.5 cm) tall; masses of deep, rich crimson flowers completely cover plants.

Red Admiral • 3 inches (7.5 cm) tall; similar to 'Crackerjack' but with carmine-red flowers.

'Starfire' is a stunning garden phlox. Its bright, fragrant flowers are offset by dark foliage and stems.

Grow garden phlox near a walkway so you can enjoy its fragrance as you pass. The variety 'David' has immense flowerheads and a strong perfume.

Garden Phlox

David • huge clusters of pure white flowers; mildew-resistant; very fragrant.

Düsterlohe • clusters of vibrant purple flowers; blooms longer than most.

Flamingo • huge clusters of flamingo-pink flowers, each with a crimson eye; plants slightly shorter than most.

Starfire • brilliant cherry-red flowers against burgundy stems and dark reddish-green foliage; striking colour combination.

TIPS

The most common type of creeping phlox is moss phlox (*Phlox subulata*). We prefer Douglas phlox because it does not brown and get patchy as does moss phlox. Douglas phlox is also lower and slower-growing.

Deadhead garden phlox to encourage a second flush of flowers.

Although some varieties of garden phlox are often listed in catalogues as blue, they bloom in a shade closer to mauve. These flowers tend to fade in full sun, so plant these varieties in a lightly shaded location.

Never crowd garden phlox. They can be prone to powdery mildew, which is warded off by good air circulation. Many of the newer varieties are mildew-resistant.

The flowers of garden phlox make a beautiful bouquet. Cut when the majority of flowers has opened. They usually last 7–10 days after cutting.

245

OTHER RECOMMENDED SPECIES

Phlox divaricata (Wild Blue Phlox): 8–12 inches (20–30 cm) tall and 24 inches (60 cm) wide; blooms in spring with icy-blue or white flowers; unusual colour; groundcover or rock garden plant.

Phlox stolonifera (Creeping Phlox): 8–12 inches (20–30 cm) tall and 24 inches (60 cm) wide; groundcover or rock garden plant; blooms in spring with flowers held well above the leaves; the only shade-loving phlox. The variety 'Blue Ridge' has lavender-blue flowers, 'Pink Ridge' has rose-pink flowers and 'Bruce's White' has snow-white flowers.

Douglas phlox is one of the best spring-flowering perennials. Use it in rock gardens, as edging and to cover sloped areas.

Pink

Dianthus deltoides
Maiden Pink

Dianthus gratianopolitanus (D. caesius)
Cheddar Pink, Pincushion Pink, Red Caesar

Dianthus plumarius
Cottage Pink

 crimson, rose, pink, salmon, white

Pinks have been prized in gardens for centuries. These charming flowers are offset by spiky, blue-green foliage, and many varieties have a delicious scent. Maiden pinks provide a blazing carpet of colour in summer. Cheddar pinks bloom mainly in spring, with fragrant flowers either single or in pairs. Cottage pinks form cushions of grassy leaves, with fragrant, carnation-like, double flowers.

Height • Maiden Pink: 6–15 inches (15–38 cm)
  Cheddar Pink: 4–12 inches (10–30 cm)
  Cottage Pink: 10–18 inches (25–45 cm)

Spread • Maiden Pink: 10–24 inches (25–60 cm)
  Cheddar Pink: 8–15 inches (20–38 cm)
  Cottage Pink: 12–18 inches (30–45 cm)

Blooms • Maiden Pink: midspring to midsummer
  Cheddar Pink: late spring to early summer
  Cottage Pink: midspring to midsummer

Many varieties of pink have a delightful, clove-like fragrance.

PLANTING

Seeding: Indoors in early February; germination 7–10 days. Cover seed lightly. Sow outdoors in early spring. Cheddar pinks started indoors will bloom the same year; others will bloom the following year.

Transplanting: Space 12–15 inches (30–38 cm) apart.

GROWING

Sun to partial shade.

Rock and cottage gardens, as edging, trailing over walls of raised beds. Front of border.

Do not cut back plants in fall or spring. Pinks are evergreen perennials, and heavy pruning prevents flowering and may harm plants.

Divide every 3 years to maintain vigour. See page 54, method B.

RECOMMENDED VARIETIES
Maiden Pink

Albus • 6 inches (15 cm) tall and 10–15 inches (25–38 cm) wide; pure white, single flowers.

Pinks earn their name not for their colour, but for their fringed petals, which appear to have been trimmed with pinking shears. The botanical name Dianthus *literally means 'flower of the gods.'*

The flowers of 'Pike's Pink' announce their presence with a strong fragrance. It's hard to resist snipping off a few short-stemmed Cheddar pinks for tiny, scented bouquets.

Brilliant • 6–8 inches (15–20 cm) tall and 10–15 inches (25–38 cm) wide; bright crimson, double flowers.

Zing • 6 inches (15 cm) tall and 10–15 inches (25–38 cm) wide; deep red, single flowers.

Cheddar Pink

Badenia • 4 inches (10 cm) tall and 12–15 inches (30–38 cm) wide; striking, rose-red flowers; light scent; long-bloomer; unusual colour.

Pike's Pink • 4–6 inches (10–15 cm) tall and 8–12 inches (20–30 cm) wide; extremely fragrant, soft pink, double flowers that almost completely cover foliage.

Cottage Pink

Roseus Plenus • 10–15 inches (25–38 cm) tall and 12–18 inches (30–45 cm) wide; clove-scented, rose-red, double flowers.

TIPS

Do not plant in low-lying, wet areas where puddles form in spring from melted snow.

Deadheading results in more flowers over a longer period. Since the flowers are small, it's easiest to give plants a 'haircut' with scissors or garden shears. Be careful to trim off only

'Roseus Plenus' is a cottage pink with spicy-scented flowers. Place it in rockgardens or border fronts.

old flowerheads and stems, not foliage. This also keeps plants neat after blooming has finished.

If spent blooms are cut off regularly and plants are fertilized, pinks will bloom much of the summer, although, in later months, less profusely than in spring. Pinks sometimes self-sow, so leave some faded flowers intact if you want plants to reseed.

Snip the flowers of cottage pinks for spicy-sweet scented bouquets. Pinks make long-lasting cutflowers.

Pinks are generally disease-free and untroubled by insects.

Maiden pinks bloom from midspring to midsummer. The variety 'Brilliant' lives up to its name with a brightly coloured display of flowers.

Plume Poppy

Macleaya cordata

apricot, white

Plume poppy is one of the largest perennials.

Plume poppy is a giant plant, with big leaves and tall, feathery plumes of flowers. Apricot-pink buds open to creamy-white flowers, followed by decorative, tawny seedpods, all on foot-long (30 cm) stems. The heart-shaped leaves are grey-green with silvery undersides, and up to 8 inches (20 cm) across. Use plume poppy as a single, stately feature plant in a border, or to fill large areas, where it will spread into a large patch.

Height • 6–8 feet (1.8–2.5 m)

Spread • 3–4 feet (0.9–1.2 m)

Blooms • summer through early fall

PLANTING

Seeding: Outdoors in spring. Plants will bloom the following year.

Transplanting: Space 3–4 feet (0.9–1.2 m) apart.

GROWING

Sun to partial shade; prefers deep, rich, moist soil.

Excellent background plant; back of the border.

Divide every 3–4 years. See page 54, method A.

Recommended Varieties

Coral Plume • 8 feet (2.5 m) tall; coral-pink flowers.

Tips

To show off the flowers, plant plume poppy against a dark background such as a wall, a painted fence or a bed of evergreen trees.

Cut plume poppy's flowers to add to bouquets.

Pests rarely bother this plant.

The species name cordata *means 'heart-shaped,' and refers to the large, grey-green leaves.*

Plume poppy makes a strong statement near the front door of a home.

Poppy

Papaver nudicaule
Iceland Poppy,
Icelandic Poppy

Papaver orientale
Oriental Poppy

 yellow, orange,
salmon, red,
pink, lavender,
white

Poppies are gorgeous. Iceland poppies are one of my favourite flowers; I love their bright colours and generous blooms. They bloom throughout the summer, though most prolifically at the beginning of the season. Oriental poppies are the most noticeable, with enormous, papery flowers carried high above coarse, hairy leaves. Many of these flowers have a black mark at the base of each petal, and they all have an unusual, black mound of stamens in the centre.

Height • Iceland Poppy: 12–24 inches
(30–60 cm)
Oriental Poppy: 24–48 inches (60–120 cm)

Spread • Iceland Poppy: 12 inches (30 cm)
Oriental Poppy: 18–24 inches (45–60 cm)

Blooms • Iceland Poppy: all summer
Oriental Poppy: late spring to
early summer

Iceland
poppies bloom all
summer long, are
drought-resistant,
grow well in poor soil
and are rarely
troubled by pests.

PLANTING

Seeding: Sow poppies indoors in February
or March. Put Oriental poppy seed in the
freezer for 48 hours prior to sowing in
order to break dormancy. Sow either
type outdoors in late fall.
Iceland poppies usually
flower the first year.

Transplanting: Space
Oriental poppies
15–18 inches
(40–45 cm) apart
and Iceland poppies
8–10 inches
(20–25 cm) apart.

Growing

Sun.

Mixed flowerbeds, in groups. Iceland poppies also in mass plantings and rock gardens. Oriental poppies toward back of border.

Oriental poppies may need staking, but many of the newer varieties don't need support because they have strong, sturdy stems.

Iceland poppies don't need to be divided. Mature plants dislike being transplanted, so just leave them in place, allow them to re-seed, and relocate the young seedlings as they appear.

Divide Oriental poppies only when plants lose vigour from overcrowding. These poppies also dislike being transplanted, so move them only if necessary. Divide in late summer, after flowering has finished and foliage has turned yellow. See page 54, method A.

Recommended Varieties
Iceland Poppy

Champagne Bubbles • flowers 2–3 times the size of others, more vibrant and produced over a much longer period.

Oriental poppies have huge flowers, up to 8 inches (20 cm) across, with silky, papery petals.

253

Oriental poppies (below) are one of the longest-lived perennials. Iceland poppies (opposite) are short-lived plants individually, but they self-seed so prolifically that they will persist in gardens for years.

Red is the original colour of Oriental poppies, but new varieties bloom in a wide array of solid and mixed colours. Recent breeding has resulted in larger flowers with stronger petals that are better able to withstand poor weather.

Extremely wide range of colours including bicolours with zoned centres; colour combinations include rose and yellow with pink and red, orange and apricot with white, as well as solid colours of each of these hues. Plants are bushier, with much stronger but shorter stems than other varieties.

Oriental Poppy

Allegro • 24–30 inches (60–75 cm) tall and 18–24 inches (45–60 cm) wide; very large, bright scarlet flowers with a central, bold, black patch; papery petals.

Picotee • 24–30 inches (60–75 cm) tall and 18–24 inches (45–60 cm) wide; pure white flowers with broad, orange edge; frilled petals.

Princess Victoria Louise • 24–36 inches (60–90 cm) tall and 24 inches (60 cm) wide; medium, salmon-rose flowers with prominent, black centres; strong stems.

Warlord • 24 inches (60 cm) tall and 18 inches (45 cm) wide; deep crimson flowers.

TIPS

After Oriental poppies finish blooming, the foliage dies to the ground and disappears by late summer. To hide the large bare spaces this creates in the garden, grow Oriental poppies with bushy filler plants, such as asters, baby's breath, statice, garden mums, sneezeweed and Russian sage.

After the flowering period, you can shear off the foliage to about 4–6 inches (10–15 cm) above the ground, and give the plants a shot of 20–20–20 fertilizer. This often encourages Oriental poppies to grow fresh new foliage and rebloom in late fall, although not as prolifically as in summer.

Allow foliage to die back naturally in fall, as this is when plants send energy to their roots.

Iceland poppies will continue to bloom until frost if dead blooms are removed, but keep in mind that these are short-lived perennials that die after 2 or 3 years. Be sure to leave a few spent flowers if you want plants to reseed. Iceland poppies self-sow readily.

Iceland poppies are often available only as a mixture, but you can sometimes find plants in individual colours. With a mix, gardeners can simply take out the plants with colours they don't want.

Oriental poppies often reseed, although not as readily as Iceland poppies. After the mother plant has flowered, seedlings often develop around its base. Transplant these while they are young. Older plants develop a long taproot, and transplant very poorly.

Poppy seedpods are somewhat like pepper-shakers; a ring of holes around the top permits the small seeds to be sprinkled out. Give the kids a few seedpods to play with, and let them spread some seeds around the garden.

Cut poppies often for bouquets; this lessens the need to deadhead and prolongs the blooming period. Cut just as petals begin to break open. To prevent the milky sap from blocking the stem, immerse the freshly cut stem end in boiling water for 20–30 seconds. Place the flowers in warm water. Poppies last 7–10 days in the vase. Iceland poppies make the best cutflowers.

Oriental poppies produce large, attractive seedpods that can be used in dried bouquets. Harvest seedheads while green, and hang stems upside-down or stand them upright to dry.

Orange and yellow are the traditional colours of Iceland poppies, but newer varieties also bloom in red, pink, white and even pastel shades. Double and semi-double flowers are also available. Iceland poppies are the famous poppies often seen in photographs of Lake Louise, in Banff National Park, Alberta.

Potentilla

Potentilla atrosanguinea
Himalayan Potentilla,
Ruby Cinquefoil

Potentilla nepalensis
Nepal Potentilla,
Cinquefoil

red, orange, yellow

256

Most gardeners know potentillas as shrubs, and are surprised to discover that there are also perennial potentillas. The perennials have similar, bright, saucer-shaped flowers, and finely cut green leaves with silvery undersides. These are tough, long-blooming plants that thrive in hot, dry areas of the garden and make wonderful additions to flowerbeds or rock gardens. Perennial potentillas also make a superb groundcover.

Height • Himalayan Potentilla: 6–12 inches
   (15–30 cm)
   Nepal Potentilla: 12–18 inches (30–45 cm)

Spread • Himalayan Potentilla: 24 inches
   (60 cm)
   Nepal Potentilla: 18–24 inches (45–60 cm)

Blooms • Himalayan Potentilla: most of
   the summer
   Nepal Potentilla: early summer and
   sporadically thereafter

PLANTING

Seeding: Indoors in February or March; germination 7–14 days. Seed needs light to germinate; do not cover with soil mix. Sow outdoors in early spring. Plants will usually bloom the first year.

Potentilla is an excellent groundcover plant.

Transplanting: Space 10–12 inches (25–30 cm) apart.

GROWING

Sun to partial shade.

Groundcover, rock gardens, edging. Front of border.

Divide every 3 years. See page 54, method B.

RECOMMENDED VARIETIES

Himalayan Potentilla

Gibson's Scarlet • 6–12 inches (15–30 cm) tall and 18–24 inches (45–60 cm) wide; dazzling scarlet flowers.

Nepal Potentilla

Miss Willmott • 12 inches (30 cm) tall; warm cherry-red flowers.

TIPS

Grow potentillas with baby's breath, blanketflower, blue sage or gasplant. Soapwort and yucca are other good companions.

Potentillas do well and bloom better in poor, dry or alkaline soil but grow more vigorously with lusher foliage if you water them during dry spells.

'Miss Willmott' puts on an impressive display of blooms.

The vivid flowers of 'Gibson's Scarlet' brighten gardens through most of the summer.

Primrose

Primula auricula
Auricula Primrose,
Dusty Miller Primrose

Primula elatior
Oxlip Primrose

Primula veris
Cowslip, Cowslip
Primrose

 brown, bronze,
orange, salmon,
red, yellow, pink,
purple, blue,
grey, white

Primroses are
beautiful flowers for
shady gardens.

Many gardeners are surprised to discover that primroses can be grown here. Common belief has it that these plants are more suited to a mild, English climate. That is true for some. Others can be grown here, but are rather fussy. The types listed on these pages are easy to grow and will thrive for years in northern gardens. Auricula primroses have rounded clusters of highly fragrant, two-toned flowers, often with a distinctive, creamy-yellow eye, and they bloom in a wide range of colours. Oxlip primroses have broad, crinkled leaves and soft yellow, nodding flowers. Cowslip primroses bloom in clusters of yellow flowers.

Height • Auricula Primrose: 6–10 inches
(15–25 cm)
Oxlip Primrose: 6–8 inches (15–20 cm)
Cowslip: 6–8 inches (15–20 cm)

Spread • Auricula Primrose: 8–12 inches
(20–30 cm)
Oxlip Primrose:
10–12 inches
(25–30 cm)
Cowslip:
10–12 inches
(25–30 cm)

Blooms • Auricula Primrose: early to late spring; sometimes again in fall
Oxlip Primrose: early to late spring
Cowslip: early to late spring

Planting

Seeding: Indoors in February; germination 14–30 days. Seed needs light to germinate; do not cover with soil. Cool temperatures improve germination rates. Sow outdoors in late spring, after blooming. Collect ripe seed from plants and sow at once. Plants started indoors may flower the first year.

Transplanting: Space oxlip primroses and cowslips 10–12 inches (25–30 cm) apart, and auricula primroses 12–15 inches (30–38 cm) apart.

Growing

Shady, moist locations. Auricula in shade to partial sun. Avoid hot locations.

Rock and woodland gardens, mixed flowerbeds. Front of border.

Most primroses need to be divided every 3–4 years. Auricula is an exception; it does not need dividing unless the centre begins to die out. See page 54, method C.

259

Auricula primroses have the widest colour range. A long row of these flowers puts on a show-stopping display in spring.

Oxlip primroses (right) bloom with delicate flowers thoughout spring. A mass of cowslips (below) is an irresistible invitation to stroll through the garden.

RECOMMENDED VARIETIES

Usually available only under one of the names listed above.

TIPS

Primroses look showiest planted in groups, and look wonderful blooming in front of small shrubs. Pulmonaria, bishop's hat and elephant-ears are also good companions.

Primroses grow well in densely shaded or moist areas of the garden. They also do well in acidic soil. Add lots of compost, peat moss or old leaves to the soil when planting.

Deadhead to prolong blooming period.

Cut primroses for miniature spring bouquets.

The botanical name
Primula *comes from a
Latin word meaning
'first.' Primroses are
often one of the first
flowers to bloom in
spring. Tibetan
primroses, however,
put on their best show
in summer.*

261

OTHER RECOMMENDED SPECIES

Primula cortusoides (Cortusa Primrose):
10 inches (25 cm) tall and 6–8 inches
(15–20 cm) wide; small clusters of purple-rose
flowers on solitary stems; spring-bloomer;
sun to partial shade; average soil moisture;
often self-seeds.

Primula florindae (Tibetan Primrose):
24–36 inches (60–90 cm) tall and 24 inches
(60 cm) wide; very fragrant, yellow, orange-
red or 2-toned flowers through most of
summer; shade to partial shade; requires
moist location.

Primula sieboldii (Siebold's Primrose, Japanese
Star Primrose): 6–10 inches (15–25 cm) tall
and 12–15 inches (30–38 cm) wide; wide
range of flower shapes and colours, including
white, purple, pink and magenta; very
attractive, often deeply notched flower petals;
blooms in late spring. Often dies to the
ground by midsummer.

Pulmonaria

**Pulmonaria
longifolia**
Long-leaf Lungwort,
Spotted Dog

**Pulmonaria
saccharata**
Bethlehem Sage

 blue, white

Pulmonaria is
one of the best
groundcovers for
shaded areas.

*Pulmonarias are remarkable for their low
maintenance requirements. Stephen Raven, who
works in the perennials area at our greenhouses,
has two Bethlehem sages growing under large trees
in his yard. For years, the only maintenance needed
was to provide water during extended dry spells.
Bethlehem sage is one of the first plants to bloom
in spring, with small pink flowers that turn blue
as they age. Throughout the summer, silver-spotted
leaves brighten shaded areas of the garden. Long-
leaf lungwort has dark green, narrow leaves with
white markings, and blooms later in spring with
vivid blue flowers.*

Height • Lungwort: 9–15 inches (23–38 cm)
 Bethlehem Sage: 12–18 inches (30–45 cm)

Spread • Lungwort: 18–24 inches
 (45–60 cm)
 Bethlehem Sage: 18–24 inches (45–60 cm)

Blooms • Lungwort: mid- to late spring
 Bethlehem Sage: early to midspring

PLANTING

Seeding: Not recommended. Hybrid varieties
 are superior to species plants, with better
 colour and longer blooming periods, but
 they do not come true from seed.

Transplanting: Space 12–18 inches
 (30–45 cm) apart.

GROWING

Partial to deep shade.

Groundcover, accent plants, mixed flowerbeds. Front of border.

Pulmonaria does not require dividing, even after several years. If you want more plants, divide using method B, page 54.

RECOMMENDED VARIETIES

Lungwort

Bertram Anderson • 9–12 inches (23–30 cm) tall and 18 inches (45 cm) wide; small, pointed, violet-blue flowers; dark green leaves spotted with silver; showy.

Roy Davidson • 12–15 inches (30–38 cm) tall and 18–24 inches (45–60 cm) wide; small pink flowers that turn sky-blue as they age; dark green leaves spotted in silver.

Pulmonaria is a striking plant for shady gardens.

263

'Bertram Anderson' is a long-leafed lungwort, with narrow, pointed leaves. It makes a striking complement to flowers as edging in a mixed bed.

Bethlehem Sage

Argentea • blue flowers; leaves with large patches of silver and overall silvery frosting.

Mrs. Moon • pink flowers that turn blue as they age; leaves have large spots of silver; makes a great groundcover.

TIPS

Grow pulmonaria with hostas, bleeding hearts or primroses. These plants are terrific companions to spring-flowering bulbs such as tulips and daffodils.

Pulmonaria makes a good groundcover, although it is not a rapid spreader. The tough foliage remains attractive all season, until a hard frost.

Pulmonaria does well in dry, shaded areas where few other plants will grow. Watering during long periods of dry weather is helpful.

These plants are rarely bothered by pests.

Experiment by snipping bits of foliage to add to your bouquets.

Bethlehem sage and bishop's hat thrive in a dry, shady bed underneath large trees (right). Small blue flowers stand out against the foliage of 'Argentea' (below) in spring. The silvery leaves of this Bethlehem sage add an uncommon accent to shady gardens.

Rayflower

Ligularia dentata
Big-leaf Rayflower,
Goldenray

**Ligularia
  stenocephala**
Narrow-spiked
Rayflower, Elephant
Ears

yellow,
orange

Rayflowers are
tall, imposing plants
that bloom most of
the summer.

*Rayflowers are wonderfully big and impressive
perennials. The big-leaf rayflower grows only 3–4
feet (90–120 cm) tall, but its leaves are up to 1 foot
(30 cm) long. Daisy-like flowers in flat clusters
adorn plants for most of the summer. Narrow-
spiked rayflower also has huge leaves (hence the
common name 'elephant ears'), but its flowers
bloom in tall, thin spikes. These plants won't suit
every garden, but those who have the proper
environment are likely to fall in love with them.*

Height • Big-leaf Rayflower: 3–4 feet
      (90–120 cm)
   Narrow-spiked Rayflower: 4–6 feet
      (120–180 cm)

Spread • Big-leaf Rayflower: 2–3 feet
      (60–90 cm)
   Narrow-spiked Rayflower: 3–4 feet
      (60–120 cm)

Blooms • summer

PLANTING

Seeding: Only species plants can be
   grown from seed; they will not
   flower the first year. Hybrids
   are far showier, but seedlings of hybrids won't
   resemble their parents.
   Professional growers
   raise hybrid plants from
   divisions.

Transplanting:
Space 18–36 inches
(45–90 cm) apart.

GROWING

Partial shade; ideally,
morning sun and
afternoon shade.
Needs constantly moist
soil.

Feature plant. Back of
border.

Do not let plants dry out, as leaves wilt quickly in dry soil and hot sun.

Divide every 3 years. See page 54, method A.

RECOMMENDED VARIETIES
Big-leaf Rayflower
Othello • showy; golden-orange flowers against purple leaves; rounded flowerheads.

Narrow-spiked Rayflower
The Rocket • 4–5 feet (120–150 cm); very thin, tall, bright, lemon-yellow flowerspikes; larger flowers on more compact plants than species.

TIPS
Rayflowers thrive in moist soil. Grow these plants in low-lying, moist or wet areas of the garden, or along a pond or stream.

Cut these unusual flowers to add to bouquets.

If you like the effect, leave the seedheads on for winter ornamentation.

OTHER RECOMMENDED SPECIES
Ligularia przewalskii (Golden Groundsel, Shavalski's Rayflower): 24 inches (60 cm) tall; narrow spires of small, bright yellow, daisy-like flowers in summer; dark green, deeply cut, heart-shaped leaves on purple-black stems; striking. Care as above. (The species name, by the way, is pronounced 'sha-val-skee-eye.')

'Othello' (above) has one of the most unusual colour combinations found in plants. Narrow-spiked rayflowers (left) are an impressive background in flowerbeds.

Rockcress

Aubrieta χ cultorum (A. deltoidea)
Purple Rockcress

red, purple, mauve

Rockcress is one of the most welcome plants in the spring garden. It begins blooming early, with masses of small, four-petalled flowers that almost entirely cover plants all spring long. Bees love these flowers and visit often, hovering from flower to flower with a soothing buzz and heralding the return of warm temperatures. The dense mat of foliage remains attractive all summer.

Height • 4–6 inches (10–15 cm)

Spread • 18–24 inches (45–60 cm)

Blooms • early spring to early summer

PLANTING

Seeding: Indoors in February or March; germinates in 15–20 days. Seed needs light to germinate; do not cover with soil. Sow outdoors in early spring. Plants started indoors may bloom the first year.

Transplanting: Space 6–8 inches (15–20 cm) apart.

Arabis is a similar-looking plant that is also known as rockcress. *Aubrieta* is somewhat easier to grow, and the plants are more compact, with brighter flower colours.

GROWING

Sun to partial shade.

Edging, rock gardens, between rocks and hanging over retaining walls. Front of border.

Rockcress is an evergreen perennial. Do not cut back foliage in fall or early spring; doing so will prevent plants from flowering.

Rockcress does not need dividing; if plants outgrow their allotted space, simply trim them around the sides. This results in thicker foliage higher up stems. If you want more plants, divide after 3 years. Use method C, page 54.

RECOMMENDED VARIETIES

Schloss Eckberg • vibrant purple; flowers larger than those of species plants; blooms longer than species.

TIPS

After blooming, shear off finished flowerspikes. This keeps plants neat and encourages the growth of fresh new shoots.

Grow rockcress at the front of raised beds so it can trail over the edge, or poke a plant into cracks in stone walls. Trailing plants may die back a bit over winter; just snip off the dead foliage in early spring.

In spring while plants are blooming, keep soil moist. After flowering, rockcress needs less water.

A southern Alberta gardener told us she grew rockcress from seed in a south-facing bed, despite common advice that these plants wouldn't do well in such heat. Lethbridge summer temperatures often reach 110°F (43°C), but with a thick mulch to keep its roots cool, the rockcress did just fine.

In winter, throw extra snow over these plants to help prevent foliage from browning.

For a splendid show in rock gardens, combine rockcress with other spring-blooming perennials. Douglas phlox and candytuft also form low mats of foliage covered in blooms through much of spring.

Rockcress is one of the first perennials to bloom in spring. Its flowers last for weeks and attract butterflies to the garden.

Russian Sage

**Perovskia
atriplicifolia**

blue, purple

Russian sage is
one of the best
perennials for hot, dry
locations.

When everyone who sees a certain plant wants one
for his or her own garden, you know you've got a
winner. Russian sage is one of those plants. It is
stunning, with tall spires of bright lavender-blue
flowers throughout the summer and into fall. It
needs little care in the garden, thrives even in
difficult, hot, dry conditions and is a bountiful
source of blooms for both fresh bouquets and dried
arrangements.

Height • 24–48 inches (60–120 cm)

Spread • 24–36 inches (60–90 cm)

Blooms • summer through fall

PLANTING

Seeding: Seed is not readily available, but if
you can find it, sow indoors in February.
Germination erratic. Sow
outdoors in early spring.
Plants started from seed
will likely not bloom
until the end of
the second
year.

Two years ago, we brought in a single flat of these plants in the fall, to test their ability to live through Alberta winters. Some were planted in a sunny area of our show garden, in conditions similar to those found in most gardens, and others in an arid, sun-baked, south-facing bed where few plants other than yarrow, cactus and sage survive. Russian sage thrived in both locations, proving itself versatile as well as hardy. The variety 'Blue Spire' has the bluest flowers.

The best varieties, however, are not available in seed; plants of these cultivars are grown from cuttings.

Transplanting: Space 18–24 inches (45–60 cm) apart.

GROWING

Sun; prefers a hot, dry location but grows well in average garden conditions.

Accent plant, mass plantings. Middle to back of border.

Water only during periods of extended hot, dry weather, except in first year after planting, when plants must be well-watered.

Do not cut back the woody stems in fall.

Dividing is not recommended, because plants grow from 1 main stem and are not easy to divide successfully.

Russian sage was named Plant of the Year for 1995 by the Perennial Plant Association.

Recommended Varieties

Blue Spire • 36–48 inches (90–120 cm) tall; large, open clusters of blue flowers; the brightest blue available.

Filigran • 24–30 inches (60–75 cm) tall; bright blue flowers on strong stems; plants bushier and more compact than other varieties; deeply cut foliage.

Longin • 24–36 inches (60–90 cm) tall; violet flowers on stiff, upright stems; a more formal appearance than the species.

Beautiful violet flowers on stiff stems are the trademark of the variety 'Longin.' Add Russian sage's flowers to fresh bouquets and dried arrangements.

TIPS

Although it is actually a member of the mint family and not directly related to culinary sages, Russian sage earns its name for the pleasant fragrance of its foliage. Plant it in a spot where you will brush the foliage on passing to best enjoy the aroma.

Russian sage is not particular about soil and will grow in poor soil, but dislikes being wet in spring. Avoid areas where snow is last to melt.

Plant with white flowers such as garden phlox and Shasta daisies, or with brightly coloured flowers such as cherry-red yarrow, purple liatris or yellow false-sunflower. Ornamental grasses or yellow-leaved shrubs also make great partners.

These flowers make beautiful additions to bouquets.

Cut flowers for drying when they are almost fully open. Place the stems upright in a vase filled with about an inch (2.5 cm) of water. They will dry slowly as the water evaporates, with the flowers remaining fuller and more brightly coloured than if air-dried. The dried flowers look a bit like long stems of English lavender.

Russian sage (top) was named for the Russian statesman B.A. Perovski. Its foliage has a pleasing sage scent, although it is not directly related to culinary sages. 'Filigran' (right) is shorter and bushier than other varieties.

Sage

Artemisia
abrotanum
Old Man,
Southernwood

Artemisia
ludoviciana
Silver King Sage,
Western Sage, White
Sage, Wormwood

274

Artemisia
schmidtiana
Silver Mound Sage,
Satiny Wormwood

Artemisia stelleriana
Perennial Dusty Miller,
Old Lady, Beach
Wormwood

green,
silvery-green,
silvery-white

Sage is
a drought-tolerant
perennial, with
delightfully
aromatic foliage.

We grow sage in the main garden and in a hot,
dry, sun-baked bed where few other plants survive.
In both spots, it produces a fine display of silvery
foliage throughout the season and thrives with
minimal attention. Old man looks somewhat like
a larger, upright version of the more common silver
mound sage, with feathery, green foliage and a
strong, lemon-pine scent. The upright and
spreading silver king sage forms thickets of slender,
woolly, silvery-white leaves on silvery stems. Silver
mound sage is a neat, rounded hill of soft, feathery,
silver-grey foliage. Perennial dusty miller is
low-growing, with light grey-green, lobed leaves.

Height • Old Man: 36–48 inches
    (90–120 cm)
    Silver King Sage: 24–36 inches (60–90 cm)
    Silver Mound Sage: 18 inches (45 cm)
    Perennial Dusty Miller: 6–12 inches
    (15–30 cm)

Spread • Old Man: 36 inches (90 cm)
    Silver King Sage: 36–48 inches
    (90–120 cm)
    Silver Mound Sage: 24 inches (60 cm)
    Perennial Dusty Miller: 36–48 inches
    (90–120 cm)

Blooms • midsummer

PLANTING

Seeding: Only perennial dusty miller is
recommended to grow from seed. Sow
indoors in February, and
outdoors in early
spring. Growing
the others from
seed is not
recommended,
because it takes
too long for
plants to reach
a good size.

Transplanting: Space old man 3–4 feet (90–120 cm) apart, silver king 3 feet (90 cm) apart, silver mound 2 feet (60 cm) apart and dusty miller 2–3 feet (60–90 cm) apart.

GROWING

Hot, dry, sunny areas. Best in poor soil.

All make stunning accent plants. Old man at back of border. Silver king and dusty miller are fast-growing groundcovers. Silver king grows well on sloped areas. Silver mound and dusty miller in rock gardens, as edging, front of border.

Do not cut back old man in fall. Wait until spring, to see where plants begin to leaf out, and trim dead stems above that point.

Divide most sages every 3–4 years or whenever plants start to look ragged. Silver mound indicates its need for dividing by becoming less vigorous; the centre often dies out. Old man may not need dividing for 10 or more years. Use method A, page 54. Allow groundcover sages to spread.

Perennial dusty miller is striking mixed with maiden pinks.

Recommended Varieties
Old Man
Usually available only under one of the names listed above.

Silver King Sage
Silver King • 30–36 inches (75–90 cm) tall; silvery-white foliage; actually a named variety but so popular that its entire species is commonly known by this name.

Silver Queen • 24–30 inches (60–75 cm) tall; silvery-white foliage; broader leaves than the variety 'Silver King.'

Valerie Finnis • 24 inches (60 cm) tall; broad, notched leaves on dense, upright stems; silvery-green foliage.

Silver Mound Sage
Silver Mound • 18 inches (45 cm) tall; finely divided, silky, silver-grey foliage; again, actually a named variety but so popular that its entire species is commonly known by this name.

Sages grow best in poor soil and are rarely troubled by pests.

Old man has been called 'the lovers' plant,' 'lad's love' and 'maid's ruin'; its leaves were once used in aphrodisiacs and love potions.

Silver mound sages are aptly named: their foliage forms a tidy ball, offsetting the spiky form of daylilies.

Perennial Dusty Miller

Silver Brocade • 6–12 inches (15–30 cm) tall; beautiful, soft, silver foliage; leaves more finely divided and plants shorter than the species; spreads extremely quickly, up to 3 or 4 feet (90–120 cm) in a single year.

TIPS

Use sage's silvery foliage to enhance flower colours. It blends beautifully with blues, lavenders and pinks, and softens oranges and reds. Plant tall sages behind, and low sages in front.

Sages do best in poor or alkaline soil and should not be fertilized, except with a little bone meal in spring. In rich soil, they tend to spread too quickly and outgrow their allotted spaces. An abundance of nutrients also causes the foliage of silver king and silver mound sages to become too lush. The plants will then split open at the centre, resulting in an unattractive shape.

Silver king sage thrives in a hot, dry location with ornamental grasses and juniper.

Do not plant sages in shade. Without full-day sun, these plants become floppy.

Silver king sages spread quickly by underground roots. Unwanted shoots are easily uprooted, but you can avoid this task by containing plants with an underground barrier to a minimum depth of 18 inches (45 cm). Left unchecked, silver king sage will quickly take over less aggressive plants.

Perennial dusty miller also spreads quickly, but is easier to control because it spreads above ground, with roots forming wherever stems touch soil. Simply chop off unwanted sections.

Old man has woodier stems than other sages. In southern areas, it grows into a huge plant but in northern gardens its stems partially die back over winter.

Silver mound sage is very effective in a border lining the driveway. Use several of these plants spaced at regular intervals between other plants.

Sage's finest feature is its silvery foliage, which looks freshest in hot, dry, sunny areas.

To keep silver mound sages more compact, trim them again in late spring as you would a hedge. Remove 1–2 inches (2.5–5 cm) of top-growth, and some branches if necessary.

Although sage is drought-tolerant, young plants need to be kept well-watered during the first growing season. After that, water sparingly. Foliage turns yellow if the soil is too moist.

Sages bloom with tiny yellow flowers in midsummer which often go unnoticed.

Deer will not eat sage. Dogs and cats are said to dislike old man and silver mound sage; these plants may keep them from your garden.

Old man is thought to repel ants and aphids. Hang its dried leaves in a net bag in closets to discourage moths. I've been told that burning its leaves to ashes in the fireplace will remove cooking smells from the house.

Snip a few stems from sage to add to fresh bouquets.

The foliage of sages can be easily air-dried for added contrast and texture in winter arrangements. Add bits of old man's aromatic leaves to potpourris. When harvesting silver king sages for drying, simply shear plants down to 4–6 inches (10–15 cm) above the ground. With other types, snip off only a few stems. Harvest perennial dusty miller in summer when leaves are small, or they will turn brown when dried. Hang the foliage upside-down in bunches for about a week.

The silvery, aromatic foliage of silver king sage can be woven into a splendid pinwheel-like wreath. Fasten the fresh foliage onto a wire frame with bits of thin wire and allow it to dry in place.

Sages are tough, long-lived perennials. In southern Saskatchewan and Alberta, old man can often be found growing near abandoned farmhouses, announcing its presence with a sweet aroma.

Saxifrage

Saxifraga arendsii
Mossy Saxifrage, Rock Saxifrage

Saxifraga cotyledon
Encrusted Saxifrage, Jungfrau Saxifrage

red, pink, white

When encrusted saxifrages are blooming at the greenhouses, the plants sell out in a matter of weeks. Staff members make quick visits to the perennials area, just to see these irresistible flowers. Encrusted saxifrages look a lot like hens & chicks until their flowers appear, rising in elegant, branching clusters up to a foot (30 cm) above the foliage. Mossy saxifrages put on their best show in gardens, forming low sheets of bright green, mossy foliage, liberally sprinkled with cup-shaped blooms in late spring.

Height (without flowers) • Mossy Saxifrage:
2–3 inches (5–7.5 cm)
Encrusted Saxifrage: 3–4 inches
(7.5–10 cm)

Spread • 10–15 inches (25–38 cm) in
2 years; ultimately up to twice as wide.

Blooms • late spring to early summer

PLANTING

Seeding: Indoors in February.
Outdoors in late spring. Plants started from seed may bloom the first season, but will put on a better show in following years.

The leaves of encrusted saxifrages are outlined with a curious silvery deposit of lime, which gives the plants their name.

Transplanting: Space 8–12 inches
(20–30 cm) apart.

Growing

Light shade to sun.

Rock gardens, groundcover, along
edges of raised flowerbeds, along paths.
Front of border.

Divide mossy saxifrage every 4–5 years, when
the centre begins to die out. Use method C,
page 54. Encrusted saxifrage shouldn't need
dividing, unless the plants outgrow their
allotted space. You won't need to dig it up.
Just hold this plant down with your hand
to keep it in place, and, with a trowel or
your fingers, gently remove rosettes at the
plants' edges. Press them on top of soil in
a new location.

Recommended Varieties
Mossy Saxifrage
Luschtintez • 3 inches (7.5 cm) tall when
blooming; deep red flowers; blooms longer
than most; forms a tight, compact bun
4–5 inches (10–12.5 cm) across.

Encrusted Saxifrage
Southside Seedling • 12 inches (30 cm)
tall when blooming; white flowers
with burgundy-red spots; larger flower
clusters than most; unbelievably beautiful
in full bloom; in our opinion, the most
stunning variety.

*Mossy
saxifrage is a
charming
addition to
rock gardens.*

Saxifraga means 'breaker of the rocks.' Saxifrage will grow in rock crevices, making it appear that the plant created the crack.

TIPS

Saxifrages are spectacular in bloom. Choose a prominent spot in the garden to display these plants.

Avoid hot locations. Although saxifrages like sun, they will be at their best in a site that receives a few hours of shade each day.

Saxifrages will grow in alkaline soil.

Remove flower stems after blooming to keep plants tidy.

The central rosette of encrusted saxifrage dies after blooming, but other rosettes quickly move in to take its place.

Snip a few blooms from encrusted saxifrages for bouquets. The flowers last about a week in a vase.

Encrusted saxifrages are easily divided in a matter of minutes. When you buy a plant, you can separate 3 or 4 small rosettes from the main plant, giving you several separate plants for your garden. The smaller ones may not bloom the next season, but after a few years, each plant will spread to 15 inches (38 cm) or more wide.

'Southside Seedling' encrusted saxifrage is stunningly beautiful in full bloom, and the perfect companion for roses.

OTHER RECOMMENDED SPECIES

Saxifraga paniculata (*S. aizoon*) (Aizoon Saxifrage): $^1/_2$–5 inches (1–12.5 cm) tall without flowers, and 3–20 inches (7.5–50 cm) tall when blooming; 8–15 inches (20–38 cm) wide. Flowers are white, pink, red, lemon-yellow, or white with red spots; some varieties have slightly encrusted leaves. Forms cushions of foliage; excellent in rock gardens and borders.

Aizoon saxifrage blooms for 3–4 weeks, from late spring to early summer.

Sea Holly

Eryngium planum
Flat Sea Holly

 blue

Sea holly has spiky, laced flowerheads, heart-shaped leaves and long, sturdy stems all in a light shade of steel-blue. As well as putting on a splendid show in the garden, this plant provides long-lasting cutflowers and attractive seedheads for drying.
Sea holly blooms all summer and thrives in hot, dry spots of the garden where few other plants will grow.

Height • 24–36 inches (60–90 cm)

Spread • 24 inches (60 cm)

Blooms • all summer

PLANTING

Seeding: Not recommended. Plants take at least 3 years to flower.

Transplanting: Space 12–18 inches (30–45 cm) apart.

GROWING

Sun.

Accent plant. Back of border.

Do not divide. Sea holly's thick taproot makes it difficult to successfully move or divide.

RECOMMENDED VARIETIES

Usually available only under one of the names listed above.

Sea holly is a large perennial that blooms all summer.

TIPS

One gardener told us he grows sea holly in combination with lavatera, an annual with showy pink flowers. The display is absolutely stunning! Another gardener favours globe thistle as a companion; both of these perennials provide flowers for fresh or dried arrangements.

Do not plant in windy, exposed areas where winter winds sweep away snow. Sea holly does best with a good snow-cover in winter.

Cut these long-stemmed flowers for bouquets when they are fully open. Once stems are cut, unopened flowers will not continue to develop. Cutflowers last up to 2 weeks.

Both flowers and stems are metallic-blue. When dried, the colour holds so remarkably well that they appear to have been spray-painted. Harvest flowers for drying before they begin to lose colour. Hang bunches upside-down for about a week.

If you are not harvesting plants for drying, leave stems standing over winter. The seedheads look attractive under frost and provide food for birds.

Sea holly does well in hot, dry locations and in poor, sandy or clay soils.

OTHER RECOMMENDED SPECIES

Eryngium alpinum (Alpine Sea Holly): 24–36 inches (60–90 cm) tall and 24 inches (60 cm) wide; dark steel-blue flowers, stems and leaves. Blooming period and care as above.

Many gardeners grow sea holly because it provides an enormous amount of flowers and seedheads for both fresh and dried bouquets. In ancient times, this plant was favoured for other reasons: according to folklore, sea holly was once a common ingredient in love potions.

Sea Thrift

Armeria maritima
Alpine Thrift, Armeria,
Common Thrift,
Sea Pink

red, pink, lilac,
white

Sea thrift is a charming plant that blooms all summer long, asks for little attention after planting, and always looks neat. Ball-shaped flowers, about an inch (2.5 cm) across, rise on slender stems above a tidy clump of grassy leaves. I like sea thrift in rock gardens, highlighted against a mulch of white rocks, or growing among low, evergreen shrubs. Try outlining a flowerbed with a row of these compact plants.

Height • 6–8 inches (15–20 cm)

Spread • 12 inches (30 cm)

Blooms • late spring through late summer

PLANTING

Seeding: Indoors in February or March; germination 14–21 days. Press seed into mix; do not cover with soil. Sow outdoors in early spring. Plants will bloom late the first season, but all summer in following years.

Transplanting: Space 9–12 inches (22–30 cm) apart.

GROWING

Sun to partial shade.

Rock gardens, along a path, edging a flowerbed, massed in groups. Front of border.

Water only when dry.

Never needs dividing. If you want more plants, divide using method C (see page 54).

Sea thrift blooms all summer long, tolerates drought, is rarely troubled by pests and grows well in poor soil.

RECOMMENDED VARIETIES

Alba • pure white flowers.

Dusseldorf Pride • bright magenta flowers; long-bloomer.

TIPS

Do not fertilize, except with bone meal in early spring. Too much fertilizer will lessen rather than increase the number of flowers.

Sea thrift does well in seaside conditions, provided soil is well drained. Plant it in beds that may be affected by road salt used to melt ice in winter.

Deadhead regularly to keep plants blooming right through to fall frosts. Snip off the entire stem of faded flowers. If you want more plants, allow some seedheads to form.

Sea thrift is an evergreen perennial. Do not cut back foliage or you will prevent flowers from forming and may even kill the plant.

These round flowers make marvellous additions to mini bouquets. Cut when flowers are almost fully open. They last about a week.

'Dusseldorf Pride' sea thrift and 'Pike's Pink' Cheddar pinks (top) are a striking combination when in full bloom. Juniper thrift (above) looks like a miniature version of sea thrift.

OTHER RECOMMENDED SPECIES

Armeria juniperifolia (Juniper Thrift): 6 inches (10–15 cm) tall; 8–12 inches (20–30 cm) wide. Blooms with masses of $1/2$-inch (1 cm) pale pink flowers in spring, and sporadically through summer. Excellent alpine plant for rock gardens. 'Bevan's Variety' has darker flowers.

Shasta Daisy

**Leucanthemum χ
superbum
(Chrysanthemum
maximum,
C. χ superbum)**

white

*Almost everyone knows the Shasta daisy. It's the
classic perennial daisy, the one that you pluck the
petals off to find out if 'she (he) loves me, she (he)
loves me not.' When I was growing up, almost
every neighbourhood garden had some of these
flowers. Shasta daisies no longer all look the same.
New varieties have huge, double or semi-double
blooms almost twice the average size. Other, more
compact varieties grow to less than half the height
of the traditional Shasta.*

Height • 12–36 inches (30–90 cm)

Spread • 12–36 inches (30–90 cm)

Blooms • late spring to early summer

PLANTING

Seeding: Indoors in February or March;
germinates in 7–14 days. Cover seed
lightly. Sow outdoors in early spring. Plants
started indoors will bloom the first year.

Transplanting: Space 12–24 inches
(30–60 cm) apart.

Shasta daisies
are tough plants
that need little
supplementary
watering and grow in
almost any type of
soil. They are rarely
troubled by pests.

GROWING

Sun to partial
shade.

Mixed
flowerbeds,
cutting gardens,
mass plantings,
in a row lining
the driveway.
Middle to back
of border.

Divide every
3–4 years to
prevent over-
crowding. See
page 54,
method A.

Recommended Varieties

Aglaia • 24 inches (60 cm) tall; beautiful, double, frilled flowers.

Alaska • 24 inches (60 cm) tall; classic single blooms, 1–3 inches (6–8 cm) across.

Sedgewick • 12–18 inches (30–45 cm) tall; dwarf plants; semi-double flowers.

Thomas Killin • 24–36 inches (60–90 cm) tall; extra-large, semi-double flowers with creamy-yellow centres.

Tips

Single-flowered varieties are somewhat hardier than double-flowered ones.

Remove finished flowers to prolong the blooming period.

Shasta daisies are short-lived plants, but by dividing them regularly or permitting self-sowing, you will have these flowers in your garden for many years.

Shasta daisies self-sow readily, with seedlings often appearing in unexpected places. My daughter-in-law's mother grows self-sown Shasta daisies between patio stones; the effect is lovely, like a backyard meadow. Let seedlings grow wherever they appear, or uproot and transplant them, and discard unwanted ones. To prevent self-seeding, remove all flowers before seeds form.

Deer will not eat Shasta daisies.

The bright, cheery flowers of the Shasta daisy are wonderful in bouquets. Cut when flowers are fully open. They usually last 7–10 days after cutting.

Shasta *is a native Indian word meaning 'white.' These daisies (above) bloom generously for a month or more in summer. 'Thomas Killin' (left) has huge, distinctive flowers. The daisies of 'Aglaia' (opposite) are smaller, with frilly, double petals.*

Shooting-star

Dodecatheon meadia
Common Shooting-star

 rose-pink, white

Children really like these flowers, which resemble shooting stars or tiny rockets taking off. Many gardeners recall seeing these plants growing in the wild. In their natural habitat, shooting-stars grow in forest clearings, in moist, rich soil sheltered from direct sunlight by leafy trees. For the best success, match these conditions as closely as possible in your own garden.

Height • 6–10 inches (15–25 cm)

Spread • 12 inches (30 cm)

Blooms • mid- to late spring

PLANTING

Seeding: Not recommended. Seed has a short period of viability, and plants will take about 3 years to bloom.

Transplanting: Space 8–10 inches (2–25 cm) apart.

GROWING

Partial shade to partial sun.

In groups in woodland, rock and shade gardens, mass plantings, mixed beds. Front of border.

Divide every 3 years, in fall when plants are dormant. See page 54, method C.

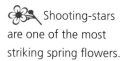 Shooting-stars are one of the most striking spring flowers.

Recommended Varieties

Usually available only under one of the names listed above.

Tips

Shooting-stars look best in groups, and blend well with spring-flowering primroses.

Avoid planting in low-lying areas where water pools in spring after snow melts. Although these plants prefer moist soil while actively growing, excessive water in early spring or while plants are dormant can be fatal.

In sunnier locations, these plants will wither and die back by mid- to late summer. To avoid this, plant them in shady, moist areas, or hide the yellowing foliage by growing a leafy perennial like elephant-ears or hosta nearby.

Shooting-stars are a delightful addition to gardens. A single stem can bear as many as 10–15 flowers, and mature plants produce 5 or more stems.

Snakeroot

Cimicifuga ramosa
Black Cohosh,
Bugbane, Silver Candle

 white

If you want a tall, dramatic plant for your shady garden, grow snakeroot. Its handsome leaves provide an attractive, dark green background for other flowers, from early spring until frost. When many other plants have finished blooming, snakeroot continues its show until late fall, with tall spires of tiny, creamy-white flowers.

Height • 3–6 feet (90–180 cm)

Spread • 3–5 feet (90–150 cm)

Blooms • midsummer to fall

Both the names 'bugbane' and *Cimicifuga* refer to this plant's reputed insecticidal properties. 'Bane' means 'poison'; the botanical name is derived from the Latin words *cimex* ('insect') and *fugo* ('to repel').

Planting

Seeding: Collect fresh seed from the plant and sow outdoors in fall. Plants will bloom the second year.

Transplanting: Space 24 inches (60 cm) apart.

Growing

Partial to full shade; moist soil. A site that receives about 4 hours of morning sun is ideal.

Shade and woodland gardens. Back of border.

Division is not necessary. If you want more plants, divide every 3–5 years using method A, page 54. Ensure each division has at least 2–3 stems.

Recommended Varieties

Atropurpurea • 4–6 feet (120–180 cm) tall and 2–3 feet (60–90 cm) wide; arching, white flowerstalks; bronze-purple foliage and stems; striking contrast; often grows taller and blooms later than the species; flowers have a tuberose-like fragrance; very showy.

Tips

The rounded leaves of hostas and elephant-ears make a nice contrast to snakeroot's vertical form.

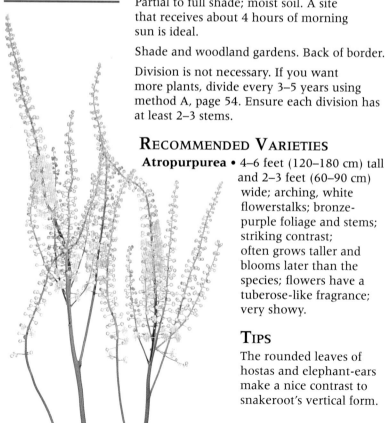

Snakeroot grows well in low-lying, wet areas of the garden.

In shady, moist areas, snakeroot grows as much as a foot (30 cm) taller than in sunny, dry locations.

We have 2 of these plants in our garden. The one that receives morning shade and afternoon sun blooms about 2 weeks sooner than the one that is shaded in the afternoon.

Add these flowering spires to mixed bouquets.

Cut stems for drying when flowerbuds are still tightly closed. Hang a few stems in a bunch upside-down. The result will be long stems covered in perfect little balls.

Children like to play with seedpod stems, because they sound like a rattlesnake when shaken.

OTHER RECOMMENDED SPECIES

Cimicifuga simplex (Kamchatka Bugbane): 3–4 feet (90–120 cm) tall and wide; upright plant with glossy, oval leaves; arching flowers like fuzzy, white bottle brushes from late summer to fall. The variety 'White Pearl' is bushier and more compact than the species.

✿ Snakeroot blooms late in the season, when many other perennials have finished flowering. This long-lived plant grows well in dense shade or acidic soil.

If you want very dark plants for your garden, look for the Latin word nigra, *meaning 'black,' or the prefix* atro, *meaning 'dark.'*
*A plant with the species name 'atropurpurea' has very dark purple colouring, like the perennial snakeroot (*Cimicifuga ramosa *'Atropurpurea'), with its deep purple leaves and stems.*

Snakeroot was not named for its snake-like appearance, but for the fact that pioneers used its roots to treat rattlesnake bites. Some people still use snakeroot medicinally, as a sedative.

Sneezeweed

Helenium autumnale
Common Sneezeweed, Golden Star, Helen's Flower

yellow, gold, orange, red, brown

With a name like sneezeweed, it's hard to become a best-selling plant. This perennial has tall sprays of daisy-like flowers in rich autumn colours—deep red, russet and bright yellow. It blooms for about a month, late in the season, carrying the summer floral show into fall. These strong-stemmed flowers are splendid in bouquets, and the plants are undemanding in gardens. So why don't more gardeners grow sneezeweed? Its flowers won't make you sneeze—this plant's rather unfortunate name comes from a medicinal use of long ago. Native American Indians used to crush dried petals into a snuff-like powder, to combat hayfever.

Height • 24–48 inches (60–120 cm)

Spread • 24 inches (60 cm)

Blooms • midsummer to early fall

PLANTING

Seeding: Indoors in February or March. Outdoors in spring. Plants will flower sparsely the first fall but better in following years.

Transplanting: Space 12–18 inches (30–45 cm) apart.

GROWING

Sneezeweed adds rich colour to the garden in late summer.

Sun.

Mixed flowerbeds, cutting gardens. Back of border.

May need staking.

Divide every 3–4 years to prevent overcrowding, or when the number of flowers decreases. See page 54, method A.

RECOMMENDED VARIETIES

Margot • 30–48 inches (75–120 cm) tall; wide, yellow-edged flowers with mahogany centres.

Moerheim Beauty • 24–36 inches (60–90 cm) tall; rich mahogany flowers with black centres; colour fades to an attractive burnt-orange; strong stems; long-bloomer.

TIPS

Pinch out the central tips of stalks when plants are about 6 inches (15 cm) tall to encourage bushiness and more flowers.

Sneezeweed is rarely troubled by pests.

Cut for bouquets when the majority of flowers in a spray has opened. Sneezeweed is an excellent cutflower, with sturdy stems up to 2 feet (60 cm) long. The flowers last about 2 weeks in bouquets.

I love sneezeweed in dried arrangements. Harvest flowers before they open fully, and hang them upside-down.

Sneezeweed is one of the best late-blooming cutflowers and makes a splendid bouquet, all on its own.

Trim off sneezeweed's faded flowers to encourage more blooms.

Snow-in-Summer

Cerastium tomentosum

white

Once you see this plant in full bloom, you will have no doubt that it is aptly named. Masses of pretty, white flowers cover the plants from late spring to early summer, creating the illusion of a mound of gleaming snow. The low, spreading mats of soft, woolly, silver foliage provide a pleasing contrast to the greenery of other plants.

Height • 6 inches (15 cm)

Spread • 24 inches (60 cm) or more

Blooms • late spring to early summer

PLANTING

Seeding: Indoors in February or March; germination 7–14 days. Seed needs light to germinate; do not cover with soil mix. Sow outdoors in early spring. Plants will bloom the second year.

Transplanting: Space 12–24 inches (30–60 cm) apart.

GROWING

Sun.

Any area of the garden where there is room to spread, trailing over walls of raised beds, groundcover, edging in borders.

Snow-in-summer is attractive throughout the season. It is one of the best groundcovers for hot, dry, windy locations, and grows well in poor soil.

These plants spread to about 24 inches (60 cm) within two years of planting, but, left unchecked, will eventually spread 8 feet (2.5 m) or more.

Snow-in-summer grows well in partially shaded areas, but blooms far more profusely in full sun.

Snow-in-summer can be left undisturbed indefinitely. Sometimes the plant centres become less vigorous. If this happens, or you want more plants, divide using method B, page 54.

RECOMMENDED VARIETIES

Usually available only under one of the names listed above.

TIPS

As with many fast-spreading plants, the key to success with snow-in-summer is control. Although many gardening books recommend snow-in-summer for rock gardens, we have found that these fast-growing plants are rather invasive and tend to take over other plants in that situation.

One gardener told us she solved this problem by installing an under-ground barrier to a minimum depth of 12 inches (30 cm), to control the underground roots. Snow-in-summer also spreads by rooting wherever its stems touch the ground, so she applied a thick layer of mulch to keep foliage away from soil. That way, whenever the plants spread too wide, she could simply lift up a mat of foliage and chop off the overgrown edges.

After blooming, shear off about an inch (2.5 cm) from the top of plants, to remove dead flowers and encourage fresh new growth. This step also helps to keep plants from spreading out of bounds.

Snow-in-summer sometimes self-seeds, but seedlings often take a long time to appear. Seeds can remain viable in soil for several years.

Deer will not eat these plants.

Soapwort

Saponaria officinalis
Bouncing Bet,
Lady-by-the-Gate

pink, white

Spicy-sweet fragrance and masses of flowers all summer should be reasons enough to grow soapwort, but this showy, old-fashioned flower also provides a solution for problem areas of the garden. It is drought-tolerant and grows well in poor soil. If you have a large area to fill, allow these long-lived perennials to spread unchecked. I particularly like the double-flowered ones, which look quite a bit like garden phlox.

Height • 24–36 inches (60–90 cm)

Spread • 24–36 inches (60–90 cm)

Blooms • all summer

Rumour has it that in the 1600s, English pub-maids known as 'Bets' or 'Betsies' used branches of this plant to clean beer bottles, hence the name 'Bouncing Bet.'

PLANTING

Seeding: Indoors in February or March; germination 10–15 days. Outdoors in early spring. Plants will bloom the second year.

Transplanting: Space 24–36 inches (60–90 cm) apart.

GROWING

Sun to partial shade.

Mixed flowerbeds. Middle to back of border.

Divide every 3–4 years. See page 54, method A. Soapwort also sends out sideshoots or suckers, which can be cut off a few inches (10 cm) below soil level, and transplanted into a new location. These take longer to reach full size than do divisions.

RECOMMENDED VARIETIES

Rosea Plena • 24–36 inches (60–90 cm) tall; double, pale pink flowers; very showy.

TIPS

Plant soapwort in rather poor soil to prevent it from spreading too rapidly. Do not fertilize plants during the growing season. A handful or two of bone meal worked into surrounding soil in early spring is all they need.

We grow soapwort in a hot, dry flowerbed against a heat-reflective wall, on the south side of the house, and it thrives there.

The leaves of soapwort contain saponin, a sudsing compound, and were once commonly used for shampoo and laundry soap. Let the kids try bruising a few leaves and agitating them in water, to create their own soap.

Cut flowers for bouquets when they are just starting to open. They last 7–10 days after cutting.

OTHER RECOMMENDED SPECIES

Saponaria ocymoides (Rock Soapwort): 6–10 inches (15–25 cm) tall and 12–18 inches (30–45 cm) wide; trailing plant smothered in pink flowers from late spring through most of the summer. Wonderful trailing over walls of raised beds and in rock gardens, where it will clamber over rocks. Cut back severely after blooming to keep plants neat. The variety 'Alba' is a rare, white-flowered form. 'Rubra Compacta' has crimson flowers; plants are more compact and non-trailing.

Soapwort blooms throughout the summer with dense clusters of fragrant flowers.

Rock soapwort is an easy-to-grow, trailing plant with dark green, oval leaves and pretty pink flowers.

Solomon's Seal

Polygonatum multiflorum
Eurasian Solomon's Seal

 white

Solomon's seal adds an exotic touch to shady gardens. In any degree of shade, and even in dry areas under mature trees, you can count on Solomon's seal to add an attractive patch of greenery. In spring, its graceful stems arch with creamy-white bellflowers edged in green. Shiny, blue-black berries follow in summer. This attractive perennial is undemanding and spreads slowly. One gardener told us that in more than ten years, his plant, which had grown to 4 feet (120 cm) across, had never needed dividing.

Height • 18–24 inches (45–60 cm)

Spread • 12–18 inches (30–45 cm)

Blooms • late spring

PLANTING

Seeding: Not recommended. Seeds take 2 or more months to germinate, and grow slowly.

Roots: Plant rhizomes in spring, 3–4 inches (7.5–10 cm) deep.

Transplanting: Space 12 inches (30 cm) apart.

GROWING

Full to partial shade.

Mixed borders, woodland gardens, under trees, as a groundcover. Middle to back of border.

The seal of biblical King Solomon was a six-pointed star, like the Star of David. A cross-section of this plant's root is said to bear a resemblance, hence the name Solomon's seal.

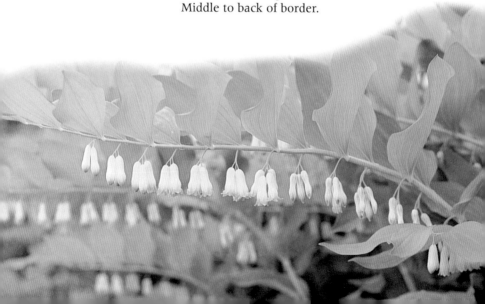

Dividing is not necessary to improve plant vigour, but if you want more plants, divide Solomon's seal in summer after flowering. See page 54, method B.

Solomon's seal is one of the few plants that grows well in either moist or dry shaded areas.

RECOMMENDED VARIETIES

Usually available only under one of the names listed above.

TIPS

Solomon's seal thrives even in heavily shaded areas, and blends well with primroses, hostas, ostrich ferns and astilbe.

These plants do well in acidic soils under evergreen trees.

Add stems of both the flowers and berries to your bouquets.

For dry, shaded gardens, Solomon's seal is a 'must-have' plant.

Speedwell

**Veronica longifolia
(V. maritima)**
Hungarian Speedwell,
Longleaf Speedwell

Veronica spicata
Spike Speedwell

blue, purple, red,
pink, white

Speedwell's
narrow spires of richly
coloured flowers are
wonderful in fresh or
dried bouquets.

Gardeners often ask for perennials that bloom
nearly all summer, have blue flowers and can be
cut for bouquets. Only a few plants can meet all
three requests, and speedwell is one of them.
Speedwell's pretty flowerspikes are also available in
purple, pink, red and white. A mix of colours and
varieties planted together looks splendid.

Height • 12–24 inches (30–60 cm)

Spread • 15–24 inches (38–60 cm)

Blooms • most of summer

PLANTING

Seeding: Indoors in February or March. Seed
needs light to germinate; sprinkle on top of
soil mix. Germination 7–14 days. Sow
outdoors in early spring. Plants started
indoors will bloom the first year.

Transplanting: Space 10–18 inches
(25–45 cm) apart.

GROWING

Sun to partial shade.

Mixed flowerbeds, cutting gardens, shorter
types in rock gardens and edging
paths. Front to middle of
border.

Divide every
3–4 years. See
page 54,
method A.

The upright blooms of spike speedwell complement other flowers.

RECOMMENDED VARIETIES
Hungarian Speedwell
Sunny Border Blue • 12–18 inches (30–45 cm) tall; intensely rich, dark violet-blue flowerspikes; blooms early summer through early fall, longer than any other speedwell; great resistance to insects and disease; the Perennial Plant Association's 1993 Plant of the Year.

Spike Speedwell
Red Fox • 12–18 inches (30–45 cm) tall; lots of rose-red flowers on erect, tapering stems; long-blooming, early to late summer.

TIPS
Offset speedwell's colourful spikes with ornamental grasses or rounded flowers, such as tickseed, daylilies, yarrow and cranesbills.

Don't be overly generous with fertilizers. Too many nutrients can cause speedwells to become floppy.

Use speedwell's flowerspikes to accent mixed bouquets. Cut stems when the lower flowers are already open. The blooms generally last 7–10 days after cutting, and longer if stems are recut regularly.

Cut flowers for drying when they are fully open. Hang several stems in a bunch and hang them upside-down for about a week.

Both 'Red Fox' (below) and 'Sunny Border Blue' (opposite) are particularly long-blooming varieties of speedwell.

Spurge

Euphorbia
polychroma
Cushion Spurge,
Yellow Spurge

 yellow

Cushion spurge earns its name by growing into a large, rounded, cushion-like mound. I always marvel at its size and perfect shape. In spring, cushion spurge is a mass of sulphur-yellow. It blooms at the same time as tulips, and looks wonderful with low-growing species of tulips blooming in front. Or, grow blue alpine asters in the foreground, with silver king sage behind. The foliage of cushion spurge remains an attractive green throughout summer and turns red in fall.

Height • 18–24 inches (45–90 cm)

Spread • 24–36 inches (60–90 cm)

Blooms • early spring

PLANTING

Seeding: Indoors in February or March; germination 28 days, often erratic. Press seed lightly into mix. Sow outdoors in early spring. Plants will bloom the second year.

Transplanting: Space 12–18 inches (30–45 cm) apart.

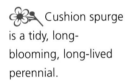 Cushion spurge is a tidy, long-blooming, long-lived perennial.

Daylilies, silver king sage and spurge all thrive in hot, dry locations.

GROWING

Sun.

Flowerbeds, rock gardens, accent plants. Front to middle of border.

Dividing is not necessary. Plants can remain undisturbed indefinitely. If you want more plants, divide using method A, page 54.

RECOMMENDED VARIETIES

Usually available only under one of the names listed above.

TIPS

What is commonly referred to as the flowers of cushion spurge are actually bracts, or coloured leaves. Cushion spurge is related to the poinsettia, another plant popular for its colourful bracts.

Cushion spurge forms a neat mound of foliage and never spreads from its allotted space.

Cushion spurge grows well in poor soil and hot, dry locations.

Gardeners often ask for deer-proof plants; cushion spurge is one. These plants are also reputed to repel mice and moles.

Spurge forms a handsome bush and is attractive throughout the season. The leaves turn red in fall.

St. John's Wort

Hypericum buckleyi
(H. perforatum)
Blue Ridge St. John's
Wort

yellow

St. John's wort
is covered in bright
yellow blooms
throughout the
summer.

I've always thought that its pretty yellow flowers were reason enough to grow St. John's wort, but, in olden days, there were far more compelling reasons. For centuries, this plant was believed to have the power to drive out evil spirits. The botanical name Hypericum *means 'above an icon.' Hundreds of years ago, common advice was to place sprigs of this plant above pictures to ward off devils. Later in history, with the spread of Christianity, this plant became associated with John the Baptist. It was said to first bloom on his birthday, June 24, a date that is now known as St. John's Day. ('Wort,' by the way, is simply an old word for 'plant.')*

Height • 10–15 inches (25–38 cm)

Spread • 24–36 inches (60–90 cm) or more

Blooms • early summer to early fall

PLANTING

Seeding: Indoors in February or March. Outdoors in early spring. Plants started indoors will bloom that season.

Transplanting: Space 18–24 inches (45–60 cm) apart.

GROWING

Sun to partial shade.

Groundcover, mixed beds. Front to middle of border.

Divide every 3–4 years. See page 54, method A.

RECOMMENDED VARIETIES

Usually available only under one of the names listed above.

TIPS

Although St. John's wort does well in moist soil, it is also drought-tolerant and can be grown in hot, dry areas of the garden.

These plants make an attractive groundcover, provided you have patience. They spread slowly.

St. John's wort is a low-maintenance plant that is rarely troubled by pests.

Statice

Limonium platyphyllum (L. latifolium, Statice latifolium)
Perennial Statice, Sea Lavender, Wide-leaf Sea Lavender

Limonium tataricum (Statice tataricum, Goniolimon tataricum)
German Statice, Caspia, Tatarian Statice

 purple, white

When it comes to filler plants, few perennials can match statice. These bushy plants fill gaps in the garden with airy clouds of flowers. In fresh bouquets, their masses of tiny flowers fill in backgrounds to enhance larger blooms, and they are unequalled for filling in large, dried arrangements. Sea lavender blooms with billowy sprays of tiny, lavender-blue flowers above dark green, leathery leaves. German statice's flowers are larger, white, and more densely packed on stiffer stems, with shiny green leaves at the plant's base.

Height • Sea Lavender: 18–30 inches (45–75 cm)
German Statice: 10–15 inches (25–38 cm)

Spread • Sea Lavender: 24 inches (60 cm)
German Statice: 15–18 inches (38–45 cm)

Blooms • summer

*Statice is one of the best flowers for fresh bouquets and dried arrangements.
Sea lavender grows into a frothy bush, with plenty of blooms for cutting.*

PLANTING

Seeding: Not recommended. Plants will take 3–4 years to flower.

Transplanting: Space 15–24 inches (38–60 cm) apart.

GROWING

Sun to partial shade.

Mixed flowerbeds. Middle to back of border.

Do not divide these plants. They have long taproots which make successful division difficult. Statice will thrive in the same location for 10 or more years.

RECOMMENDED VARIETIES

Usually available only under one of the names listed above.

Plan for variety in dried arrangements by adding annuals to the garden. Here, annual statice grows with German statice. Both make excellent dried flowers.

TIPS

Statice is a great plant for narrow flowerbeds, like those alongside driveways. It grows into an airy, rounded bush that adds fullness.

Use statice to hide the foliage of plants that die back midseason, such as Oriental poppies.

Statice earns the name sea lavender because it grows well in the salty soil of coastline gardens. Grow these plants in spots where soil may be affected by winter road salt. They are also drought-tolerant.

Fertilize statice regularly. The richer the soil, the larger statice's flowerheads will be.

Both types make superb cutflowers and are often used as filler or as a substitute for baby's breath. Cut stems for bouquets when most of the flowers are open and showing colour. They usually last well over 2 weeks.

German statice is often used in bridal bouquets. Try to plan ahead if you want to grow it for an upcoming wedding, because most perennials don't put on their best show the year they are planted.

Statice is one of the best dried flowers.

Cut for drying when flowers are fully open and at their peak of beauty. Hang bunches upside-down in a shady, airy place, or simply plunk fresh stems into a big basket or vase to dry. You can harvest almost the entire plant, as long as you allow the leaves at its base to remain.

The flowers of German statice have a curious habit of appearing to change colour. On close inspection, when flowers first open, they are tinged in pink. As they age, they look white or even pale sky-blue, when viewed from farther away.

Sea lavender is showy enough to use solo in a dried arrangement.

Stonecrop

Sedum acre
Gold-dust Stonecrop,
Goldmoss Stonecrop,
Yellow Stonecrop

Sedum kamtschaticum
Kamschatca Sedum,
Russian Stonecrop

Sedum spectabile
Showy Sedum, Showy
Stonecrop

Sedum spurium
Two-row Sedum,
Dragon's Blood
Stonecrop

pink, red,
orange, yellow

Showy
stonecrop attracts
butterflies.

Stonecrops are one of those wonderful plant families that, on their own, could fill an entire flowerbed, blooming from spring right through until frost with a rainbow of colours in both foliage and flowers. These perennials are undemanding and rewarding. All have succulent, fleshy foliage.

Goldmoss stonecrop is a low, creeping mat of tiny, bright green, pointed leaves with masses of brilliant yellow, star-shaped flowers. It makes a great groundcover. Russian stonecrop is a beautiful, ball-shaped plant with trailing stems, little, golden-orange flowers and small, dark green leaves that sometimes turn bronze in fall. Showy stonecrop is one of the most spectacular perennials, with enormous pink or red flowerheads from late summer until heavy frosts. Dragon's blood stonecrop has open clusters of pink or white flowers and rounded leaves crowded at the ends of wiry, creeping stems. It grows into a thick, low mat; use this one in rock gardens or cascading over walls.

Dragon's blood stonecrop (opposite) is a good companion to pinks. Showy stonecrop 'Autumn Joy' has huge flowers in varying shades of colour.

Height • Goldmoss Stonecrop: 2–3 inches (5–7.5 cm)
    Russian Stonecrop: 5–10 inches (12–25 cm)
    Showy Stonecrop: 12–18 inches (30–45 cm)
    Dragon's Blood Stonecrop: 6 inches (15 cm)

Spread • Goldmoss Stonecrop: 2–3 feet (60–90 cm) within 2 years,
    and ultimately, as wide as you allow
    Russian Stonecrop: 12–18 inches (30–45 cm)
    Showy Stonecrop: 18–24 inches (45–60 cm)
    Dragon's Blood Stonecrop: 18–24 inches (45–60 cm)

Blooms • Goldmoss Stonecrop: late spring to midsummer
    Russian Stonecrop: all summer
    Showy Stonecrop: late summer to late fall
    Dragon's Blood Stonecrop: early to late summer

PLANTING

Seeding: Indoors in February. Outdoors in early spring. Most creeping stonecrops will bloom the first year.

Transplanting: Space creeping types 12 inches (30 cm) apart, and upright ones 15–18 inches (38–45 cm) apart.

GROWING

Hot, dry, sunny location.

Creeping stonecrops for edging borders, trailing over walls or growing in cracks between stones, in rock gardens or as a groundcover. Goldmoss also between patio bricks or stepping stones. Upright types in flowerbeds; middle to front of border.

Stonecrops are one of the least demanding perennials. They are virtually maintenance-free, and most pests will have nothing to do with them. Russian stonecrop blooms all summer.

Water only when plants are dry.

Creeping types do not need dividing, but if you want more plants, divide using method C, page 54, or simply break off a piece of stem with leaves attached, and poke it into the soil in a new location. Divide upright types every 3–4 years. Use method B, page 54.

RECOMMENDED VARIETIES

Goldmoss Stonecrop
Usually available only under one of the names listed above.

Russian Stonecrop
Variegatum • 8–10 inches (20–25 cm) tall; pink buds open to apricot-orange flowers; green leaves with cream, yellow, pink and red markings.

Showy Stonecrop
Autumn Joy • 15–18 inches (38–45 cm) tall; massive flowerheads turn from salmon-pink to bronze-red.

Brilliant • 18 inches (45 cm) tall; huge flowerheads of rich raspberry-carmine.

These versatile plants grow well in poor or alkaline soil and hot, dry areas of the garden, but they also do well in average flowerbed conditions.

Dragon's Blood Stonecrop
Dragon's Blood • red-tinted foliage and brilliant rose-red flowers; one of the showiest stonecrops and so popular that the entire species is commonly known by this name.

TIPS

When shopping for plants, keep in mind that tall stonecrops often won't look great in pots, where they may appear twisted or floppy. Once planted in your garden, they will regain their sturdy, upright posture the following year.

Cut off flower stems when creeping stonecrops finish blooming, to keep plants attractive. Goldmoss stonecrop is 'self-cleaning'; faded flowers drop cleanly from the plant, so it needs no deadheading. Many of the upright stonecrops have attractive seedheads that can be left on for winter ornamentation.

315

Even the tiniest broken-off bit of goldmoss stonecrop is likely to grow into a new plant. A heavy rainfall can knock off a few leaves, which will quickly sprout where they land. Unwanted sprouts are easily uprooted.

For an unusual bouquet, cut the flowers of showy stonecrop when most flowers in the cluster have begun to open. The flowers last up to 2 weeks after cutting.

OTHER RECOMMENDED SPECIES

Sedum telephium ssp. *maximum* (Great Stonecrop): 24 inches (60 cm) tall; thick, oval leaves and creamy-white flowerheads up to 6 inches (15 cm) across; may need staking. The variety *atropurpureum* 'Moorchen' is particularly striking, with deep burgundy foliage and clusters of pink, star-like flowers with bright red stamens.

Sedum ewersii (Ewer's Stonecrop): 4–6 inches (10–15 cm) tall; blue-green foliage with purplish-pink flowers in late summer and early fall; forms a spreading mound; great in rock gardens.

A hot, dry, sun-baked bed is perfect for stonecrop and old man sage.

The pink-flowered strawberry is unique for the colour of its large flowers.

Strawberry

Fragaria frel 'Pink Panda'
Ornamental Strawberry, Pink-flowered Strawberry, Pink Panda Strawberry

 pink

The pink-flowered strawberry is the showiest of all strawberries, and is grown as much for its large, pink flowers as for its small, sweet fruit. This plant is actually a cross between a potentilla and a strawberry, and this accounts for the colour of its flowers. Pink-flowered strawberries make a nice groundcover. Grow them at the base of clematis plants to shade clematis's roots, or plant several in a row to edge flowerbeds.

Height • 6–10 inches (15–25 cm)

Spread • 18–24 inches (45–60 cm)

Blooms • all summer

PLANTING

Seeding: Seed of these plants is not available.

Transplanting: Space 12–18 inches (30–45 cm) apart.

GROWING

Sun to partial shade; the sunnier the location, the more flowers and fruit are produced.

Edging, groundcover, rock gardens, trailing from raised beds. Front of border.

Pink-flowered strawberries (opposite-top) produce small, sweet, juicy berries. All strawberries except 'Pink Panda' (opposite-bottom) have white flowers.

Divide every 3 years. See page 54, method
C. You can also remove runners and replant
them in new locations.

RECOMMENDED VARIETIES

'Pink Panda' is one of a kind; there are no
other pink-flowered strawberries.

TIPS

It is hard to force yourself to remove all of
the blossoms the first year, but if you do, the
result will be more vigorous plants in
following years.

Allowing runners to form on plants detracts from berry production.
If fruit is most important to you, remove runners as they form.
If you want more plants, allow runners to remain.

Pink-flowered strawberries look wonderful in hanging baskets and
patio pots. We often grow them in a large planter, with a clematis or
other tall plant against a trellis for height. In northern gardens, any
perennial grown in a planter will need to be transplanted into the
ground to survive the winter, but the splendid show throughout the
summer is worth the extra effort.

OTHER RECOMMENDED SPECIES

Fragaria vesca 'Variegata' (Variegated Strawberry): 6 inches (15 cm)
tall and 18–24 inches (45–60 cm) wide; white flowers and sweet
berries about the size of a thumbnail; strongly variegated leaves with
as much green as white; wonderful groundcover; trails to over 6 feet
(1.8 m) in a hanging basket.

Fragaria virginiana (Wild Strawberry): 4–12 inches (10–30 cm) tall
and 12–18 inches (30–45 cm) wide; white flowers in spring followed
by small red strawberries throughout the summer; very sweet, juicy
fruit; considered a delicacy in France.

Thyme

Thymus pseudolanuginosus
Woolly Thyme

Thymus serpyllum
Creeping Thyme,
Mother-of-Thyme

318

purple, red, pink, white

Although it is closely related to the culinary herb, perennial thyme is grown solely for ornament. Woolly thyme has pink flowers and quickly spreads into a low, dense mat of soft, fuzzy, silvery-grey leaves. Mother-of-thyme is more like a miniature, mounded bush, with masses of tiny flowers in red, pink, white or rosy-purple. Both have aromatic foliage with a pleasing, savory-sweet scent.

Height • Woolly Thyme: 2–4 inches
(5–10 cm)
Mother-of-Thyme: 3–6 inches (7.5–15 cm)

Spread • Both: 12–18 inches (30–45 cm)

Blooms • Woolly Thyme: late spring to
early summer
Mother-of-Thyme: late spring to
late summer

PLANTING

Seeding: Indoors in February or March. Cover seed lightly; germination 3–14 days. Sow outdoors in early spring. Plants started indoors may bloom the first year.

Transplanting: Space 6 inches
(15 cm) apart.

Thyme spreads into a fragrant mat of dense foliage covered in tiny flowers.

Plant woolly thyme between paving stones. These plants do not mind being walked on, and they release a pleasing fragrance with each step.

GROWING

Sun to partial shade.

Rock gardens, between stepping stones, front of border, groundcover for slopes, in crevices.

Divide every 3 years. See page 54, method C.

RECOMMENDED VARIETIES

Woolly thyme is usually available only under one of the names listed above. In mother-of-thyme, the varieties 'Albus,' with white flowers, 'Coccineus,' with bright-red blooms, or 'Roseus,' which is pink, may be easiest to find. There are other varieties, but they are not commonly available.

Mother-of-thyme is a bright carpet of colour thoughout the summer.

TIPS

The easiest way to deadhead thyme is to trim it with shears after flowering, or even to run the lawnmower over it.

These plants do well in poor soil, and, once mature, are fairly drought-tolerant.

In a rock garden, woolly thyme forms a flat mat of foliage around the bases of rocks. The effect is gorgeous—the rocks appear to be floating in a silvery pool.

Dry creeping thyme flowers for miniature arrangements. The little, purple spikes retain their colour remarkably well.

Tickseed

Coreopsis lanceolata
Lance Coreopsis,
Lance Tickseed

Coreopsis verticillata
Butter Daisy,
Coreopsis, Threadleaf
Tickseed

 yellow

With over 1500 choices in perennials alone, it's quite a feat for a plant to be selected as a personal favourite. Ernie Onyskiw, a long-time staff member at the greenhouses, absolutely loves these plants. Tickseed is a long-blooming perennial and has a profusion of bright yellow flowers in summer. The plants form tidy, airy mounds. They need little care and are rarely troubled by pests.

Height • Lance Tickseed: 4–24 inches
　　　(10–60 cm)
　　Threadleaf Tickseed: 15–24 inches
　　　(38–60 cm)

Spread • Lance Tickseed: 8–12 inches
　　　(20–30 cm)
　　Threadleaf Tickseed: 24 inches (60 cm)

Blooms • early summer to frost

PLANTING

Seeding: Indoors in February; germination 2–4 weeks. Sow outdoors in early spring. Plants may bloom the first year.

Transplanting: Space 12 inches (30 cm) apart.

GROWING

Sun to light shade.

Rock gardens, flower beds, sloped banks. Lance tickseed as edging, front of border. Threadleaf tickseed front to middle of border.

Cut back in fall, tickseed does not usually need dividing. If you want more plants, divide after 3 years using method B, page 54.

Tickseed blooms throughout the summer.

Recommended Varieties
Lance Tickseed

Rotkelchen • 4–6 inches (10–15 cm) tall;
bright yellow flowers with burgundy
centres; plants more compact and
longer-blooming than the species.

Threadleaf Tickseed

Moonbeam • 15–24 inches (38–60 cm) tall;
icy-yellow, lightly scented flowers;
exceptional disease-resistance; blooms
longer than species; the Perennial Plant
Association's 1992 Plant of the Year.

Zagreb • 15 inches (38 cm) tall; masses of
bright, golden-yellow flowers; plants fuller
and more compact than others; the longest
bloomer, from late spring to frost.

Tips

Avoid planting in spots where puddles form
after snow melts in spring. These plants may
die if their roots sit in water.

Have patience in spring. Tickseed is often
one of the last perennials to emerge through
the soil.

Tickseed is drought-tolerant and grows well
in average or poor soil.

*The sunny, bright
yellow flowers of
'Zagreb' tickseed look
stunning combined with
blue sage or speedwell.*

'Zagreb' (right) is the longest-blooming variety of threadleaf tickseed. Shorter-growing pink tickseed is a good partner.

While admiring a flat of 'Rotkelchen' lance tickseed (below), a German woman exclaimed to a staff member over the variety name. She told us that rotkelchen is the name of a little songbird commonly found in European gardens. The bird has a bright red breast and throat and is loved for its sweet songs.

Tickseed blooms all summer, but less profusely as summer wanes. For more flowers then, I usually just pinch the dead ones out with my fingers, but you can cut plants back to at least half their size and get a second show of flowers. Tickseeds are tough plants; our perennials manager, Bob Stadnyk, sometimes deadheads his plants by cutting them with a lawnmower. Use a high setting, so about 4 inches (10 cm) of growth remains. The plants respond with fresh foliage and rebloom that season.

Remove tickseed's spent flowers often to prolong blooming.

Tickseed makes a superb cutflower. Cut for bouquets when flowers have fully opened. They generally last 7–10 days.

'Moonbeam' blooms in a shade of icy-yellow rarely found in flowers, and was cited by the Perennial Plant Association as one of the ten best varieties ever developed. 'Moonbeam' tickseed looks particularly striking with pastel flowers. Garden phlox, irises and coneflowers are good companions.

Yarrow

Achillea millefolium
Common Yarrow

yellow, red, pink,
lavender, white

Yarrow is one of those plants that gives a lot in return for very little care. Showy, flat-topped flowerheads provide months of colour in the garden, even in hot, dry weather. These brightly coloured flowers are long-lasting in bouquets, and air-dry effortlessly for year-round displays. As a child, I used to pick wild yarrow for bouquets. Those wildflowers bear little resemblance to the sturdy, colourful varieties now available.

Height • 12–30 inches (30–75 cm)

Spread • 30 inches (75 cm) or more

Blooms • midsummer through fall

Yarrow is a tough plant that blooms all summer long and thrives in poor, dry soil.

PLANTING

Seeding: Indoors in February or March; germination 7–15 days. Seed needs light to germinate; do not cover with soil. Sow outdoors in early spring. Plants will bloom the first year.

Transplanting: Space 24–36 inches (60–90 cm) apart.

GROWING

Sun to partial shade. Afternoon sun is best.

Mixed flowerbeds, cutting and wildflower gardens. Middle to back of border.

Divide every 3–4 years. See page 54, method A.

Recommended Varieties

Cerise Queen • 18–30 inches
(45–75 cm) tall; large clusters of
shell-pink to deep cherry-red flowers;
the best of the cherry-red cultivars.

Debutante Mix • 18–24 inches
(45–60 cm) tall; mixture of strong pastel
shades including peach, apricot, lavender,
coral, salmon and cream; large flowers.

Lavender Lady • 18–24 inches
(45–60 cm) tall; soft, pastel lavender—
a shade not often seen in these flowers;
blooms earlier than others.

Paprika • 12–24 inches (30–60 cm) tall;
bright coral-red flowers; one of the nicest
colours available.

Tips

We grow yarrow in a hot, dry, south-facing
flowerbed with Russian and silver king sages.
Few other plants do well in this sun-baked
location, but these ones thrive.

Deadhead to extend blooming period.

The species name *millefolium* means 'thousand
leaves' in Latin and refers to the finely
divided foliage. Yarrow's ferny leaves are
aromatic when crushed and can be added
to potpourris.

Heat-loving liatris grows well with 'Paprika' yarrow in a sunny flowerbed.

Yarrow, blue sage and annual cosmos provide a bountiful source for bouquets throughout the summer.

Deer will not eat yarrow and it is rarely bothered by pests.

Cut yarrow's flowers for bouquets when most blooms are open. They generally last 7–10 days in a vase.

Yarrow's flowers are marvellous dried. Cut when flowers are just beginning to open. We've found that flower colour remains brightest when stems are placed upright in a vase filled with just a bit of water. The flowers dry slowly as the water evaporates, and they remain fuller than when air-dried.

The botanical name *Achillea* honours Achilles, the famous warrior of Greek mythology. When Achilles was a child, his tutour taught him the healing properties of this plant, which was then regularly used in medicine. During the Trojan War, he packed yarrow leaves on his comrades' wounds to stop the bleeding.

OTHER RECOMMENDED SPECIES

Achillea ageratifolia (Greek Yarrow): 8 inches (20 cm) tall and 12–18 inches (30–45 cm) or more wide; downy, silvery leaves and clusters of white flowers in spring; excellent for rock gardens and border fronts.

Achillea tomentosum (Woolly Yarrow): 6–12 inches (15–30 cm) tall; 18 inches (45 cm) wide; small, yellow flowers in flat clusters from late spring to fall; good groundcover or rock garden plant.

Fossils of yarrow pollen have been found in Neanderthal burial caves, suggesting that this plant's association with the human race is some 60,000 years old.

Yellow and white are the only pure flower colours of wild yarrow. Hybrid varieties now bloom in a wider colour spectrum, from pastel shades of salmon and pink to intense deep red, orange and fuchsia. 'Cerise Queen' is an outstanding cherry-red variety.

Yucca

Yucca filamentosa
Adam's Needle Yucca,
Desert Candle, Spanish
Bayonet

Yucca glauca
Native Yucca, Small
Yucca, Soapweed

 white

Yucca looks deceivingly tropical, but these plants are amazingly hardy and survive for years—even through winters of -40°. Although the small yucca is reputed to be slightly hardier than Adam's needle, both plants have been growing in local gardens for more than 10 years. In midsummer, long-lasting, stately spikes of creamy-white bellflowers rise above the sword-shaped leaves.

Height (without flowers) • Adam's Needle:
18–24 inches (45–60 cm)
Small Yucca: 18 inches (45 cm)

Spread • Adam's Needle: 36 inches (90 cm)
Small Yucca: 24–36 inches (60–90 cm)

Blooms • mid- to late summer

PLANTING

Seeding: Sow indoors in February; germination 3–4 weeks. Sow outdoors in late fall. Plants take several years to bloom from seed.

Transplanting: Space 24 inches (60 cm) apart.

Yuccas are long-lived perennials.

Yucca's tough, sword-shaped leaves make striking silhouettes in sunny gardens.

GROWING

Hot, dry, sunny location.

Feature plant, in mixed flowerbeds, with shrubs and groundcover plants. Middle to back of border.

Yuccas are evergreen perennials. Do not cut back the leaves.

Yuccas do not need to be divided; they remain attractive and vigorous for 10 or more years. If you want more plants, you can separate some of the offset rosettes from the mother plant and transplant them into a new location. See page 54, method B.

RECOMMENDED VARIETIES

Usually available only under one of the names listed above.

TIPS

Yuccas thrive in poor or alkaline soil. They are one of the most drought-tolerant perennials and need little care after planting.

Grow yuccas with other heat-loving perennials, such as soapwort, blue sage or Russian sage. Yucca's sturdy, sword-shaped leaves provide a fine contrast to these flowers.

Have patience; yuccas take a long time to bloom. Adam's needle may not bloom for 2–3 years after planting, and one gardener told us her 10-year-old small yucca had bloomed for the first time that season!

Yucca's waxy, bell-shaped flowers are said to be fragrant at night, although I have never smelled them myself. Small yucca has larger, more open flowers than Adam's needle.

Don't be surprised if your yucca doesn't produce seed after blooming; they won't unless a certain species of moth is present during pollination.

Yuccas are striking plants, even when not blooming. Their foliage remains attractive year-round. The leaves poke through snow, adding interest to gardens in winter.

Yuccas grow rosettes of leaves, with offsets or suckers forming around the main plant. The centre rosette of Adam's needle dies after blooming, but offset rosettes quickly grow in to take its place.

While it seems to me a shame to remove yucca's flowers from the garden, they can be cut for bouquets. Do this when most of the flowers on the spike are open. The blooms last about 10 days.

Small yucca is native to the northern United States and the badlands of southern Alberta. It is less common than Adam's needle, and may be available only on the Prairies.

The species names tell how these two yuccas differ. Long, fine, hair-like threads curl from the edges of the Adam's needle's leaves (above); the name filamentosa *means 'bearing filaments or threads'.* Glauca *means having a 'bloom,' as grapes do; the foliage of small yucca has a dull, hazy, greyish-green tinge (opposite).*

Appendix

LISTING OF PERENNIALS BY HEIGHT

Heights given include the approximate height of flowers. Perennials which rarely flower, or which are grown mainly for their attractive foliage, such as sage, elephant-ears and hostas, are exceptions; the height given for these plants includes only the leaves. Plants suited to shady areas are marked with an asterisk(*).

Short (under 1 foot / 30 cm)

Anemone*	Cranesbill	Lamium*	Sage
Aster	Creeping Jenny*	Lily-of-the-Valley*	Saxifrage
Baby's Breath	Flax	Ornamental Onion	Sea Thrift
Bellflower	Fleeceflower	Pasqueflower	Shooting-star*
Bishop's Hat*	Gentian*	Phlox	Snow-in-Summer
Bitterroot	Goutweed*	Pink	Stonecrop
Blanketflower	(sun or shade)	Potentilla	Strawberry
Campion	Hens & Chicks	Primrose*	Thyme
Candytuft	Hosta*	Rockcress	Tickseed
Catmint	Iris		

Medium (1-2 feet / 30-60 cm)

Anemone*	Campion	Goldenrod	Pulmonaria*
Aster	Coralbell*	Hosta*	Sage
Astilbe*	Cranesbill	Iris	St. John's Wort
Beardtongue	Daylily	Lily	Shasta Daisy
Bellflower	Elephant-ears*	Lupin	Solomon's Seal*
Black-eyed Susan	(sun or shade)	Masterwort*	Speedwell
Blanketflower	Evening Primrose	Ornamental Onion	Spurge
Bleeding Heart*	Flax	Painted Daisy	Statice
Blue Fescue	Fleabane	Pink	Stonecrop
Blue Oat Grass	Garden Mum	Poppy	Tickseed
Blue Sage	Globeflower*	Potentilla	Yarrow

Tall (over 2 feet / 60 cm)

Anemone*
Astilbe*
Aster
Baby's Breath
Beebalm
Bellflower
Black-eyed Susan
Blanketflower
Bleeding Heart*
Blue Himalayan
  Poppy*

Astilbes bloom all summer long.

Campion
Checker Mallow
Clematis
Cornflower
Daylily
Delphinium
False-sunflower
Foxglove
Foxtail Lily
Gasplant
Globe Thistle
Goatsbeard*
Goldenrod
Hollyhock
Honeysuckle*
  (sun or shade)

Hops
Iris
Jacob's Ladder
Joe Pye Weed
Liatris
Lily
Lupin
Meadow Rue
Meadowsweet*
Monkshood*
Moor Grass
Obedient Plant
Ornamental Onion
Ostrich Fern*
Peony

Phlox
Plume Poppy
Poppy
Rayflower*
Russian Sage
Sage
Sea Holly
Shasta Daisy
Snakeroot*
Sneezeweed
Soapwort
Statice
Yarrow
Yucca

Rayflowers reach up to 6 feet (180 cm) in height and do best in partial shade.

Plant Listings by Colour of Bloom

Red 🏵

Aster
Astilbe
Beebalm
Bishop's Hat
Bitterroot
Blanketflower
Bleeding Heart
Campion
Checker Mallow
Clematis
Cranesbill
Coralbell
Daylily

Elephant-ears
Foxglove
Garden Mum
Hollyhock
Honeysuckle
Iris
Lily
Lupin
Masterwort
Ornamental Onion
Painted Daisy
Pasqueflower
Peony

Phlox
Pink
Poppy
Potentilla
Primrose
Rockcress
Saxifrage
Sea Thrift
Sneezeweed
Speedwell
Stonecrop
Thyme
Yarrow

Orange 🏵

Blanketflower
Bitterroot
Campion
Daylily
Foxtail Lily
Garden Mum
Globeflower
Honeysuckle
Iris
Lily
Phlox
Plume Poppy
Poppy
Potentilla
Primrose
Rayflower
Sneezeweed
Stonecrop

Oriental poppies have enormous flowers.

Pink

Anemone
Aster
Astilbe
Baby's Breath
Beebalm
Bitterroot
Bleeding Heart
Checker Mallow
Clematis
Coralbell
Coneflower

Cranesbill
Daylily
Delphinium
Elephant-ears
Fleabane
Fleeceflower
Foxglove
Foxtail Lily
Garden Mum
Gasplant
Hens & Chicks
Hollyhock

Iris
Joe Pye Weed
Lamium
Lily
Lupin
Masterwort
Meadowsweet
Obedient Plant
Ornamental Onion
Painted Daisy
Peony
Phlox

Pink
Poppy
Primrose
Saxifrage
Sea Thrift
Shooting-star
Soapwort
Speedwell
Stonecrop
Strawberry
Thyme
Yarrow

Purple

Anemone
Aster
Astilbe
Beardtongue
(foliage)
Beebalm
Bellflower
Blue Sage
Checker Mallow
Clematis

Coneflower
Coralbell
(foliage)
Cranesbill
Daylily
Delphinium
Fleabane
Foxglove
Garden Mum
Gasplant
Hollyhock

Hosta
Iris
Lamium
Liatris
Lily
Lupin
Meadow Rue
Monkshood
Obedient Plant
Ornamental Onion
Pasqueflower

Phlox
Poppy
Primrose
Rockcress
Russian Sage
Sea Thrift
Snakeroot (foliage)
Speedwell
Statice
Thyme
Yarrow

Blue

Bellflower
Blue Fescue
(foliage)
Blue Oat Grass
(foliage)
Blue Himalayan
Poppy
Catmint

Clematis
Cornflower
Delphinium
Flax
Gentian
Globe Thistle
Hosta (foliage)
Iris

Jacob's Ladder
Lupin
Monkshood
Primrose
Pulmonaria
Russian Sage
Sea Holly
Speedwell

Plant garden mums for late-season colour.

334

Yellow

Bitterroot
Black-eyed Susan
Blanketflower
Clematis
Creeping Jenny
Daylily
Evening Primrose
False-sunflower
Flax
Foxglove
Foxtail Lily
Garden Mum
Globeflower
Goldenrod
Hens & Chicks
Hollyhock
Hops (foliage)

Hosta (foliage)
Iris
Lady's Mantle
Lily
Lupin
Moor Grass
    (foliage)
Poppy
Potentilla
Primrose
Rayflower
Sneezeweed
Spurge
St. John's Wort
Stonecrop
Tickseed
Yarrow

*Rayflowers are striking
plants for shady, moist sites.*

White 🏵️

Anemone
Aster
Astilbe
Baby's Breath
Beardtongue
Beebalm
Bellflower
Bitterroot
Bleeding Heart
Candytuft
Catmint
Checker Mallow
Clematis
Coneflower
Coralbell
Cornflower

Cranesbill
Daylily
Delphinium
Flax
Fleabane
Foxglove
Foxtail Lily
Garden Mum
Gasplant
Gentian
Globeflower
Goatsbeard
Goutweed
Hens & Chicks
Hollyhock
Hosta
Iris

Jacob's Ladder
Lamium
Liatris
Lily
Lily-of-the-Valley
Lupin
Masterwort
Meadowsweet
Monkshood
Obedient Plant
Ornamental Onion
Painted Daisy
Pasqueflower
Peony
Phlox
Pink
Plume Poppy

Poppy
Primrose
Pulmonaria
Saxifrage
Sea Thrift
Shasta Daisy
Shooting-star
Snakeroot
Snow-in-Summer
Soapwort
Solomon's Seal
Speedwell
Statice
Thyme
Yarrow
Yucca

Silver 🏵️

Sage (foliage)
Snow-in-Summer
    (foliage)

Black 🏵️

Daylily
Hollyhock
Iris
Lily

*Shasta daisies bloom
profusely in early summer.*

BLOOMING PERIODS

Plant	Spring	Summer	Fall
Anemone	Woodland / Snowdrop	Japanese	
Aster	Alpine	Others	
Astilbe			
Baby's Breath	Creeping	Common	
Beardtongue			
Beebalm			
Bellflower		Carpathian	
	Clustered		
	Peachleaf		
	Spiral		
Bishop's Hat			
Bitterroot	Columbia	L. cotyledon	
	Lewisia		
Black-eyed Susan			
Blanketflower			
Bleeding Heart	Common		
		Fernleaf	
Blue Fescue			
Blue Himalayan Poppy			
Blue Oat Grass			
Blue Sage			
Campion			
Candytuft			
Catmint			
Checker Mallow			
Clematis	Alpine		Alpine
		Solitary	
	Big-petal		Big-petal
		Golden & Hybrid	
		Viticella	
Coneflower			
Coralbell		American Alumroot	
	Coralbell		
Cornflower			
Cranesbill		Grey-leaf	
	Endres		
	Bigroot		
		Armenian	
Creeping Jenny			
Daylily			
Delphinium			
Elephant-ears			
Evening Primrose			
False-sunflower			
Flax			
Fleabane			
Fleeceflower			
Foxglove			
Foxtail Lily			
Garden Mum			
Gasplant			
Gentian	Stemless	Crested	Chinese
Globe Thistle			
Globeflower	Common / Hybrid		
Goatsbeard			
Goldenrod			
Goutweed			
Hens & Chicks			
Hollyhock			
Honeysuckle			
Hops			

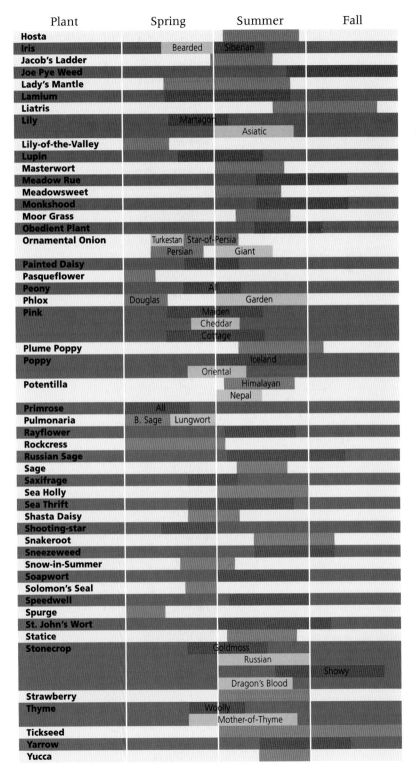

The Best Perennials for Cutflowers

Almost all perennials can be used as cutflowers, but the best ones have showy blooms, strong stems and last as long as two weeks in a vase. I like to add a few stems of attractive foliage, such as sage, meadow rue or moor grass, to bouquets. These are my favourite cutflowers:

Aster	Fleabane	Lily-of-the-Valley	Russian Sage
Astilbe	Foxglove	Lupin	Shasta Daisy
Baby's Breath	Goldenrod	Monkshood	Sneezeweed
Bellflower (tall ones)	Hollyhock	Obedient Plant	Soapwort
	Iris	Ornamental Onion	Speedwell
Blue Sage	Lady's Mantle	Peony	Statice
Delphinium	Liatris	Phlox (tall ones)	Tickseed
False-sunflower	Lily	Pink	Yarrow

The Best Perennials for Fragrance

Make the most of fragrant flowers by planting them along a walkway, near the back deck, close to a doorway, or under a window that is often open. Perennials with fragrant foliage should be planted where you will brush them as you pass by, releasing the aroma of their leaves.

Beebalm (foliage)	Pink
Daylily (some varieties)	Primrose (auricula types)
Gasplant	Russian Sage (foliage)
Lily-of-the-Valley	Sage (foliage)
Peony	Soapwort
Phlox (garden phlox)	Thyme (foliage)

The Best Perennials for Dried Flowers

Jan Goodall, who works at our greenhouses, dries almost everything in her garden, and spends the winter creating arrangements. She recommends that you pick flowers or foliage in midmorning, after the dew has dried from their petals and leaves, and place them in a location out of direct sunlight to prevent fading. (See individual listings for instructions on whether

Peonies are splendid in dried arrangements.

they should be hung or stood upright.) Through experimenting, Jan has found the best results from the following perennials:

Astilbe	False-sunflower	Obedient Plant (seedpods)	Shooting-star (seedpods)
Baby's Breath	Globe Thistle	Ornamental Onion	Sneezeweed
Blanketflower	Goldenrod	Peony	Speedwell
Blue Oat Grass (seedheads)	Iris (seedpods)	Poppy (seedpods)	Statice
	Masterwort	Russian Sage	Thyme
Clematis (golden)	Moor Grass (seedheads)	Sage (foliage)	(for miniature arrangements)
Delphinium		Sea Holly	Yarrow

339

The Best Perennial Groundcovers

A groundcover is a massed group of a single type of plant that covers the ground with thick foliage. These plants are low-growing and tough; they may provide a solution for areas where little else will grow. Many gardeners like groundcovers simply because they require so little maintenance! Groundcovers spread quickly, reduce water loss and soil erosion on slopes, and retard the spread of weeds.

To cover an area, space plants one square foot (900 cm²) apart. Most groundcovers are attractive and useful plants; they have beautiful foliage, texture and, sometimes, flowers. An asterisk(*) indicates plants best suited to shady areas.

Anemone*	Hops
Clematis (species types)	Lady's Mantle*
	Lamium*
Cranesbill	Lily-of-the-Valley*
Creeping Jenny* (sun or shade)	Potentilla
	Sage
Elephant-ears* (sun or shade)	Snow-in-Summer
Fleeceflower	Solomon's Seal*
	Stonecrop
Goutweed* (sun or shade)	Thyme

Lily-of-the-valley flourishes in shade.

Perennials that Attract Hummingbirds and Butterflies

One of the best things about summer mornings for my family is watching the hummingbirds. Hummingbirds can easily be attracted to your garden by bright red or tubular flowers. Once in your garden, though, these tiny birds will visit flowers of any colour in search of nectar. The best perennials for attracting hummingbirds are:

Beardtongue	Daylily	Hollyhock	Monkshood
Beebalm	Delphinium	Honeysuckle	Phlox (garden phlox)
Campion	Foxglove	Lily	Pink
Coralbell			

Butterflies seek flowers for nectar, but they need sunlight almost as much as food. They are cold-blooded creatures and need the sun's warmth to help them fly. This is why you often see butterflies basking in the afternoon sun, but few in mornings and on cloudy days. A flower garden that is sheltered and sunny for most of the day will attract an abundance of butterflies. In additon to those on the preceding list, these flowers are among the best for butterflies:

Aster	False-sunflower	Joe Pye Weed	Sneezeweed
Black-eyed Susan	Globe Thistle	Ornamental Onion	St. John's Wort
Coneflower	Goldenrod	Rockcress	Tickseed

THE BEST WOODLAND PERENNIALS

Woodland perennials are plants which are happiest in dappled sunlight and rich, moist soil. Grow them in spots where sunlight is filtered through tree leaves, so that the garden is rarely either fully sunny or shady at any time in the day. In their natural habitats, woodland plants thrive in acidic soils that contain a high percentage of rotted leaves. Match these conditions as closely as possible in your own garden.

Anemone	Jacob's Ladder	Ostrich Fern
Astilbe	Lily (martagon types)	Primrose
Bishop's Hat		Shooting-star
Bleeding Heart	Lily-of-the-Valley	Snakeroot
Gentian	Masterwort	Solomon's Seal
Goatsbeard	Meadowsweet	

A martagon lily produces up to 200 flowers.

THE BEST PERENNIALS TO GROW ON SLOPES

Steep slopes are challenging areas because water runs off faster than it penetrates them, often taking soil with it. Some gardeners sow grass seed as a solution, but I think that just creates another problem: how do you cut that part of the lawn easily? If you've ever watched someone trying to mow a steeply-sloped lawn, you will probably agree that it is much easier to

Fleeceflower is an attractive solution for problem areas.

choose perennials whose roots develop quickly into heavy root-systems that reduce soil erosion. Plants suited to shady areas are marked with an asterisk (*).

Anemone*	Fleabane	Hops	Snow-in-Summer
Blue Fescue	Fleeceflower	Lady's Mantle*	Soapwort
Catmint	Goatsbeard*	Lamium*	Speedwell
Clematis	Goldenrod	Lily-of-the-Valley*	St. John's Wort
Cornflower	Goutweed*	Potentilla	Stonecrop
Cranesbill	(sun or shade)	Russian Sage	Thyme
Daylily	Honeysuckle*	Sage	Yarrow
Evening Primrose	(sun or shade)		

341

'DEER-PROOF' PERENNIALS

Grow the following perennials if deer are a problem in your yard; they will not eat these plants:

Aster	Lamium
Beardtongue	Lupin
Beebalm	Meadowsweet
Bishop's Hat	Monkshood
Black-eyed Susan	Sage
Blanketflower	Shasta Daisy
Bleeding Heart	Snow-in-Summer
Catmint	Spurge
Daylily	Yarrow
Foxglove	

Fast-growing hops vines do well in sun or partial shade.

'Sunny Border Blue' blooms longer than other speedwells.

THE LONGEST-BLOOMING PERENNIALS

I love irises and peonies, so I grow them even though their flowers last for only a few weeks. To carry the floral show between my favourite flowers, I plant a few perennials with longer blooming periods. The following perennials bloom for six or more weeks, some beginning in late spring and others starting in midsummer and continuing through fall. The ones marked with an asterisk(*) will grow in shade.

Baby's Breath	Bitterroot	Bleeding Heart* (fernleaf)	Catmint
Beebalm	Black-eyed Susan	Blue Sage	Checker Mallow
Bellflower	Blanketflower		Clematis

Coneflower
Coralbell*
Cranesbill (some)
Daylily (some)
Evening Primrose
False-sunflower
Flax
Fleabane
Foxglove
Garden Mum
Goldenrod
Honeysuckle*
  (sun or shade)
Lady's Mantle*
Liatris
Monkshood*

Obedient Plant
Phlox (garden
  phlox)
Pink
Poppy (Iceland)
Rockcress
Sea Holly
Sea Thrift
Shasta Daisy
Soapwort
Speedwell (some)
St. John's Wort
Stonecrop
Strawberry
Thyme
Tickseed
Yarrow

*Soapwort has masses of
fragrant flowers all summer.*

PERENNIALS WITH INTERESTING FOLIAGE

Think not only of flowers when planning your garden, but also of
foliage. Include perennials with various leaf shapes, colours, sizes and
textures to both unify and diversify the overall effect of your garden.
Many of these perennials also have glorious flowers, but even when
they are not blooming, their foliage enhances the flowers of other
plants. I grow some of these plants solely for their handsome leaves!
Plants marked with an asterisk(*) are suited to shady areas.

Bishop's Hat*
Blue Fescue
Blue Oat Grass
Coralbell*
  (some types)
Daylily
Elephant-ears*
  (either sun
  or shade)
Flax
Goutweed*
  (sun or shade)
Hens & Chicks
Hops
Hosta*
Iris
Lady's Mantle*

Lamium*
Lupin
Moor Grass
Ostrich Fern*
Plume Poppy
Pulmonaria*
Rayflower*
Russian Sage
Sage
Saxifrage*
Sea Holly
Snakeroot*
Snow-in-Summer
Stonecrop
Thyme
Yucca

*The glossy leaves of
elephant-ears turn bronze-red in fall.*

BOTANICAL NAMES
LEARNING A LITTLE LATIN

Why should anyone be bothered to learn the botanical names of plants, when there are common names which are much easier to pronounce?

Well, for one, because the botanical or Latin name often provides useful information. Without ever seeing a plant, you may be able to tell its height, texture, blooming period, fragrance or colour just by knowing its Latin name. You may also find a plant's name contains the key to its preferred growing conditions, or tells who or what the plant was named after.

This internationally accepted system of plant naming was masterminded in the 1700s by Swedish botanist Carl Linneaus. Each plant name consists of at least two words. The first word, which is always capitalized and derived from either Latin or Greek, is the genus—a group of closely related plants.

The second word is the species. It is usually written in lower case letters, often provides some clue to the plant's behaviour in the garden, and indicates how one plant differs from another of the same genus. For example, flax plants are of the genus *Linum*. *Linum perenne* is the common perennial blue flax, while *Linum flavum* has yellow flowers. *Perenne* means 'perennial' and *flavum* means 'pale yellow.'

Often there is a third name, which may indicate a hybrid variety or cultivar. *Alba* means 'white,' so we know that *Linum perenne alba* is the white-flowered perennial flax.

Any plant with *officinalis* in its name is, or was at one time, listed in the official *Pharmacopoeia*, a book containing standard formulas and methods for the preparation of medicines and drugs. *Paeonia officinalis*, the common peony, for example, was at one time valued as much for the reputed healing power of its roots as for its beautiful flowers.

343

MEANINGS OF A FEW COMMON PLANT NAMES

Suffixes follow the Latin rules of grammar; the Latin word for white, for example, may be *albus* (masculine), *alba* (feminine) or *album* (neuter), depending on the gender of the species or variety name.

Colours
(may refer to flowers or leaves)

album: white; *Dictamnus albus* (gasplant)

atropurpureum: dark purple, purple-red or purplish-black; *Cimicifuga ramosa* 'Atropurpurea' (snakeroot)

aureum: golden-yellow; *Lysimachia nummularia aureum* (creeping Jenny)

caeruleum: sky-blue; *Polemonium caeruleum* (Jacob's ladder)

coccineum: scarlet; *Tanacetum coccineum* (painted daisy)

flavum: pale yellow; *Linum flavum* (yellow flax)

purpureum: purple; *Eupatorium purpureum* (Joe Pye weed)

roseum: pink or rose; *Alcea rosea* (hollyhock)

rubrum: red; *Filipendula rubrum* (meadowsweet)

sulphureum: sulphur-yellow; *Epimedium χ sulphureum* (bishop's hat)

variegatum: variegated leaves (marked, striped or blotched with a colour other than green); *Aegopodium podagraria* 'Variegatum' (goutweed)

Growth Habit

acaulis: stemless flowers, resting in the centre of a clump of leaves; *Gentiana acaulis* (stemless gentian)

alpinus: a plant native to the Alps or other mountainous region; usually low- growing; *Aster alpinus* (alpine aster)

cordifolia: heart-shaped leaves; often wide-leaved as well; *Bergenia cordifolia* (elephant-ears)

flore-plena: a double-flowered form; *Saponaria officinalis flore-plena* (soapwort)

paniculata: having an open flower cluster (panicle); *Phlox paniculata* (garden phlox), *Gypsophila paniculata* (baby's breath)

repens: creeping habit, often rooting; *Gypsophila repens* (creeping baby's breath)

spicata: having flowers in spikes; *Veronica spicata* (speedwell), *Liatris spicata* (liatris)

Select Glossary

acidic soil • a soil with a pH reading below 7; peaty soils, soil in areas of high rainfall and areas underneath evergreen trees, such as spruce and pine, are often acidic; very acidic soil inhibits the growth of many plants.

alkaline soil • a soil with a pH reading above 7; very alkaline soil also inhibits plant growth. Most perennials prefer soil that is close to the neutral pH of 7.

alpine plant • generally refers to any very small, low-growing, compact plant, many of which are native to areas above the tree-line in mountains; popular for rock gardens.

annual • a plant that completes its life-cycle, from seed to flower to seed, within a single growing season; petunias and marigolds are common annuals.

basal leaves • leaves growing at the base of a plant, either directly from the crown or from the lowest section of the stem; statice and bitterroot have basal leaves.

biennial • a plant that grows evergreen leaves the first year, blooms the second year, and then dies; perpetuates in gardens by self-seeding; hollyhocks and foxgloves are biennials.

bract • a modified leaf below a flower or flower branch; sometimes brightly coloured; the yellow 'flowers' of cushion spurge are actually bracts, as are the red 'flowers' of poinsettias.

calyx • whorl of sepals forming the outer case of the bud covering the flower.

crown • the thickened junction of the stem and root of a perennial; daylilies and peonies have obvious crowns.

cultivar • an abbreviation for 'cultivated variety'; plants with special characteristics created by plant breeders—for example, *Heuchera americana* 'Ruby Veil' or Ruby Veil coralbell.

cutting • part of a plant cut off to be rooted for vegetative propagation; commercial growers often raise plants from stem or root cuttings.

evergreen perennial • a plant with foliage that remains green year-round, even under snow; pinks and thyme are evergreen perennials.

fiddlehead • a new fern frond, shaped like the head of a fiddle. Some fiddleheads are considered delicacies.

frond • the expanded leaf of a fern.

genus • classification for a group of closely related plant species.

globular • shaped like a ball or globe; ornamental onions and globe thistle both have globular flowerheads.

harden off • to acclimatize plants from an indoor to an outdoor environment, typically by a gradual reduction in temperature and moisture.

herbaceous perennial • a plant whose leaves and stems die to ground level during winter, but whose roots survive. Most perennials fall into this category.

humus • well-decomposed, relatively stable, organic matter; often added to soil to improve nutrient levels and composition.

hybrid • the cross-bred, offspring plant of parents of different species or varieties, with some characteristics of both parents. Usually indicated with an 'χ' in its botanical name— *Aconitum χ bicolour* (bicolour monkshood), for example.

inflorescence • a botanical term for the collective parts of a flower; the entire flower.

leaf mould • partially decayed leaves; traditionally added to improve garden soil; particularly good for woodland plants.

loam • balanced soil mixture of sand, silt, clay and organic matter; the ideal garden soil.

mulch • a material spread on soil surface for plant protection, beauty or erosion reduction; compost, leaves, gravel and bark chips are common mulches.

panicle • flower cluster with flowers on individual stalks attached along a branched stem; astilbe, baby's breath and phlox bloom in panicles.

pistil • the female, seed-bearing organ of a flower.

raceme • flower cluster with flowers on individual stalks attached along an unbranched stem; lupins and delphiniums have racemes.

rhizome • a thickened, horizontal, underground stem which produces roots on its lower side and leaf shoots on its upper side; bearded irises have rhizomes.

rock garden • a garden with closely spaced rocks interspersed with plants.

rosette • a cluster of leaves radiating from a plant's base, as with primroses and hens & chicks.

sepal • one of the divisions of the calyx, located just below the flower.

species • a closely related group of plants which can interbreed; a group of related species form a genus.

spike • a flower cluster with stalkless or nearly stalkless individual flowers closely attached to an unbranched stem, e.g., speedwell and liatris; often, however, also used generally as a description of long, tall flowers, like delphiniums (which are technically racemes).

stamen • the male, pollen-bearing organ of a flower. The yellow centres of single-flowered peonies are showy stamens.

succulent • a plant with thick, fleshy leaves and stems; e.g., stonecrop, hens & chicks, yucca.

taproot • a long, descending, main root; perennials with taproots are difficult to transplant once mature; baby's breath and gasplant are examples.

tender perennial • a perennial that has difficulty surviving winters without protection.

top-dressing • a thin layer of organic matter or fertilizer spread over and around plants, to enrich soil.

umbel • flower cluster in which individual flowers have stalks of the same length that seem to emerge from the same place on the stem, forming a flat-topped or rounded cluster. The flowers of ornamental onions and yarrow are umbels.

variety • a plant within a species that has developed one or more characteristics that set it apart from other plants within the species. For example, *Linum perenne* var. *alba* is a white-flowered variety of flax ('var.' is an abbreviation for 'variety').

whorl • a circle of leaves, branches or flowers around the stem; the candelabra-like flowers of Tibetan primrose are a whorl.

woody perennial • a perennial with hard-tissue stems that do not die to the ground at the end of the growing season. Russian sage is a woody perennial.

Select Index

A

Achillea
see yarrow
Aconitum
see monkshood
Adam's needle
see yucca
Aegopodium
see goutweed
Alcea
see hollyhock
Alchemilla
see lady's mantle
Allium
see ornamental onion
alpine thistle
see sea holly
alpine thrift
see sea thrift
Althea
see hollyhock
alumroot
see coralbell
American alumroot
see coralbell
anemone 62
see also pasqueflower
arabis
see rockcress
archangel
see lamium
Armeria
see sea thrift
Artemisia
see sage
Aruncus
see goatsbeard
Asiatic lily
see lily
aster 64
astilbe 68
Astrantia
see masterwort
Aubretia
see rockcress

B

baby's breath 72
bachelor's button, perennial
see cornflower
barrenwort
see bishop's hat
bear hops
see hops

bearded iris
see iris
beardtongue 76
beebalm 78
bellflower 80
Bergenia
see elephant-ears
Bethlehem sage
see pulmonaria
biennials 11
bishop's hat 84
bishop's weed
see goutweed
bitterroot 86
black cohosh
see snakeroot
black-eyed Susan 90
blanketflower 92
blazing star
see liatris
bleeding heart 94
blue clips
see bellflower
blue fescue 98
blue flax
see flax
blue grass
see blue fescue, blue oat grass
blue Himalayan poppy 100
blue oat grass 102
blue sage 104
boneset
see Joe Pye weed
bouncing Bet
see soapwort
bugbane
see snakeroot
bulbs 20, 21
burning bush
see gasplant
butter daisy
see tickseed
button snakeroot
see liatris

C

Campanula
see bellflower
campion 106
candle larkspur
see delphinium
candytuft 108

Canterbury bells
see bellflower
caspia
see statice
catmint 110
Centaurea
see cornflower
Cerastium
see snow-in-summer
chalk plant
see baby's breath
charity
see Jacob's ladder
checker mallow 112
Cheddar pink
see pink
Chrysanthemum coccineum
see painted daisy
Chrysanthemum maximum
see Shasta daisy
Chrysanthemum χ morifolium
see garden mum
Chrysanthemum χ superbum
see Shasta daisy
Cimicifuga
see snakeroot
cinquefoil
see potentilla
clematis 114
common thrift
see sea thrift
coneflower 120
see also black-eyed Susan
Convallaria
see lily-of-the-valley
coralbell 122
Coreopsis
see tickseed
cornflower 126
cottage pink
see pink
cowslip
see primrose
cranesbill 128
creeping Jenny 132
cushion mum
see garden mum
cushion spurge
see spurge

D

daisy
see painted daisy, Shasta daisy
daylily 134
deadheading 47
deadnettle
see lamium
delphinium 138
Dendranthema
see garden mum
desert candle
see foxtail lily, yucca
Dianthus
see pink
Dicentra
see bleeding heart
Dictamnus
see gasplant
Digitalis
see foxglove
dittany
see gasplant
Dodecatheon
see shooting-star
dragon's blood
see stonecrop
dropwort
see meadowsweet
dusty miller, perennial
see sage

E

Echinacea
see coneflower
Echinops
see globe thistle
elephant-ears 142
see also rayflower
Epimedium
see bishop's hat
Eremurus
see foxtail lily
Erigeron
see fleabane
Eryngium
see sea holly
Eupatorium
see Joe Pye weed
Euphorbia
see spurge
evening primrose 144

347

F

fairy thimble
see bellflower
false dragonhead
see obedient plant
false goatsbeard
see astilbe
false hens & chicks
see hens & chicks
false houseleek
see hens & chicks
false lion's-heart
see obedient plant
false spirea
see astilbe
**false-
sunflower 146**
fern
see ostrich fern
fertilizing 46, 47
Festuca
see blue fescue
feverweed
see Joe Pye weed
Filipendula
see meadowsweet
flax 148
fleabane 150
fleur-de-lis
see iris
flowering onion
see ornamental
onion
foxglove 154
foxtail lily 156
Fragaria
see strawberry
funkia
see hosta

G

Gaillardia
see blanketflower
garden mum 158
gasplant 162
gayfeather
see liatris
gentian 164
Gentiana
see gentian
Geranium
see cranesbill
German iris
see iris
German statice
see statice

giant rockfoil
see elephant-ears
globe thistle 166
globeflower 168
goat's foot
see goutweed
goatsbeard 170
golden star
see sneezeweed
goldenray
see rayflower
goldenrod 172
groundcovers 339
groundsel
see rayflower
goutweed 174
Greek-valerian
see Jacob's ladder
Gypsophila
see baby's breath

H

hardening off 37
harebell
see bellflower
heart-leaf bergenia
see elephant-ears
Helen's flower
see sneezeweed
Helenium
see sneezeweed
Helictotrichon
see blue oat grass
Heliopsis
see false-
sunflower
helmet flower
see monkshood
Hemerocallis
see daylily
hens & chicks 176
Heuchera
see coralbell
Himalayan poppy
see blue
Himalayan poppy
hollyhock 180
honeysuckle 182
hops 184
hosta 186
houseleek
see hens & chicks
Humulus
see hops
Hypericum
see St. John's
wort

I–J–K

Iberis
see candytuft
Iceland poppy
see poppy
iris 190
**Jacob's
ladder 194**
Jerusalem cross
see campion
Joe Pye weed 196
Jovibarbas
see hens & chicks
knotweed
see fleeceflower

L

lady's mantle 198
lady-by-the-gate
see soapwort
lamium 200
leather-leaf
see elephant-ears
Leucanthemum
see Shasta daisy
Lewisia
see bitterroot
liatris 202
Ligularia
see rayflower
Lilium
see lily
lily 204
**lily-of-the-
valley 210**
Limonium
see statice
Linum
see flax
Lonicera
see honeysuckle
lungwort
see pulmonaria
lupin 212
Lupinus
see lupin
Lychnis
see campion
Lysimachia
see creeping
Jenny
Lythrum
see purple
loosestrife

M

Macleaya
see plume poppy
maiden pink
see pink
mallow
see checker
mallow
Maltese cross
see campion
martagon lily
see lily
masterwort 214
Matteuccia
see ostrich fern
meadow rue 216
meadowsweet 218
Meconopsis
see blue
Himalayan poppy
mistflower
see Joe Pye weed,
meadow rue
Molinia
see moor grass
Monarda
see beebalm
moneywort
see creeping
Jenny
monkshood 220
moor grass 222
Morden mum
see garden mum
mother-of-thyme
see thyme
mountain bluet
see cornflower
mulch 49

N–O

Nepeta
see catmint
**obedient
plant 224**
Oenothera
see evening
primrose
old lady
see sage
old man
see sage
Oriental poppy
see poppy
ornamental grass
see blue fescue,
blue oat grass,
moor grass

ornamental
  onion **226**
Orostachys
  see hens & chicks
ostrich fern 230
Oswego tea
  see beebalm

P

Paeonia
  see peony
painted daisy 232
Papaver
  see poppy
pasqueflower 234
Penstemon
  see beardtongue
peony 236
perennial bachelor's
  button
  see cornflower
perennial dusty
  miller
  see sage
perennials
  blooming periods
    of 336–337
  by colours 333–
    335
  by height 332
  definition of 10
  for
    cutflowers 338
  for foliage
    effects 342
  for
    fragrance 338
  for dried
    flowers 338, 339
  for hot, dry
    areas 27
  for shady
    areas 26
  for wet areas 26
  for woodland
    gardens 340
  longest
    blooming 341
Perovskia
  see Russian sage
Persicaria
  see fleeceflower
phlox 242
Physostegia
  see obedient plant
pink 246
pink panda
  see strawberry
plantain lily
  see hosta
plume poppy 250

Polemonium
  see Jacob's ladder
Polygonatum
  see Solomon's seal
Polygonum
  see fleeceflower
poor man's orchid
  see iris
poppy 252
  see also blue
  Himalayan poppy,
  plume poppy
potentilla 256
prairie crocus
  see pasqueflower
primrose 258
  see also evening
  primrose
Primula
  see primrose
pulmonaria 262
Pulsatilla
  see pasqueflower
purple coneflower
  see coneflower
purple loosestrife,
  alternatives to 203
purple rockcress
  see rockcress
pyrethrum daisy
  see painted daisy

Q–R

queen-of-the-
  meadow
  see meadowsweet
queen-of-the-prairie
  see meadowsweet
rayflower 266
red Caesar
  see pink
rockcress 268
rockfoil
  see elephant-ears
rock gardens 41, 42
roots 34
Rudbeckia
  see black-eyed
  Susan
Russian sage 270

S

sage 274
  see also blue sage,
  pulmonaria,
  Russian sage
Salvia
  see blue sage

Saponaria
  see soapwort
Saxifraga
  see saxifrage
saxifrage 280
  see also elephant-
  ears
scarlet lightning
  see campion
sea holly 284
sea lavender
  see statice
sea pink
  see sea thrift
sea thrift 286
Sedum
  see stonecrop
Sempervivum
  see hens & chicks
Shasta daisy 288
sheep's fescue
  see blue fescue
shooting-star 290
Siberian iris
  see iris
Sidalcea
  see checker
  mallow
silver candle
  see snakeroot
silver king
  see sage
silver mound
  see sage
snakeroot 292
sneezeweed 294
**snow-in-
  summer 296**
snow-on-the-
  mountain
  see goutweed
soapweed
  see yucca
soapwort 298
soil 37
soldier's coat
  see campion
Solidago
  see goldenrod
**Solomon's
  seal 300**
southernwood
  see sage
Spanish bayonet
  see yucca
speedwell 302
spotted dog
  see pulmonaria
spurge 304

**St. John's
  wort 306**
star-of-Persia
  see ornamental
  onion
statice 308
stonecrop 312
strawberry 316
sundrops
  see evening
  primrose
sunflower heliopsis
  see false-
  sunflower
sweet bergamot
  see beebalm

T

Tanacetum
  see painted daisy
Thalictrum
  see meadow rue
thrift
  see sea thrift
thyme 318
Thymus
  see thyme
tickseed 320
transplanting 38
Trollius
  see globeflower
Turk's cap lily
  see lily

V–W

valentine flower
  see bleeding heart
Veronica
  see speedwell
watering 44
white clips
  see bellflower
windflower
  see anemone,
  pasqueflower
winter protection
  57–59
wolfsbane
  see monkshood
wormwood
  see sage

Y–Z

yarrow 324
yucca 328
zone ratings 23

349

References

Coombes, Allen J. *Dictionary of Plant Names*. Portland, OR: Timber Press, Inc., 1993.

Davies, Dilys. *Alliums: The Ornamental Onions*. Portland, OR: Timber Press, Inc., 1992.

Kowalchuk, Claire & Hylton, William H., eds. *Rodale's Illustrated Encylopedia of Herbs*. Emmaus, PA: Rodale Press, 1987.

Neal, Bill. *Gardener's Latin: A Lexicon*. Chapel Hill, NC: Algonquin Books, 1992.

Riotte, Louise. *Roses Love Garlic*. Pownal, VT: Storey Communications, Inc., 1983.

Searles, James D. *The Garden of Joy*. Great Falls, MT: Medicine River Publishing, 1990.

Trehane, Piers, ed. *Index Hortensis, Volume 1: Perennials*. Wimborne, Dorset: Quarterback Publishing, 1989.

Wyman, Donald. *Wyman's Gardening Encyclopedia*. New York, NY: Macmillan Publishing Company, 1986.

About the Author

Lois Hole and her husband Ted started selling vegetables out of their red barn over 30 years ago; today Hole's Greenhouses & Gardens Ltd. is one of the largest garden centres in Alberta. It remains a family business, owned and operated by Lois, Ted, their sons Bill and Jim, and Bill's wife Valerie.

Through her books and gardening columns in more than 35 weekly newspapers, Lois provides helpful information and tips to gardeners across Canada. During the summer months, she is a regular guest on CBC Radio's 'Wild Rose Country' and travels the province as a guest speaker.

Gardeners Around the World
Enjoy Lois Hole's Gardening Series!

Recipient of the
Professional Plant Growers Association
1995 Educational Media Award

Lois Hole's Bedding Plant Favorites

by Lois Hole with Jill Fallis
Turn your bare patch of soil into a glorious garden full of color with annual flowers and advice from Lois Hole, gardening expert and greenhouse operator. This book is bursting with ideas about how to make your favorite flowers thrive. Lois's good advice helps make your gardening easy, successful and enjoyable!
5.5" x 8.5" • 272 pages • over 350 color photographs
Softcover • $19.95 CDN • $15.95 US• ISBN 1-55105-074-9

Lois Hole's Vegetable Favorites

by Lois Hole
With growing tips, variety recommendations, recipes and nutritional hints, Lois Hole describes how to grow, harvest and prepare more than 30 of her favorite vegetables. Suggestions for composting, fertilizing, pest control and small-space gardening make this inspirational guide a horn of plenty.
5.5" x 8.5" • 160 pages • 44 color photographs •
51 B & W illustrations • 33 color illustrations
Softcover • $14.95 CDN • $11.95 US• ISBN 1-55105-072-2

Lois Hole's Tomato Favorites

by Lois Hole with Jill Fallis
Home-grown tomatoes are one of the great joys of our gardens. Lois Hole provides you with all the secrets of a great tomato harvest, including planting and growing for the entire season, growing large tomatoes, treating tomato problems and how to extend the growing season. Richly illustrated and organized by size for easy reference, this book also includes sumptuous recipes from renowned chefs from world-class restaurants and from the kitchens of devoted tomato fans.
5.5" x 8.5" • 160 pages • over 258 color photographs •
Softcover • $16.95 CDN • $12.95 US • ISBN 1-55105-068-4

> *"This author's collective attributes, from gardening to writing (and several in between), touched with an aura of sincere warmth and affection for the subject she loves so much, and integrated with some solid, down-to-earth tomato gardening advice, all kindle together and radiate profusely from the pages."*
> —Bob Ambrose, Publisher, *The Tomato Club Newsletter*

Praise for Lois Hole's Gardening Series

> *"Beginner and experienced gardeners alike benefit from Lois's years of experience."*
> —Wayne Gale, President, Stokes Seed

> *"Not only are Lois Hole's books packed with useful information, they're great to read and follow, guaranteeing success…"*
> —David Harrap, Garden Writer, *The Edmonton Sun*

CANADA		USA
206, 10426-81 Avenue	202A, 1110 Seymour Street	16149 Redmond Way, #180
Edmonton, AB T6E 1X5	Vancouver, BC V6B 3N3	Redmond, WA 98052
Ph (403) 433-9333	Ph (604) 687-5555	Ph (206) 343-8397
Fax (403) 433-9646	Fax (604) 687-5575	

1-800-661-9017